If These WALLS *Could* TALK:
BOSTON BRUINS

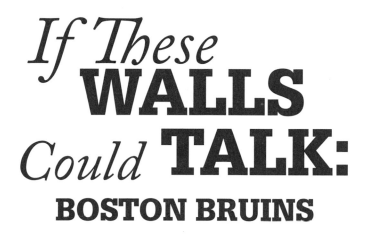

If These WALLS Could TALK:
BOSTON BRUINS

Stories from the
Boston Bruins Ice, Locker Room,
and Press Box

Dale Arnold with Matt Kalman

TRIUMPH
BOOKS

Library of Congress Cataloging-in-Publication Data

Names: Arnold, Dale author.
Title: If these walls could talk : Boston Bruins : stories from the Boston
    Bruins ice, locker room, and press box / Dale Arnold, with Matt Kalman.
Description: Chicago, Illinois : Triumph Books LLC, [2018]
Identifiers: LCCN 2018004175 | ISBN 9781629375342
Subjects: LCSH: Boston Bruins (Hockey team)—Anecdotes. | Boston Bruins
    (Hockey team)—History.
Classification: LCC GV848.B6 A76 2018 | DDC 796.962/640974451—dc23
LC record available at https://lccn.loc.gov/2018004175

This book is available in quantity at special discounts for your group or organization. For further information, contact:

Triumph Books LLC
814 North Franklin Street
Chicago, Illinois 60610
(312) 337-0747
www.triumphbooks.com

Printed in U.S.A.

ISBN: 978-1-62937-534-2

Design by Amy Carter

Page production by Nord Compo

Photos courtesy of the author unless otherwise indicated

This is for my home team—Susan, Taylor, Lauren, Alysha, and Brianna—who always believed in me, even when I didn't. They make me better than I am, and I'm forever grateful.

—D.A.

For Mason and Amy

—M.K.

CONTENTS

Foreword *by Ray Bourque*   ix

Introduction   xiii

Chapter 1: **How I Got Here**   1

Chapter 2: **Announcers**   39

Chapter 3: **Mike Milbury**   79

Chapter 4: **Boston Garden**   93

Chapter 5: **TD Garden**   99

Chapter 6: **Coaches**   103

Chapter 7: **Harry Sinden**   137

Chapter 8: **Nate Greenberg**   153

Chapter 9: **Bobby Orr**   159

Chapter 10: **Ray Bourque**   169

Chapter 11: **Hal Gill**   183

Chapter 12: **Joe Thornton**   193

Chapter 13: **The Boston Bruins and the Sports Talk
Radio Wars**   205

Chapter 14: **Tales from the Room**   215

Chapter 15: **Marc Savard**   223

Chapter 16: **Patrice Bergeron**   233

Chapter 17: **Zdeno Chara**   241

Chapter 18: **Andrew Ference**   253

Chapter 19: **Goalies**   261

Chapter 20: **Tough Guys**   273

Chapter 21: **Shawn Thornton**   283

Chapter 22: **Patriots' Day**   293

Chapter 23: **Greatest Games**   307

Chapter 24: **Current Players**   313

Chapter 25: **Bruins in the Community**   325

Acknowledgments   349

FOREWORD

I was born and raised in the Montreal suburb of Saint-Laurent, Quebec. It probably goes without saying that I was a big fan of the Montreal Canadiens.

In 1979, I was playing for the Verdun Eperviers of the Quebec Major Junior Hockey League, and Verdun hosted the Memorial Cup that year. This was before the current system, when the host city gets an automatic berth, and we had been eliminated from contention.

The night of May 10, 1979, I went to our home arena to watch Brandon beat Trois-Rivieres 6–1 in Game 6 of that series. I didn't have a car, so I had to take the subway home, and had to change trains at the Atwater Station, right near the Forum.

I arrived at Atwater just minutes after the conclusion of the infamous "too many men on the ice" game, when the Canadiens beat the Bruins 5–4 in overtime to win Game 7 of the Stanley Cup semifinals, and I remember pumping my arm in celebration because the Canadiens had once again beaten Boston. Ninety-two days later I was drafted eighth overall in the first round...by the Bruins! My days of rooting for the Canadiens were over forever.

In fact, I learned to hate them pretty quickly. And when I say hate, I mean with the respect you have for a great organization, and how much you want to beat them. I would go home every summer, and I would have to hear from everyone, "What happened? They beat you again?" But then, after the playoffs in 1988, it was the quietest summer I ever had back home. No one wanted to talk to me at all!

I arrived at my first Bruins training camp, with guys like Cheesy, Cash, Jean Ratelle, Brad Park, Terry O'Reilly, Don Marcotte, Gary Doak—and there was so much history and so much tradition. Everyone said I couldn't speak English. I spoke plenty of English. I grew up in a bilingual home. I just chose to listen and watch and keep my mouth shut. I was a little shy, but I was trying to earn my way.

I will always remember how Brad Park took me under his wing and taught me the proper way to be a Bruin. His knees were pretty bad by that time, and he was kind of in and out of the lineup, but it was still crazy how good he could play, and the things he could do. After practice, he would take the wooden bench from our bench onto the ice and work with me. Sometimes he would stand it up and I would have to jump back and forth around the bench, trying to get my shot away. Other times he would lay it down on the ice, and make me jump over it to shoot. Brad did so much for me, and I'll never forget that.

My wife, Christiane, and I made a home in Boston and, later on, the suburbs. We grew to love it here. My children, Melissa, Ryan, and Christopher, were all born here, went to school here, played sports here, and never wanted to leave. People sometimes ask if I ever thought of leaving after I retired, and going back to Quebec, but we never even thought about it.

I was fortunate enough to play most of 21 seasons for the Bruins. Most of the time, we had really good teams and were always competitive. A couple of seasons, especially at the end of my time playing in Boston, we weren't very good, but those years were pretty rare. I had great teammates, and made wonderful friends, and many of those relationships will be with me forever.

The only regret I ever had was never winning a Stanley Cup in a Bruins uniform. In fact, when we won the Cup in Colorado in 2000–01, one of the things I thought was, "What would this have been like if we had done it in Boston?" When the Bruins won the Cup in 2011, and I saw what it meant to the people of Massachusetts and the city of Boston, I thought again about how I missed the chance to win in Boston.

I got to know Dale when he came to Boston and started doing the Bruins games in 1995. He loved the sport, and we began a friendly professional relationship. In fact, Dale was the one who introduced me to Larry Bird when we sat in on his radio show.

When the mayor of Boston asked me to bring the Stanley Cup back to the city for a rally in 2001, I asked Dale to host the event in City Hall Plaza.

Dale might be the perfect guy to tell some of these stories from behind the scenes with the Bruins. He has been a part of the sports broadcasting industry in Boston for almost 30 years, and part of the Bruins scene for more than 20 years. He was there for many of these stories, and he'll even share a few of mine later in this book.

The Bruins are a very special organization, with the history of an Original Six franchise. I hope you enjoy reading about them as much as we players enjoyed playing in the city of Boston.

Ray Bourque played 21 seasons with the Boston Bruins and was the team's longest-serving captain. He currently holds records for the most career goals, assists, and points by a defenseman in NHL history. He won the Norris Trophy as the NHL's best defenseman five times and won his only Stanley Cup in his final NHL game, with the Colorado Avalanche. In 2017, he was named one of the 100 Greatest NHL Players.

INTRODUCTION

I don't have to tell hockey fans. They already know the sport is just different. I never played the game, but I love it just the same.

I love the speed and the physicality. I love the constant motion. I love the feeling of walking into an arena with a light snow falling and a crispness in the air. But I also love the feeling of leaving the arena after a late spring playoff game with temperatures hinting at a possible late Stanley Cup run.

I love that my daughter, Alysha, played through high school and college, and I had the opportunity to experience the game from the grassroots level. I even loved that it was only friends and family in the building (except when Mount Saint Charles Academy was winning back-to-back state championships!). I love when I was watching the movie *Miracle* with my daughter and she said, "Hey, Dad—Taylor's father, my coach, is named Jim Craig, too! Isn't that something? Wait...what? No! No way!" Of course, Alysha was born 10 years after the gold medal in Lake Placid.

I love knowing every rink from Orono to Amherst. I love seeing a mom and dad coming into TD Garden with a son and a daughter, all of them covered in black and gold from head to toe. I love that I'm blessed to watch a game I love, and have since I was young—and even get paid to do it!

I love that it's a sweater, not a jersey...that it's a dressing room, not a locker room...that it's a coach, not a manager...that it's a toque, not a hat...that guys pitch in and carry their own bags, not complaining about how tough travel is.

But most of all I love the players. I've dealt with professional athletes in every sport in Boston, and there are good people in all of them, but hockey players are just different. It probably has to do with leaving home at a young age and playing junior or club hockey. It might have something to do with not getting an inflated sense of self, like athletes in other sports do from time to time. It likely has to do with an advanced maturity level, even when some players turn professional at the age of 18, 19, or 20.

But just watch young hockey fans when Zdeno Chara fist-bumps them on his way to the ice, when David Pastrnak photo-bombs them at the glass during warmup, when Brad Marchand tosses a puck over the glass, or when Patrice Bergeron hands a fan his stick on the way to the dressing room. Hockey players know they have to fight for every fan, and they're willing to do that every single day.

I always wanted to write a book, and it just seems fitting that the Boston Bruins would be the subject for my first one. I also love learning about things behind the scenes, and my goal is to tell you stories you might not know about the team and the players you love. I'll tell you about how I came to know and love the sport, and I'll tell you about the team that means so much to you.

I hope you have as much fun reading this as I had writing it.

CHAPTER 1
HOW I GOT HERE

It's such a simple concept. In the broadcasting business you don't want to be the man who follows The Man. There is too much pressure, expectations are too high, and the probability for success is low. If you can work it out, you want to be the man who follows the man who followed The Man.

It pushes you. You say to yourself, "I can't suck. I've got to be good." I'm not sure I've succeeded, but I have survived.

I began my hockey broadcasting career because I initially failed as a college student. I had packed everything I owned in my 1964 Ford Galaxy and driven south to matriculate as a proud student at the University of Miami. As the oldest of five children growing up in a mobile home in rural Maine, the money for a campus visit was out of the question, so the first time I ever set eyes on Coral Gables, Florida, was when I arrived on campus. I thought I wanted a school that was big and warm and with a strong broadcast program. What I really wanted to do was follow Fred Lynn as the center fielder for the Red Sox, but that was somewhat (okay, very) unrealistic. The next step was for me to find a way I could make a living in the sports world, and I came to the conclusion that sports broadcasting was the way to go. I was one for three.

What I quickly realized was that there were more kids in my dorm than there were in my hometown (Bowdoin, Maine: current population 3,061, but in 1974 probably less than 2,000). My roommate, who I think I saw for a total of 15 minutes, was taking the family jet back home to Long Island for the weekend to pick up some more stuff. I was woefully overmatched.

I was basically on a full-boat academic scholarship, and I remember calling my father and making up a phony story about not having enough money to purchase the books I needed. He told me to not worry, that he would find a way to send me the money. It was then that I broke down and tearfully told him that I didn't want him to find the money for me; I wanted to come home. My father was always a man of few words, and he had only three for me at that time: "So come home."

Not only did I feel overwhelmed, I had also left my girlfriend (and future wife), Susan, back in Maine. We were high school sweethearts. We met when my friend and I were doing a 50-hour fundraising marathon on the local radio station to raise money for the high school scholarship fund. Susan worked at the local Dunkin Donuts, and she brought an urn of coffee to our remote site to help us stay awake. She certainly woke me up! The first girl I ever kissed, I married. I always joked that I was from Maine, so I thought I had to.

After a four-day career as a Hurricane, I drove back to Maine with my tail tucked between my legs, completely humiliated and wondering what my career path would be. I had been the commencement speaker at Mt. Ararat High School and was even voted by my classmates as most likely to succeed, and yet my college career lasted four days.

Obviously, it was too late in the academic year for me to enter college locally, so I returned to work, managing the sporting goods store in Brunswick (yes, it really was called The Good Sports) and broadcasting high school football on the local radio station. WKXA AM-FM was a "leaves are falling on Maine Street" small town radio station with a monster signal. The FM was 80,000 watts and could be heard over most of the coast of Maine.

The station had just been purchased by two couples from Minnesota and was under new management. They didn't really know me or that I had been doing play-by-play on the station since I was 15. My friend Bruce Biette and I had talked our way into part-time weekend jobs at the station, and slowly but surely worked our way onto the air. While I lettered in four sports in high school (soccer, cross country, basketball, and baseball), I never played football or hockey, two of the three sports that the WKXA broadcast in the community.

So at the high-pitched age of 15, I was the play-by-play announcer for the Brunswick High School Dragons football games, and Bruce was the color announcer. Later we talked the station into adding broadcasts of Bowdoin College football, as well. I broadcast football games through my senior year, and also did basketball games for a while. As a sophomore, I would play in the junior varsity game, then rush to shower and change and broadcast the varsity game.

After my short stint at the University of Miami, I returned to Brunswick and picked up where I had left off, broadcasting the high school and college football games. In late November, the new owners suddenly decided, at the last minute, to add Bowdoin College hockey to the lineup. They realized they were missing a play-by-play announcer and asked if I could do the games "until we can hire a grown-up."

My first hockey broadcast was in December 1974 at the Matthews Arena in Boston as Bowdoin College played Northeastern University. I had a lot of experience (relatively speaking, doing football and basketball games), but I had never broadcast a hockey game. Ever. I was working with a salty, crusty Maine legend by the name of Frank Gibbs. I was supposed to be his gopher. Carry the equipment, set it up, do color for Frank, and give him a break when he needed it.

4

But Frank had other ideas. He was fairly uncomfortable broadcasting hockey games and he wanted me to do more than the station owners had in mind. Suddenly I was sitting in a press box in Boston, broadcasting back to Brunswick and feeling like I was speaking a foreign language. And it was the most fun I had ever had broadcasting a game.

Doing hockey play-by-play was like verbal gymnastics. The challenge of keeping up with the speed of the players, talking at a rapid rate, and the excitement of the game itself was fun. I loved every minute, and suddenly was worried that my fill-in position was not going to last. Thankfully, it was apparently enough to convince the new owners they didn't need a grown-up, and I finished the season schedule. I had no idea, at the time, that I would ultimately graduate from Bowdoin College, as well.

Thankfully, my boss at The Good Sports, Rob Jarrett, was a Bowdoin alum and was understanding about giving me the time I needed to travel with the team, because suddenly I was the voice of the Bowdoin College Polar Bears for the next five years, learning the game from legendary coach Sid Watson. He was patient beyond words and knowledgeable about every aspect of the sport. There could be no better first tutor.

My first memories of Sid Watson were not as the Bowdoin hockey coach. I went to Brunswick High School with several of Sid's children: Nancy, John, and Susan. I knew Sid as John's father, and I had absolutely no idea that Sid was an athletic legend in his own right.

Sid was a running back at Northeastern University and actually averaged more than seven yards per carry for his college career. His 1951 Huskies team was undefeated, and he was captain of the team in 1954. I certainly didn't know that he still holds the Northeastern school record for points in a single season, or that he had also lettered in basketball and hockey. He was simply my friend's dad. I also didn't know that he played for the Pittsburgh Steelers from 1955 to 1957 and the Washington Redskins in 1958.

I ultimately learned that Sid was also a legendary figure in college hockey circles. The Division III Player of the Year Award was named the Sid Watson Award following his death in 2004. The arena at my alma mater is called the Sid Watson Arena. And one of the greatest honors of my professional life was when his wife, Henrietta, asked me to speak at his memorial service at Bowdoin.

Sid Watson, quite honestly, taught me the game. I had not been to many hockey games as a youngster. And the first Bowdoin game I ever saw, I broadcast. I mimicked the terminology and cadence of broadcasters like Bob Wilson, but I didn't really understand what I was watching. Sid took the time to talk to me, one-on-one, and teach me the nuances of the sport. I never had the feeling that he thought I was asking a stupid question. When I began broadcasting the games, I was driving to the away sites with my color announcer, Fred Harlow. Once I transferred to Bowdoin, and was a student there, Sid invited me to ride on the team bus with them. Then he told me to sit in the second seat, right behind him, and talked to me about the sport on many long bus rides. Even when he probably preferred reading a book, or taking a nap, he took the time to teach me the game. I will be forever grateful.

Just to complete the whole college story, after returning to Maine I enrolled at the University of Maine at Portland-Gorham (now the University of Southern Maine). My color man on the Bowdoin games was another Polar Bears alum, Fred Harlow, and he was convinced I needed to attend the college. I explained that they accepted about four transfer students a year, so Fred issued a bet. I would apply to Bowdoin, and if they accepted me I would attend. If they didn't, then Fred would pay the application fee. I became one of those four transfer students accepted, but then I had another problem.

In June 1975, after returning from the University of Miami, and working a couple of different jobs, Susan and I got married and both of us were working full time. I made an appointment with the Bowdoin director of student aid, Walter Moulton. I explained to him my bet with Fred, and expressed my appreciation at being admitted, but had to tell the truth — there was no way I could possibly afford to attend Bowdoin College. Mr. Moulton listened, looked me in the eye, and simply and quietly said, "Dale, we wouldn't have let you in if we weren't going to let you stay."

Between scholarships and grants, my total indebtedness for my Bowdoin education was less than $5,000. Susan and I were able to work my way through my final three years of college and earn my Bachelor's Degree in Psychology. But even as a student at Bowdoin, I knew I really wanted to be a play-by-play announcer in professional sports. That led to my second "heart to heart" talk at the college.

I met with the Dean of Students, a terrific woman named Alice Early. I explained that I was enrolled in a college without a broadcast department, and basically no class offerings leading me to my ultimate career goal. Alice said to me, "Dale, do you know what my major was at Harvard? Creative writing. Do you know how much creative writing I do here at Bowdoin? Almost none."

Then Dean Early started to question me. "Dale, what's the least offensive academic offering we have here at Bowdoin?" I answered, "Psychology." She said, "You are now a psychology major! But I want you to take everything this college has to offer. I want you to take archaeology classes, and anthropology, and English, and history. Get an education. Learn how to learn. You'll be fine after that." It might be the single best piece of advice I've ever received. I'm not sure where Alice Early is now, but I hope she knows how much she helped the kid from Maine who was trying to figure out his path in life.

I am forever indebted to Bowdoin College for the opportunity to earn a world-class education. Later in life, I was proud and happy to pay the complete tab for my son, Taylor, to also attend Bowdoin. He was a much better student than me. His name is on the wall in the Mathematics Department and he went on to earn his Ph.D. in statistics from Yale University. It all became possible because I lost a bet and was admitted to Bowdoin College.

In fall 1977, when I was a junior at Bowdoin, the Philadelphia Flyers placed an American Hockey League franchise in Portland called the Maine Mariners. At the time, it was the only professional franchise of any kind in my home state, and they started as a juggernaut, winning the Calder Cup championship in each of their first two seasons. Pete Peeters, who would go on to play almost 500 NHL regular-season games and was a First Team NHL All-Star for the Bruins in 1982–83, was part of a goaltending tandem with Rick St. Croix, who spent almost a decade as an NHL backup. Ken Linseman, "The Rat," who went on to score 125 goals and rack up 744 penalty minutes in 389 games over six seasons with the Bruins as part of an 860-game NHL career, actually contributed 17 goals in 38 games for the Mariners during the 1978–79 season.

The Mariners were dubbed "A Major Among the Minors" in an article by *Sports Illustrated*. I knew who they were, but was too busy with my college studies to pay much attention. I never attended a Mariners game, because I was trying to keep my head above water as a student at Bowdoin and working two jobs. I may have never attended a Mariners game, but it was hard to not know what they were doing. And if you were a hockey play-by-play announcer, it was hard to miss the voice that was coming out of my radio. It was a voice, and a career path, that was beckoning.

To the best of my knowledge, I was the only married student at Bowdoin. Susan and I lived in a mobile home about two miles from campus (it was all we could afford) and approximately 30 feet from her parents' home. Now *that* is pressure!

I was still able to be a student at the school and made friends despite the fact that I never lived on campus and never attended a college party. My friends got to know Susan, and I think they came to love her almost as much as I did. I worked two jobs (The Good Sports and WKXA Radio) and kept my grades at a respectable level. It was hard, but it was worth it.

When I graduated from Bowdoin in May 1979 I became the first person in my family to receive a college degree, and it was from an institution I thought I could only dream about. I started to think about the next step. I knew I didn't want to use my psychology degree but wanted to become a professional play-by-play announcer. I started to put together an audition tape, and scour the trades for positions at the lower levels of the hockey world. Then I received a call from Ed Anderson, the president of the Maine Mariners.

Ed had heard my college play-by-play work and the message he delivered was short and simple: the Mariners had a broadcaster who was too good to be there very long. I didn't really know Ed that well. Prior to working for the Mariners, he had worked for the *Portland Press Herald* and covered Bowdoin hockey from time to time. I certainly never considered contacting him because I knew all too well how talented their play-by-play announcer was. But, completely out of the blue, Ed Anderson was contacting *me*.

Ed wanted me to work with that announcer for the 1979–80 season and then replace him on play-by-play if things went as planned going forward. Remember what I said about not being the man who followed The Man? Well, I certainly was in no position, under the circumstances, to follow that advice and spent the most educational year of my life learning the world of hockey broadcasting from future Hall of Famer Mike "Doc" Emrick, who has been the national television voice of hockey for decades.

I certainly didn't know Mike before that. I don't think I had ever met him prior to going to work for the Mariners. But as someone who hoped to someday do what he was doing, I was an unabashed admirer of his work. Mike was given his nickname "Doc" because he earned his Ph.D. in Communications from Bowling Green University. He had worked for Port Huron in the International Hockey League, and was given the chance to take that next step to the AHL.

At times I worried about what Doc thought about me. I was fresh out of college, and while certainly no threat to his position, I never really knew if he was on board with Ed Anderson's plan. Doc was in the early stages of an eventual Hall of Fame career, which is still going strong. Thankfully, Doc was very generous, sharing his knowledge and love of the game with a kid right out of college. I was incredibly lucky.

The single greatest lesson I learned from Doc was preparation, and no one I've ever met, in any field, prepares as much or as well as he does. I learned about voluminous note-taking, memorization, and multi-colored game and score cards—the colors making it easier to find things more quickly and with no assistance.

Let me give you an example. This was the early stages of media relations in professional hockey, and there was no Internet to make life simple. So Doc took it upon himself to keep his own set of league statistics. He would find the box scores from every AHL game in the newspaper, and would update every single player in the league's statistics in real time. Every goal, every assist, every point, every penalty minute. Doc knew the stats for every player in the league, and knew every scoring streak before each team's media relations people did.

And Doc didn't just keep individual statistics, he also kept team statistics and knew every team's home and road records, shots for and against, power play and penalty kill. Doc was the first person I ever saw who kept every team's record (home and away) with *every* referee in the league. And Doc could tell you what each referee was most likely to call. It's hard to describe how much work this was, and how unerringly accurate Doc was. If Mariners coach Bob McCammon wanted to know how the penalty killing team was for the Hershey Bears when they were on the road, Doc could tell him within minutes. Can you imagine following that act? Well, actually I didn't. At least not right away.

I spent that entire year working with Doc and learning the broadcasting part of the business from one of the best who has ever done it. He taught me about game prep, cadence, emotion, pacing, and information. After that season, I felt that I had done *nothing* during my five years of doing college games. I was more ready than I had ever been to properly be a hockey play-by-play announcer. And then suddenly, I wasn't.

Ed Anderson had hired me to replace Mike Emrick, and then he changed his mind. Ed decided I would be more valuable to the Mariners if I worked in the front office. After he talked me into accepting his plan, the Mariners hired a guy named Hal Maas, from the IHL, to replace Doc. I'm not sure who was more miserable that season—Hal because he missed his old job in the IHL or me because I missed doing play-by-play. At the end of the 1980–81 season, Hal returned to his former position, and I stepped back into the broadcast booth.

Look, I am not going to lie. Working in the front office of the Maine Mariners was miserable. I was a play-by-play announcer, but I understood that at the minor league level, other things were expected. I was expected to help sell advertising and group and season tickets. I was also responsible to all of the team's publications. I designed and printed everything from schedules to season ticket brochures to advertising rate cards. I wrote and printed the game program, and later we became the first minor league team to add a yearbook, which I was also responsible for writing and printing.

But none of that mattered to me without the games to broadcast. I think Ed felt I could be more productive if I didn't have to travel for 40 road games a year, but he didn't understand my passion was broadcasting. I was willing to do all of those other duties, as long as I got to do the games.

The Mariners continued to be incredibly successful. They lost in the Calder Cup Finals one year, losing the deciding game in Portland to the Rochester Americans. The next year, they returned the favor, winning the deciding game in Rochester and returning the Calder Cup to Portland.

I can tell you, from experience, some of the best relationships you ever develop in professional hockey come as a result of 12-hour bus rides. And I relished the opportunity to get to know some legendary names from the American Hockey League. I got to know guys like Gordie Clark, Bob Froese, Ron Flockhart, and Dave Poulin. In fact, Dave and I joke that I signed him to his first professional contract. When Dave joined the Mariners on an Amateur Tryout Agreement after a season in Europe, he sat at my desk as I typed his contract and he signed it in front of me. Dave played 16 games for the Mariners before the Flyers made him a regular NHLer. He went on to score 205 goals in 724 NHL games, including 34 goals in 165 games for the Bruins. He won the Selke Trophy in 1987 as the league's best defensive forward and the King Clancy Trophy in 1993 as the player who best exemplifies leadership.

It's easier now, because I lived to tell the tale, but I remember the Mariners' regular bus driver and an issue he had. We'll call him "Billy," because there is no need to use first and last names here. As equipment manager Peter Henderson used to say, Billy seemed to have see-through eyelids. You see, Billy had a hard time keeping his eyes open.

We used to take turns standing on the steps right in front of the head coach's seat. Our job was to keep Billy awake—and all of us alive. I remember the bus bombing up an exit ramp around

Bangor about two hours into a late night postgame trip from Portland to Fredericton, New Brunswick. As Tom McVie bellowed, "Billy!" from the front seat, the bus came to a screeching halt at the top of the ramp.

Billy looked left and looked right, then simply said, "Shit!" Then he bombed back down the other side of the ramp, and returned to Route 95.

Did you know that in far northern Maine, the big green signs along Route 95 that say, WELCOME TO... don't have town names on them, but map coordinates? I remember spending the night in a ditch in T2-R6, Maine, when our 49-passenger bus slid off the highway in an ice storm. First we slid sideways down a small incline, and the bus was sitting across two lanes of traffic. The entire team climbed off the bus and pushed it back to a more normal position, facing down the highway. About 10 minutes later we just slid off the road and into the ditch. We were there until a sanding truck helped us out early the next morning.

In addition to the many players I got to know, I also had the chance to work with three outstanding coaches. I began my career working with Bob McCammon (a.k.a. "Cage" or "Cagey Mentor") until his successes at the AHL level led him to a promotion to the NHL. Late in my AHL career, I worked with John Paddock, who graduated at the last minute from the player ranks and led the Mariners to a Calder Cup championship. But most of my time in the AHL was learning at the feet of Tom McVie.

All of us learned, quickly, the meaning of McVie Standard Time, which meant very simply that if you're 10 minutes early, you're late. If Tommy said the bus left at 2:00 PM, it would leave at 2:00 PM if there were only three people on it.

Tommy was also a brilliant hockey mind. He'll tell you he's not very smart, but he's lying when he says it. He's a lot like my father. Neither guy had an impressive academic career, but both guys are as street smart as anyone I've ever met. Both men had an incredible ability to read people, and both had as much common sense as any person I've ever met. Both might give the impression of being cold and calculating, but both cared tremendously about people they are close to. I was blessed to call one my father and lucky to call one my friend. Both helped me get to where I am today. If Sid Watson at Bowdoin helped me earn my bachelor's degree in hockey and Doc helped me with my master's, I earned my hockey Ph.D. with Tom McVie.

McVie is a hockey lifer and a force of nature. He is 83 years old and has been in professional hockey for 63 years. He's been with the Bruins for more than a quarter of a century over two stints, including most recently more than 20 years as a scout.

He has the body of an incredibly fit man half his age, and never, ever misses an opportunity to work out like a mad man. With his basso profondo voice and deep-throated belly laugh, he doesn't so much enter a room as he invades it, leaving virtually everyone happier for the encounter.

Before he came to the Bruins, Tommy was in the Devils' organization, and he became the head coach of the Maine Mariners after I got there.

Other than my father, no other man has had a greater impact on my life and career. Anyone who has worked with Tommy, player or broadcaster, ends up quoting him and remembering the lessons he taught.

I found out about McVie Standard Time the hard way on two occasions, both in Baltimore.

15

After a game against the Baltimore Skipjacks, Tommy wrote on the whiteboard in the dressing room that he was moving the departure time of the bus up 15 minutes, from 6:30 AM to 6:15 AM. Unfortunately, I did not check the board after the game and came waltzing down from my room the next morning to see the bus pulling away from the hotel. I chased it down the street, and was actually surprised that Tommy had the driver stop and let me on. He then proceeded to blister me in front of the entire team.

After flying back to Portland, I dejectedly went to my desk to get some work done. An hour or so later, Tom came into my office and sat at the chair next to my desk. He said, simply and quietly, "D, if I can't trust you, who can I trust?" Lesson learned.

After another game in Baltimore, the team bus was scheduled to leave at 10:00 AM the next morning, heading for Hershey. The entire team was on the bus, with the exception of Tommy. Technically, I was the No. 2 in charge, and as the clock kept ticking toward the top of the hour, the players started teasing me. They wondered if I would have the courage to leave Tom McVie and take off. I didn't.

None of us knew it, but Tommy was on a phone call with the owner of the New Jersey Devils, Dr. John McMullan. At about 10:05, Tom jumped onto the bus and didn't say a word as it pulled away from the curb. Tommy walked to the back of the bus, and quietly handed $100 to player Larry Floyd. It was the amount of the fine for being late. Then he came back to the front of the bus and sat down across the aisle from me. After about 30 minutes, Tommy leaned across the aisle and said to me, "D, if I say the bus leaves at 10:00 AM then the f—g bus leaves at 10:00 AM!" He was mad at me for *not* leaving him in Baltimore.

Those stories pale in comparison to what Tom did in Winnipeg in 1979. The Winnipeg Jets had made the move from the World Hockey Association to the National Hockey League. This big news was made even bigger a couple of months into the season when it was announced that Bobby Hull was going to make a comeback and play again for the Winnipeg Jets. The date was set for December 15, 1979, and Winnipeg was ready to make it a gigantic event.

The Jets decided to celebrate by making it Tuxedo Night. That meant 15,000 fans, coaches, trainers, and everyone else would wear tuxedos. It was also Hall of Fame Night, honoring former Winnipeg players who were in the Hall of Fame. There were Hollywood-style spotlights in front of the building, swinging back and forth. *Hockey Night in Canada* did away with its normal regional telecast and brought the game from Winnipeg against the mighty Montreal Canadiens to hockey fans from coast to coast. The game time was altered slightly to benefit the audience from Newfoundland to British Columbia. Unfortunately, no one bothered to tell Bobby Hull.

Tommy's rule was simple: you have to be in the dressing room at least 90 minutes before faceoff, but Bobby missed the deadline. He arrived and began to take off his tie and begin to get dressed for the game, when McVie informed him he could not play. Tom McVie had just benched Bobby Hull on Bobby Hull Night.

When the players went out onto the ice for warmups, Tommy stayed in his office. Soon general manager John Ferguson, McVie's boss, came bursting into the office. *Where was Hull?* he asked. Tommy told him Hull would not be playing because he got to the arena late.

Ferguson exploded. He yelled at McVie, "Stop f—g around here! Where is Hull? You do know this is Bobby Hull Night, right?" He stormed out of the office, but came back in minutes later. Unfortunately, he also put his foot completely through McVie's hollow office door. Tommy described him as hopping around as he started in on his lifelong friend again.

"Do you know it's Tuxedo Night? Do you know it's Hall of Fame Night?"

Tommy, who has a bit of a temper himself, responded, "I don't care if I'm going in the Hall of Fame, the guy came in late!" Ferguson stormed back out the battered door.

He came back minutes later, and said quietly to McVie, "I'm going to ask you one more thing, then I'm going to leave you on your own, okay?" With his voice rising back to volcanic levels, Ferguson blasted, "Do you know he's one of the f—g owners of this team?!"

So what happened on Bobby Hull Night? The Winnipeg Jets played without Bobby Hull and beat the mighty Montreal Canadiens 6–2, outshooting them 46–18. Tommy remembers Ferguson interrupting his session with reporters and saying, "When we were growing up, I knew you had big balls. I just didn't think you carted them around in a wheelbarrow!"

It was that same John Ferguson who helped McVie get his first coaching job in the Bruins organization. Ferguson had worked with Bruins general manager Harry Sinden on the famous Canada Cup team that culminated in the historic Paul Henderson goal that gave Canada the come-from-behind series win against the Soviet Union in 1972.

Not long after that series, Ferguson told Sinden he needed to give McVie a job. After being assured that McVie was not quite as crazy as he had been during his earlier playing days, Sinden hired McVie to be the player/coach for the Dayton Gems, the Bruins' affiliate in the International Hockey League.

McVie was getting ready for his first training camp with the Gems when Sinden called and gave him another assignment. The Bruins had seven players who were coming off of injury and would be working out a week before the start of training camp. That group included Johnny Bucyk, Phil Esposito, and the incomparable Bobby Orr.

"I was a player/coach for Dayton," said McVie. "But I was no longer a very good player and probably a horse— coach! I couldn't do either. I was too old to be a good player, and not smart enough to be a good coach."

Coaches were not allowed to be on the ice with the players until training camp, and the Players' Association was just beginning to flex its muscle on rules like this. So Sinden figured out a way around those rules—Tom McVie would report to Fitchburg as a player, to work with the injured group. He stayed in the hotel with the players, and had a coaches' office, but he would be on the ice in full Bruins uniform.

"Harry wanted me to go work with these seven guys for a week before training camp. Remember, in those days, players didn't work as hard in the offseason as they do now, plus those guys were coming off injury. So I get to Fitchburg, and I'm in tremendous shape, because I was worried about my new job as player/coach for Dayton. I had no education and no trade, so I needed this hockey thing to keep going."

Tommy started working the players through drills he had learned during his days as a player, but he was leading them as a player himself in full uniform.

19

"I'm running Orr and Espo through these killer drills, and I'm thinking any minute now they're going to get together and tell me to f— right off. They never did, and seven days later when the real training camp opened, those seven guys looked like the Russian Red Army team!

"So I'm running the guys through these drills, and I'm skating them pretty hard. There's enough snow on the ice for a ski jump. Now, here comes No. 4 skating up to me, and I'm thinking I'm in trouble now. They've sent him to tell me off. Bobby quietly says, 'Coach, I've got brand new skates on, and my feet are just killing me. I don't want to say anything in front of the other guys, but can I go to the dressing room and change into my other skates?'"

As I watched McVie coach throughout the years, I noticed no player ever left the ice to go to the dressing room—at least not more than once. Tommy would be waiting for them when they returned to the ice, and tell them to take their gear off and go home for the day. He would simply say, "If the great Bobby Orr can check with me before leaving the ice, you can f—g check with me!"

As it turned out, McVie and Orr had another little something worked out, and it brought down the house every single time. You have to remember that while McVie was going to be the player/coach for the Dayton Gems, at Bruins training camp he was simply a player. McVie told me the team would practice in the morning, then have a black/white scrimmage in the afternoon. They would charge Bruins fans 50 cents and would have a standing-room-only crowd of more than 3,400 people every day. McVie says, to this day, they were some of the best hockey games he ever saw in his life. But McVie and Orr had something to help keep the fans entertained.

"Bobby would start that thing where he started behind his own net, and would come charging to the offensive end. He's going about a hundred miles an hour, like Orr would, and I would skate toward him, then back off to the front of the net, in front of the opposing goaltender. Bobby would wind up and shoot the puck straight into my gut, and I would fold up down on the ice. I would take the puck and put it into my glove, and, after a few minutes, the others players would help me to my feet. Bobby would clap me on my back, and I had another puck in my mouth that I would spit onto the ice, while the whole crowd went, 'Ohhh!' Terry O'Reilly was down on his hands and knees he was laughing so hard. He couldn't even breathe. He still says it was the funniest thing he's ever seen in the game!"

Tom McVie is like a Marine drill instructor: you might hate his guts while he's putting you through hell, but you come to learn he's trying to get the best out of you. Almost every guy who ever played for him thinks back fondly on the experience. You also end up quoting him forever.

Andy Brickley played for Tommy, and I work with Andy. We find ourselves quoting "McVie-isms" to each other all the time.

"Catch up hockey is losing hockey."

"If you think you're going someplace, you probably are."

"Can you believe they pay us to do this? Meal money and everything!"

"Every player who has ever played knows more than the coach. I know. I was one."

"Be someone your coaches and teammates can rely on."

You also learn that McVie cares about "his guys" like a father cares for his son. I remember a night in Halifax, Nova Scotia. The

Maine Mariners had just beaten the Nova Scotia Voyageurs in a crucial playoff game, and we were flying back to Portland the next morning. Like everyone else in the minor leagues, I had plenty of other duties besides simply calling the game. I went right back to my hotel room after the game to begin working on material that had to be turned in when we got back home.

I heard a knock on my hotel room door, and when I opened it, there was McVie (unfortunately wearing nothing but his trench coat), holding a paper plate. He knew I wasn't going to be able to get anything to eat after the game, so he had gone to a store that afternoon. He showed up at my door with a plate full of sandwiches and some chips. He simply said, "I was afraid you wouldn't eat anything."

There was another time when he was looking out for me. I worked for the Mariners, but my dirty little secret was that I had never played the game and couldn't skate. I asked the equipment manager for an old pair of skates (thanks, Wayne Schaab!), and I would sneak out into the darkened arena late in the afternoon and try to teach myself to skate. One day, I heard the doors behind the penalty boxes open, and it was McVie. He simply put a helmet and some gloves down on the dasher, and said, "I don't want you to hurt yourself." I didn't even know he was aware of my late afternoon efforts.

When the Bruins won the Stanley Cup in 2011, I was happy for a lot of people. There were many players, such as Patrice Bergeron, Shawn Thornton, and Zdeno Chara, who had put so much into winning that Cup. But I was also so happy for Tom McVie. The hockey lifer finally had his Stanley Cup ring, and the picture in Vancouver of Tommy holding the Cup over his head was the happiest I've ever seen him. He had always given the game of hockey everything he ever had. It was nice to see the game give something back to him.

Robert Hughes, the legendary high school basketball coach from Texas, was inducted into the Hall of Fame with the Class of 2017. Mac Engel, writing in the *Fort Worth Star-Telegram*, said of Hughes, "If you were respectful, if you cared, if you tried, you did what was asked, you always had a home in his gym. You had a mentor. You had a teacher. You had a coach. You had a secondary parent. And, eventually, you had a friend." Just change the word gym to rink and you have the perfect description of Tom McVie. Both longtime, legendary coaches are Hall of Fame worthy. One is in now. One should be.

After serving my apprenticeship for seven years with the Mariners in the American Hockey League, I finally had my opportunity to make the move up to the National Hockey League. The New Jersey Devils had allowed me to call several preseason games over the years, and I guess I never realized that they were, in effect, auditions.

I think the Devils had decided they were ready to move on from their original play-by-play announcer, Larry Hirsch. Larry was "energetic" to the point that after calling a Devils goal (and there weren't always a lot of them in those days) he would sometimes take off his headset and run up and down the aisle, high-fiving fans. The Devils were aware of my work with the Mariners, and maybe they felt that allowing me to call preseason games was a bit of a reward, but they came to the opinion that I might be the next guy in line.

When Devils team president Bob Butera decided he was ready to move on from Hirsch, I received a call. It was my time; I was offered the chance to jump to the National Hockey League.

23

But I've got to be honest; I almost said no to my big opportunity. My father-in-law, John, had just passed away after a valiant battle with cancer. My wife, Susan, wanted to be there for her mother, and I had a big decision to make. I could stay with the Mariners and never know if I would receive another chance at the NHL. Or I could take the Devils job and leave my wife and three-year-old son back in Maine. After much soul-searching and countless discussions, Susan and I decided I had to grab this chance. I followed Hirsch as the new radio voice of the Devils.

I was living in a hotel near the team's practice rink at South Mountain Arena in Totowa, New Jersey, and trying to slip home to see my wife and son as often as I could. The Devils were incredible and basically said I could fly home any time, on their tab, or my wife and son could fly to New Jersey any time, again with the Devils paying the way.

As gracious as they were and as accommodating as they tried to be, it was painful being away from my family. I would fly to Maine for a couple of days, and when my wife and son would drop me off at the airport, Taylor would begin sobbing uncontrollably. After a few of those airport runs, I finally had to tell my wife she couldn't bring him to the airport anymore. It was simply too hard.

I had been living in that hotel for a few months when I was contacted by the Conte family. Judge John Conte, his wife, Lucille, and their family had been the host family for the Devils' first-round draft picks for several years. They had an amazing home in Mahwah, New Jersey, and sent word to the Devils that they had a place for me to live if I wanted it. That was how I ended up living, for several months, across the hall from defenseman Craig Wolanin, the Devils' 1985 first-round pick who was already being

With my son, Taylor, in 1988, my first year as the voice of the New Jersey Devils.

hosted by the Contes. Judge Conte and his family became my second family, as they had for several Devils players before. They were just as accommodating to Susan and Taylor when they would visit New Jersey.

Oh, and a side story about my friend Judge Conte. Remember coach Jim Schoenfeld and the infamous "have another donut, you fat pig" playoff episode with referee Don Koharski in 1988? Remember that Schoenfeld was suspended by the NHL and Devils president Lou Lamoriello was unable to find NHL president John Ziegler to appeal the suspension? The Devils needed a court order to sidestep the league punishment to Schoenfeld, and it just so happened I knew a judge who was able to issue that order. So, I guess I was part of that scene with Devils off-ice officials in colored practice jerseys refereeing and calling the lines for a playoff game. I was not living with the Contes in my second season with the Devils, but they were still my second family. Devils president Lou Lamoriello felt that his team was being done wrong with no possibility of appeal. Lou never wanted to go the legal route, but felt his first obligation was to his team, his fans, and his players. So the call was made to The Judge, and a temporary restraining order was granted. The full-time NHL officials felt they had to strike, in support of Koharski, and the replacement officials were born. I knew all those guys. I worked the home games every night and knew them as official scorers, goal judges, and penalty box time keepers. But for that night they were NHL officials, even if some of them couldn't skate very well.

That second season with the Devils was exciting, with the team making an improbable first-time run to reach the Stanley Cup playoffs in 1988. The Devils had been 29–45–6 my first year and were just a few years removed from back-to-back 17-win seasons. In the final game of the 1988 regular season, they were playing on the road against the Chicago Blackhawks. They knew a tie or a loss kept them out of the playoffs and would put the Rangers in after their victory earlier in the day. Only a win would get that elusive first postseason berth. As Schoenfeld was contemplating when to pull his goalie in overtime (think about that type of desperation for a minute), John MacLean scored the game-winning goal on a rebound of a Joe Cirella shot at 2:21 for a 4–3 victory—the biggest goal in Devils history to that point.

I was working with Larry Brooks. Larry worked for the team in a public relations management position and, as a cost-cutting measure, also served as color announcer for the broadcasts. By the way, this is the same Larry Brooks who returned to his newspaper roots after leaving the Devils and had epic encounters with then-Rangers coach John Tortorella and player Dan Boyle, among others, over the years. He was every bit as ornery and acerbic as my color announcer, but at least he was on my side. I never keep tapes of things I've done, and almost never listen to tapes of my work, but I sincerely wish a tape existed of the call of that John MacLean goal.

It's hard to describe what this meant to the organization and their fans. The many years of frustration melted away on a single goal. I remember vividly the jubilation on the plane ride back to New Jersey. And I also remember seeing a sports story on TV when we returned with Rangers goaltender John Vanbiesbrouck, practically in tears, saying how everyone knew the Rangers would be a better playoff representative than the Devils. I've laughed about that VBK scene ever since.

Hockey fans who've grown up in the aftermath of the Devils winning the Stanley Cup three times in their history would have a tough time fathoming how big a deal it was for the Devils just to reach the playoffs. But Wayne Gretzky didn't call them a "Mickey

Mouse organization" just the season before to get a laugh. He was making a statement that too many people knew was all too true. The Devils *had been* Mickey Mouse—until that day in Chicago.

But there the Devils were, suddenly in the Stanley Cup playoffs. What happened next was mind-boggling. After beating the New York Islanders in six games and the Washington Capitals in seven, the Devils suddenly found themselves in the Wales Conference Final against the Boston Bruins. And they didn't just play the Bruins; they battled them all the way to Game 7. That series ended with a 6–2 loss at Boston Garden, but it gave the Devils hope that they could become the model franchise they would turn into less than half a decade later.

Meanwhile, while the Devils were battling for their playoff lives, I was planning for my career future.

During the playoffs series between the Devils and the Bruins, I received a call from Cary Pahigian, the general manager for WHDH radio in Boston and the man who ran the Maine Mariners flagship in Portland (WGAN radio), where I had worked for seven seasons. I am not going to lie; his call shocked me. I hadn't spoken to him in years. Cary had remembered my work in Portland and reached out to me. He wanted to know if I ever thought about broadcasting in the NFL.

I had not given a single thought to the possibility of broadcasting in the NFL. I had established myself in the hockey world, with nearly a decade of work, and I would not have even thought of applying for a job in football. But I discussed the idea with my wife, and we felt I had nothing to lose. I had a job in New Jersey for the foreseeable future, but the idea of moving back to New England was appealing to both of us, probably even more for Susan. When the Devils would head out on the road for a long trip, Susan and Taylor would hop in the car and drive back to Maine. Boston was absolutely enticing, but I just couldn't wrap my head around actually getting the job.

Cary asked if I would be interested in submitting a tape to become the new voice of the New England Patriots. I explained I didn't have a football tape to give him (the last football game I had done was at Bowdoin 10 years before) and assumed that would end the discussion. But he told me to give him what I had. I sent him a tape of a Devils game against the Edmonton Oilers from that season. The Devils had upset the Oilers in the game, so my excitement level and enthusiasm was very high. I felt that kind of audition tape gave me my best opportunity for what I still saw as a long shot.

While in Boston for the Devils' series against the Bruins, I interviewed with Cary. I wanted to prepare properly for the interview, but we were also in the middle of a surprising playoff run and the Devils were my primary focus. I went in and did my best, then WHDH surprisingly offered me the job.

The Sullivan family, who owned the Patriots, had approval rights for the announcer and they approved my hiring based on just that hockey play-by-play tape featuring Gretzky, Mark Messier, and the amazing Oilers. So in a way Gretzky, the guy who insulted the Devils a year earlier, helped *me* get a job in the NFL and move back to New England.

And who did I follow as the voice of the Patriots? Another future Hall of Famer, Curt Gowdy. Smart move, huh? I had once told the *Portland Press Herald* that I wanted to be Curt Gowdy, and now I was replacing him. It was another tough challenge, but my family and I were overjoyed to be heading closer to home.

The first NFL game I ever saw live in my life, I broadcast. I had never even attended a Patriots game as a fan. Thank god my color announcer was Patriots legend Gino Cappelletti. Gino was one of the most gracious and elegant men I have ever known. He could have buried me, with my obvious lack of knowledge, but it was just the opposite. He helped me, and taught me, and gave so much of his time and knowledge.

It is hard to explain how much I felt like a fish out of water. I really didn't know the sport, nor the players, at that point, and I always felt like I was playing catch-up. I had spent the previous 15 years broadcasting hockey games at the college, AHL, and NHL levels, and I felt confident I knew that sport and the participants inside and out. I worked hard at it, and Gino really helped, but I knew I wasn't as good at football as I had been at hockey. It was a good move, both from a personal and professional position, but I had left my first love, and missed it greatly. Oh, and the Patriots stunk the three years I broadcast their games, too.

Even after I replaced Gowdy, he became a mentor and a friend. The 1988 Summer Olympic Games were in Seoul, South Korea, and with most of the NBC announcer staff there, some longtime network legends were brought back for the month of September to call the NFL on NBC. You don't get more legendary than Curt Gowdy, who was the voice of the Red Sox for many years and called some great moments in just about every sport. He called Ted Williams' final-at-bat home run, Super Bowl III, the "Heidi Game," the "Immaculate Reception" game, and 24 NCAA men's basketball Final Fours. The Naismith Memorial Basketball Hall of Fame calls its media award the Curt Gowdy Award.

Gowdy was assigned to broadcast a Patriots–Green Bay Packers game during those 1988 Olympics. The Patriots were happy to offer Gowdy a ride home on the team charter, and you can imagine my excitement when they assigned Curt the seat next to me for the flight to Boston. We talked the entire ride home, and at one point he said, "I've been listening and you're doing great." It was one of the highlights of my entire career, as was his continuing friendship.

After three seasons calling the Pats games, the station lost the broadcast rights to WBZ Radio. At that exact time, the first all-sports radio station was preparing to start in Boston, trying to follow the astronomical success of WFAN in New York. I was offered a position as midday talk show host and made the jump. At about the time I was thinking of getting an audition tape ready and hoping to make a return to hockey, I was offered the chance at a whole new profession, and I jumped at it.

My new job at WEEI led to a stint as play-by-play announcer for Boston College football, where I followed the legendary Gil Santos (I am an idiot). I also took any other jobs that became available, including the Beanpot, Boston College basketball. You name it, I did it. When I speak to young people looking to get their start in the business, I always tell them that the more they can do, the better their chances in the broadcasting world. I loved doing play-by-play, so any chance I was given to sit in front of a microphone and broadcast a game, I accepted. I enjoyed being a talk show host, but doing games was always my first love.

My big break and chance to get back into play-by-play for an NHL team came in the form of the 1994 lockout.

The New York Rangers had won the Stanley Cup in June, ending a 54-year drought, and the NHL was riding high after its team in the media capital of the world won a championship. But the league, in its infinite wisdom, locked out the players for the start of the 1994–95 season because of several disputes involving a new collective bargaining agreement. The bottom line was that revenue in professional sports (remember Major League Baseball was on strike at the same time) was going through the roof, and owners and players everywhere were trying to figure out how to divvy up an astronomical amount of cash.

A lot of people were hurt by the work stoppage, but it ended up working to my advantage. When the lockout ended in December, the NHL reduced the regular-season schedule to 48 games. During the lockout, longtime radio voice Bob Wilson had decided he didn't miss the game as much as he expected and he decided he was ready to retire. When the shortened season started, somewhat unexpectedly, I was asked to follow another future Hall of Famer in the broadcast booth (I know, I know; I did it again!).

The games were on WEEI at the time, so management, in conjunction with the team, decided to ask me to take over. It was similar to when I got the job broadcasting Bowdoin College games. They needed someone with little advance notice, and I was given the opportunity.

Bob Wilson was and is a broadcasting legend. He was the voice I listened to when I first fell in love with Bruins hockey, and was probably that for many people around New England. To even think about following him as the radio voice of the Bruins was beyond my wildest dreams. And it was just the beginning.

Wilson, the Bruins' radio voice for nearly 30 years, was one of the greatest voices I ever heard. There are a few people who you hope narrate the movie of your life. Morgan Freeman and Bob Wilson are the two I think of first.

His deep baritone became synonymous with the Bruins, and it made fans feel warm to hear his voice coming through their radios. I could pick him up all the way in Maine and it was always appointment listening. When I got to meet and later become friends with Bob, I simply referred to him as "Voice," as in, "Hello, Voice."

WEEI management wanted me to do the Bruins games, but they also wanted me to continue to host my midday radio show. When the Bruins were at home, it was easy. I would broadcast my show from Charlestown, then head over to the Boston Garden at night. It was less than a 10-minute trip over. It was a long work day, but I loved every minute of it.

When the team was on the road, it was much more difficult. I would do my show from either my hotel room or the arena. I remember once doing my radio show from a telephone closet at The Pond in Anaheim...and other just as glamorous locations.

When I was tabbed to replace Bob for that 1994–95 season, it was such an honor. And I bet it was an adjustment for the listeners, as well. I always joked that, compared to Bob's baritone, my voice kind of sounded like Mickey Mouse—"Hi, Mr. Disney."

In the same way that I never intended to mimic the style of my original mentor, Mike Emrick, it was impossible for me to sound like Bob Wilson. Even without the obvious differences in vocal tone, Bob had established a style all his own.

Bob Wilson was born as Robert Henry Castellon on March 9, 1939, in Stoneham, Massachusetts. Bob worked at various radio stations in Boston, and ultimately succeeded Jim Laing as the voice of the Bruins in 1967. In 1969, the Bruins broadcast rights shifted from WHDH to WBZ and Bob was suddenly out of a job. It was eerily similar to my experiences when my Patriots broadcasting job disappeared after the rights shifted...also from WHDH to WBZ. Bob went to Midwest powerhouse KMOX and worked there until 1971.

That was the year that Fred Cusick moved from radio play-by-play to TV, and Wilson moved back to Boston to take over the radio call. It meant he was in place to call the team's Stanley Cup championship victory over the New York Rangers, and he was there for every season until 1995.

I've always described hockey play-by-play as verbal gymnastics, and that's even truer for radio than for television. It's the job of the radio announcer to bring the listener to the game, and describe every moment of the action. The TV announcer can often let the pictures tell the story, but the radio guy has no such luxury. He has to not only tell the listener who has the puck, and where it is, but he also has to take them on the same emotional trip they would experience if they were in the arena. No one was better than Bob Wilson.

Nate Greenberg, who was with the Bruins as the head of public relations, and later as the assistant to the president, from 1973 until his retirement in 2007, knew Bob better than most. He said there were a number of reasons that hockey fans everywhere were drawn to Wilson's descriptions.

"First of all, he had a voice that was second to none. His voice was deep and compelling. He grew up around here and had a deep love for the Bruins from birth. For so many years, radio was the way for Bruins fans to connect with their team, even more than TV was. And when the games were on WBZ, you could pick them up anywhere. They used to advertise 38 states and Canada. He had the voice, and the passion. And everyone listened to him."

Bob's descriptions were crisp and precise, and you were always positive of what was going on. It wasn't just names and locations; Bob understood that he knew the roster better than most of the listeners, and he was always helpful. Instead of saying, "Pass intercepted by Clarke," Bob would say, "Pass intercepted by Clarke of Philadelphia," and the listener immediately knew about the change of possession. This was something that legendary announcer Gene Hart of the Flyers once told me about, but that Wilson already knew. He understood that he saw more than the listener did, and he tried to help the listener along.

Vocal inflection was another of Wilson's strengths. I always tell younger announcers that they can't ever do the game in a monotone inflection. If the listener were at the game (and it's the job of the truly gifted announcer to bring them there) he or she should be going through emotional phases—excitement when something great was happening and disappointment when something bad was occurring. Wilson's inflections were enough to tell the listener what was going on even if he wasn't speaking English.

There wasn't anything Bob couldn't bring to life as a play-by-play announcer, but if he had a particular gift, it was calling hockey fights. This was the thing I attempted to borrow from him, although probably unsuccessfully. He was the voice of the "Big, Bad Bruins" and he relished that. His description of a battle between Stan Jonathan and Pierre Bouchard wasn't just play-by-play, it was performance art.

Bob Wilson never used nicknames, and he rarely used just last names. The play was usually, "Bobby Orr headmans the puck to Phil Esposito" because Bob knew that was the proper way to make the call. A goal was a "blast from Raymond Bourque" not "a blast from Bourque," because he never wanted the listener to be unsure. I know it seems self-evident, but you also never heard Bob refer to numbers. He had memorized the roster and only used names, because the person listening on the radio wasn't looking at a numerical roster either.

Bob Wilson also straddled the line perfectly between sounding like a local announcer and a national announcer. Network announcers have an audience split, more or less, down the middle. The local announcer has an audience that is likely 95 to 5 percent in favor of that team. Bob understood that, and clearly was more excited when the Bruins did something positive. But he also respected the game, and was always willing to give opposing players credit for a good play.

I simply cannot overstate how much it meant to me to have Bob Wilson as a friend and a mentor. In 1995, when I followed him as the radio voice of the Bruins (because no one could ever replace him), Bob would stop by the games and come up to the booth. He was always positive about the work I was doing, telling me I sounded great and was doing a great job. I never sensed any regrets from him about stepping away from the game when he did.

Bob Wilson was named recipient of the Foster Hewitt Memorial Award in 1987, enshrining him in the Hockey Hall of Fame. He was inducted into the Massachusetts Broadcasters Hall of Fame in 2007.

Bob succumbed to lung cancer on January 15, 2015, in Arlington, Massachusetts. He was 85 years old. But memories of his voice and his calls live on in Bruins history.

Following the 1994–95 season, the Bruins decided to split their television broadcast teams—they would use one play-by-play man and color analyst for home games and another duo for road games starting in 1995-96. General manager Harry Sinden called me into his office and said the team wanted me to take over one of those teams, but Harry made it clear that Fred Cusick, as the veteran, would have first choice. Harry also said, "But I'm pretty sure Fred will want the road games." As was usually the case, Harry was right. Fred chose to broadcast the road games on TV and I became the TV voice of the Bruins for home games, allowing me to keep my "day job" as midday host on WEEI. I then embarked on 11 seasons as the play-by-play television voice for Bruins home games.

Bob and Fred were the direct link between the team and their legion of fans. If you weren't able to attend the Bruins game in person, both of those guys made you feel as if you were in the arena. They brought the game to you, and they made you feel a part of the team. It was, and is, an honor to have followed in their footsteps.

CHAPTER 2
ANNOUNCERS

Let's be honest; no fan ever says, "I want to watch or listen to this game because so-and-so is calling the game."

The only reason anyone ever watches or listens to a game is because they can't be there in person. The reasons may be financial (tickets are *very* expensive these days), familial, or time-related, or the game may simply be on the road.

Having said that, there have been and continue to be some very talented people bringing Boston Bruins hockey to their fans through the television and radio.

In this chapter, I wanted to bring you the inside story of many of them.

Kathryn Tappen

If not for Kathryn Tappen, I would not have had the opportunity to return to Bruins telecasts on NESN. And when she was named the host of the Bruins games, she thought she was being demoted. Kathryn was an athlete in college, running track at Rutgers University. She is a native of Morristown, New Jersey, and her father's company had season tickets for the New Jersey Devils, but she used them only sporadically. At one time she dated a soccer goalie at Rutgers and was a huge Buffalo Sabres fan, so she used that as an excuse to go to the Meadowlands for games. But hockey was far down her list of preferred sports.

After starting at College Sports Television, she joined WJAR Television in Providence, Rhode Island, where she was both a weekend sports anchor and weekday sports reporter. She was hired by NESN and served a similar role as sports reporter and weekend anchor. It was clear to anyone who watched her work that she wasn't going to be at NESN very long. That's how talented she is and was already back then.

Let's fast-forward to 2007. Kathryn was serving as the beat reporter for the New England Patriots, and the team was a wagon. They were 16–0 in the regular season and then won their two playoff games before falling to the New York Giants in the Super Bowl.

Joel Feld was the executive vice president of programming for NESN, and he approached Kathryn on the Tuesday before the Bruins season began and told her he wanted her to host Boston Bruins hockey.

"I probably couldn't have named seven players on the team at that point," Kathryn told me. "But I had helped out on Mike Milbury's audition that summer, and my producer said, 'Oh you nailed that! You're going to be the Bruins host.' I truly didn't even know who Mike was at that time, and never gave it another thought. I knew football and was covering the Patriots, and that's what I wanted to do."

Kathryn worked her first season with Milbury, Barry Pederson, Gord Kluzak, and Rick Middleton as studio analysts. By her own admission, her hockey knowledge was minimal and she felt her job was simply to tee up her analysts, get to commercials on time, and stay out of the way. But she also said they helped the rookie out, and she did her part too.

"After that first season, and the Bruins didn't make the play-offs, I just took on a crash course on the National Hockey League. I was contacting general managers, player personnel guys, agents, and team presidents. I just wanted to learn the league, knowing I was going into Season Two as host."

Kathryn quickly came to love the people around the game, and appreciate the passion of hockey fans everywhere, but especially in New England. She continued to work and grow. She was working with many of the team's charitable endeavors, like the Wives' Charity Carnival, and NESN was developing ancillary programming as the team improved.

During the 2010–11 season, the team's fortunes changed, and so did Kathryn's career. Suddenly the team was one of the best in the NHL, and Kathryn was the television host for a team that ended up winning the Stanley Cup championship.

It was fortuitous for me that Kathryn's profile was growing just as WEEI Radio made a change in their programming lineup in March 2011. Suddenly I found myself with only part-time work and an uncertain future. I was trying to figure out what I was going to do to continue to make a living and put my children through college. I was watching the improbable Bruins run to a title from the outside, worrying about my options.

Late in the playoff run I got word through the grapevine that Kathryn was going to be leaving NESN. I reached out to her to make sure this was true before I did anything to pursue a job that she was so proficiently filling.

Her reply to me was immediate and emphatic: "Nothing has been announced, but I am leaving. You've got to call NESN and you've got to be the next host for the Bruins games!"

After Kathryn's suggestion and with her support I called NESN. Sean McGrail asked me to meet him in the NESN offices the next day. I sat across the table from him in his office, and he laid out the duties of Bruins host and what they expected the person in that job to do.

Sean then told me exactly what he planned to pay for the position and that concluded the easiest contract negotiation in television history. Sean asked if I wanted to take a couple of days to think about it and talk it over with my wife. I stood up, stuck out my hand, and said, "There's nothing to think about. I want to come home."

Sean McGrail and NESN literally saved my family at that moment. We had been discussing what our next professional move would be, where we might have to move, and what it would be like to interrupt my daughter's high school years by relocating. After I left Sean's office, I sat in my car and called my wife, Susan, and simply said, "We don't have to move. We can stay here and I have a job to pay our bills." I can't describe in simple words the relief and gratitude I felt. Everything fell into place for me, and ultimately I was given my old job back at WEEI as well.

Things have worked out unbelievably for Kathryn too. Talent usually leads to that. She moved on to the NHL Network and then to NBC. She has become one of the bright, young voices in sports television, working telecasts for the National Hockey League, Notre Dame football, *Football Night in America*, and the Olympic Games. I truly believe there is nothing in the medium she couldn't do, and do spectacularly. She is that talented.

The Bruins had the little matter of a Stanley Cup parade to enjoy after they defeated Vancouver, and before she could move on to bigger things, Kathryn had that parade to cover. She was originally scheduled to host the NESN coverage from the studios in Watertown, Massachusetts, along with Tom Caron. But she was upset about the assignment, pointing out that she had hosted the telecast when the team was at the bottom of the league and she wanted to be on the scene when their ultimate success was being celebrated. After speaking with McGrail, Kathryn's assignment was changed, and she did all the one-on-one interviews with the triumphant players at the TD Garden.

"I was so emotional at the Garden, *for* them. I had covered David Krejci when he was with the Providence Bruins. Patrice Bergeron was in Providence during the lockout year, and I had known him then. I was so proud of all of them, and I felt such a connection to those players and their success."

Kathryn pointed out the prominence of the Bruins in the New England market and the quality of the telecast on a nightly basis.

With my NESN predecessor, Kathryn Tappen.

"When I was at the NHL Network, we would have all the telecasts up on the monitors, and the regional sports networks who do the local telecasts. I would put the quality of the NESN telecast at the very top of what the league has to offer in terms of the broadcast quality and the people on the broadcast. NESN became the standard for regional sports networks for hockey, and I loved being a part of that."

Many people who have heard Mike Milbury's work and his acerbic nature may find this surprising, but Kathryn is quick to give Milbury much of the credit for her connection to hockey, and says it was his unflagging support of her work that led directly to her position with the NHL Network. That position led to her hiring at NBC Sports Network, and ultimately NBC to work at the Olympic Games in Sochi, Russia; Notre Dame football; and *Football Night in America*.

When you see the career successes of Kathryn Tappen, it's easy to forget it all began with a job she didn't want to do.

Barry Pederson

There may be nicer people in hockey than Barry Pederson, but I haven't met them. He was a skilled and talented player, and he's gone on to a strong career as a broadcaster, as well.

Barry was born in Big River, Saskatchewan, and grew up in British Columbia. He was selected in the first round, No. 18 overall, by the Bruins in 1980 from the Victoria Cougars of the WHL. He finished second to future Hall of Famer Dale Hawerchuk in Rookie of the Year voting in 1981–82 and still holds the Bruins records for goals (44) and points (92) by a rookie.

I understand that many younger Bruins never got the chance to see Barry play. I always wonder if younger Bruins players know who he is and what he did. After one telecast, Barry and I were interviewing Anders Bjork, a skilled offensive player out of Notre Dame University who was an NHL rookie in 2016–17. As we were talking to Bjork, who wears No. 10, I wondered if he even knew that Barry wore that same number for the Bruins, and with such distinction. Sometimes I think people only know Barry as the guy who brought the Bruins Cam Neely.

I'm not always great at figuring out which player reminds me of another player. My NESN analysts are great at that, so I leave it to them most of the time. But if I was pressed to pick a player who reminds me of Barry it might be Adam Oates, a playmaker from a decade later who's in the Hockey Hall of Fame. Although Barry had a better scoring touch than Oates, both were magicians with the puck on their sticks and were perfect partners for their All-Star linemates.

Barry followed his remarkable rookie season with a couple of other All-Star-caliber years. In 1982–83 he had 46 goals and 61 assists for 107 points, which was fifth in the NHL that season. He had magical chemistry with linemate Rick Middleton and the two combined for 65 points in just 17 playoff games before falling to the New York Islanders in the conference finals. Barry finished third in playoff goals and points, even though the team did not reach the Stanley Cup Final.

In 1983–84 Barry had 39 goals and 77 assists for 116 points, finishing sixth in league scoring and third in assists to Wayne Gretzky and Paul Coffey. He was an All-Star and played in the Canada Cup. He was on track to being one of the best players in the NHL.

Then Barry was shocked by a cancer scare. In summer 1984 he was diagnosed with a benign tumor in his shoulder. He was able to play 22 games in the 1984–85 season and had 12 points. But his medical issues required further surgery. Part of his shoulder muscle had to be removed and he missed the rest of the season.

When Barry was finally able to return to the team on a full-time basis, his shoulder issues had taken their toll. He had 29 goals and 76 points, but he wasn't able to produce the type of numbers he had been putting up pre-surgery. At the end of the 1985–86 season, general manager Harry Sinden engineered a trade sending Barry to the Vancouver Canucks for a first-round draft pick in 1987 (used to select Glen Wesley) and a rather unheralded right wing—Cam Neely. As he was being buried on the Canucks' bench at the time, Neely's Hall of Fame career was just a dream when he landed in Boston.

The irony is not lost on Barry that he is now friends and colleagues with the guy the Bruins got in what was at the time considered the "Barry Pederson trade."

"I really had mixed feelings about the Cam Neely trade. I was going home [to British Columbia], which was good, and I never thought of it in any other way than as a simple business deal. I had the cancer scare, and I wasn't playing as well as I would have liked at the time, so we kind of looked at it as a fresh start. Obviously, I couldn't control what was on the other side of the trade, and Cam came to Boston and took his career to the next level. It's not like Cam or I decided to make the trade, but we went on to become great friends."

Barry eventually came back to Boston.

"After finishing up my career in Pittsburgh, Hartford, and Boston—for a cup of coffee—it was time to retire. [My wife] Patty

47

is from here and I was able to get into the financial services industry here, so it made all the sense in the world to settle here. It's such a hockey mecca. It's a wonderful area to live—really one of the best in the country. Fans here are so passionate about sports. It becomes a natural place for guys to retire."

After a season doing color on the radio broadcasts on WBZ, Barry decided his day job in the financial industry wouldn't allow a full-time travel schedule and he gave up the position, which ultimately went to Andy Brickley. Barry, as well spoken and passionate about the game as anyone working, was given the chance to join NESN as one of several studio analysts.

When Barry started, the NESN studios were in the bowels of Fenway Park. Even when the network built a studio setup at TD Garden for home games, it was in an arena restaurant called Legends. The host of the telecast was Tom Caron, who now fills that same role so ably for the Boston Red Sox. They were forced to watch the games on a small monitor away from the actual action. It was not a good way to do the game, and not much fun for the guys working the telecast. Finally, NESN built a set in the arena bowl (just about after the NHL came back from the 2004-05 lockout), and that look has been imitated by many other telecasts around the NHL.

"The beauty of our set is it gives you a perfect feel for the game. The ninth floor, where the press box is, doesn't give you a true sense of the speed of the game. It slows the game down. We have far and away the best setup for what we do. It also brings the fans into the telecast with their energy and intensity. You think of the playoff games we've been blessed to work over the years, and you just can't replicate that feeling from another broadcast position."

Pederson has a true feel for the game, and the people who play it. He knows as well as anyone how difficult it is to play at the highest level, but I have never heard him compare the efforts of a current player to his performance. He is not one of those, "I would have done this..." kind of guys. He respects the game, and he respects those that play the game. Hockey has been a large part of his life since he was a youngster growing up in British Columbia, and he has never lost his enthusiasm for what we do. He also works as hard at his role as analyst as anyone in the game, despite the fact that he has a full-time job in the financial world as well.

I don't want to make it sound as if Barry likes everything about the game as played today. He has legitimate concerns for the direction the game has taken over the past several seasons.

"Hockey has to careful. As they've become so intent on creating more offense, they have to make sure they don't do away with the physicality and the intensity. The best game I ever saw was the 1–0, Game 7 win over Tampa Bay. There wasn't a single penalty, and the action was up and down all night long. The intensity, the respect on both sides—you just felt that no one deserved to lose."

Gord Kluzak

When I made the move from Bruins radio to television, my first color analyst was Gord Kluzak. He was as green as grass, but so smart and so willing to learn, it just didn't take long for him to become a superb broadcaster.

Gord was a former No. 1 overall pick in the NHL draft, and his talent was beyond question. He had size and skill and could beat you with either skill or truculence. Many younger Bruins fans only know Gord as a broadcaster, but let me tell you—he was one heck of a player, and had his career not ended early because of injuries, he and Ray Bourque might've made one of the greatest defense pairs in the NHL on Boston's back end. I'm not going to say he was as good as Ray Bourque—there are not a lot of those—but he was really good.

Gord started out fine. He was voted the most outstanding defenseman at the 1982 World Junior Championships and he starred for two years of junior hockey with the Billings Bighorns. Gord's play convinced Bruins general manager Harry Sinden to take him No. 1 overall in the 1982 NHL draft instead of Brian Bellows. Gord had missed half the season in 1981–82 because of a knee injury but he seemed no worse for wear as an NHL rookie, skating in 70 games for the 1982–83 Bruins without ever going to the minors.

He played 80 games and had 10 goals and 27 assists in 1983–84. He was solid as a rock at 6'4" and he could hit, shoot, fight; he had it all. But I was memorably at the last exhibition game of the 1984 preseason in Portland, Maine, working for the New Jersey Devils when everything went crashing down. Dave Lewis, who would later go on to be a forgettable Bruins head coach in 2006–07, was a Devils defenseman and he hit Gord low at the blue line. Gord suffered a torn ACL, MCL, and medial meniscus. He missed the entire 1984–85 season and was never the same, in and out of the lineup.

Gord had 11 knee surgeries in his four NHL seasons, and this was the late '80s and early '90s. Surgeries weren't as advanced as they are now. He played his 299th and last game in November 1990.

Gord took some time away from hockey. He'd been taking business courses at Salem State while he was still an active player, and after retirement he graduated from Harvard Business School with highest honors. What a way to make good after being dealt such a severe blow as an athlete. It had to be tough for Gord to think about what could've been.

Fortunately for me, Gord came back to the game and joined me in the booth, and later on in the studio. He's an astute hockey mind and I could sense that once he started doing games again and connected with the team and the sport, he realized how much he missed it. You could see Gord's emotion as he reconnected to the game he loved so much, but had been taken from him far too soon. He had some emotional scars to heal.

I'll never forget one of our first games, in San Jose in October 1995. We set up to do our standup for the game open and we looked comical standing next to each other. Like I said, he's 6'4"; I'm, well, not 6'4". I had to stand on one of those big, heavy camera cases so I didn't look like an eight-year-old. From then on any time Gord and I were on camera together, we did it sitting down so it didn't look absurd.

I had done thousands of hockey games and he had done none when we started, but it didn't matter. It ended up being fine just because our relationship was good. He's such a smart guy; it didn't take him long to learn when to jump in and when to stay out. That can be the toughest adjustment for a guy going from playing to analyzing. But he's so intelligent. He was pretty good at it almost from the jump.

Gord also seemed to enjoy his return to the game of hockey. It had simply been too painful for him to be around the game, and as a result, he retreated. Gord worked on his MBA from Harvard and his career with Goldman Sachs, but he seemed to welcome a chance to return as well.

"I have so enjoyed working with you from the very beginning," Gord told me. "I really appreciated your support those first few months in 1995 when you were patiently, perhaps nervously, waiting for me to say 'something, anything!' You are a consummate professional; so prepared, dedicated, articulate and entertaining."

While I sincerely appreciated Gord kind words, I also loved working with him and bringing out his innate sense of humor.

Once Gord and I were discussing what it's like to get traded. I knew from his brief career in the NHL that he had never been traded. Gord remembered that he had been traded when he was 12 years old. That's what it's like being a hockey player in Canada. I joked, "What did they get for you? A bicycle and a wagon?"

Our rapport grew and there were challenges. We had to call games during the 1996–97 season, when the Bruins went 26–47–9, dead last in the NHL standings (a horrible showing that would earn them the right to draft Joe Thornton No. 1 overall in the 1997 NHL draft).

Gord also gave me a once-in-a-lifetime opportunity. When I was a student at Bowdoin College, I majored in psychology and minored in archaeology. I liked to joke that I knew more about the Acropolis than any sports announcer on the planet. Thanks to Gord, I got a chance to finally see it.

Gord and his beautiful wife, Tania, were married in Athens in August 2004. Ray Bourque, Cleon Daskalakis, and I were among those who made the trip from Massachusetts to be part of the festivities. I took advantage of the opportunity to spend a week in Greece and traveled extensively, finally seeing the archaeological sites I had only known through my college studies. The wedding was certainly the highlight, but the chance to tour Delphi, the

Acropolis, and, specifically, the Parthenon were experiences I'll never forget. And the wedding reception, at an outdoor restaurant at the base of the Acropolis, was magical for me...and for the Kluzak's, as well.

While there wasn't a lot to talk about on the ice, we found ways to make the games entertaining. They pay you the same, win or lose, so you owe your employers and the fans the same effort. You have to keep the fans involved and the advertisers happy. We both loved the game, and we found ways to laugh, even when the hockey wasn't always the best. I remember a helmet being knocked off a player on a big center-ice hit, and our director cutting to a shot of the helmet, spinning near the blue. I wondered to Gord, on the air, if we should check to see if the head was still in it.

One thing Gord and I often debated on the air was fighting. I was for it; he was against it, especially the staged kind where two goliaths who skate just a couple shifts a night stare each other down, drop the gloves simultaneously with the drop of the puck, and then brawl. Fans agreed with me more than Gord—after all, these are fans of the Big, Bad Bruins. But that didn't bother him much, and of course he knew firsthand what he was talking about. He had played in the junior ranks when bench-clearing brawls were a regular occurrence. He once fought Detroit brawler Bob Probert (a lengthy bout during which he held his own—the YouTube video proves it). Being on the wrong end of some knuckles in the NHL could change one's perspective on fighting.

I remember calling a goaltender fight between Byron Dafoe and Olaf Kolzig. Okay, even Byron told me we were overstating things by calling it a "fight". He said it was more of a "dance." But I was amused by the sight of two best friends (Dafoe had been the best man at Kolzig's wedding the previous summer) squaring off and attempting to fight with each other. This was a full-fledged line brawl, and everyone on the ice was squared off. Gord, with that experience factor, was more worried that someone would fall over a piece of fallen equipment and get hurt in that manner, not necessarily in the fight.

Gord eventually cut back on his schedule and became exclusively a studio analyst. In our years in the studio on the pre- and post-game shows and between periods, Gord continued to prove he was an astute hockey mind. His particular expertise is looking at video and breaking it down. He breaks it down as well as anyone I've ever seen. When we're watching one thing, he's pointing out something behind the play, a failure to back-check or something else that made the play happen.

In that way, Gord probably would've made a great coach. But in the years immediately after his playing days it was probably too painful for him to be around the game. In the years since, he's been so successful in his non-hockey life he couldn't afford the pay cut to join the coaching ranks.

Gord made the decision before the 2017–18 season to step away from analyzing games. I'll miss him, but we'll always have all those memories we shared from the start of his broadcasting career through now.

Billy Jaffe

Billy Jaffe broke the mold for Bruins broadcasters. While hosts like me and Kathryn Tappen never played the game, analysts are usually ex-players who played for the Bruins. Billy is the first analyst I can think of who didn't play for the team, but there is a reason he got the job. He's just that damn good.

Billy, a Chicago native, played college hockey for two years at the University of Michigan for the venerable Red Berenson. He went on to officiate in the CCHA for four seasons (and to this day, defends officials over the protests of Barry Pederson and me). He tried out for the Muskegon Fury of the Colonial Hockey League with Bruce Boudreau, who would soon embark on a lengthy career as a successful NHL coach, behind the bench. After a few long bus rides, and thinking of the $274.00 weekly pay rate, Billy decided to use his Michigan education in another way.

In his own words, he "fell into" broadcasting for the Chicago Blackhawks radio network in 1997–98, doing pre- and post-game analysis and a weekly coaches show. That same season he was given the chance to do two games on television, and his career began to roll. In 1999 the newly born Atlanta Thrashers offered Billy an opportunity to make the move into a full-time roll. The call from Atlanta came in September of that season, but it was just a precursor to how his career would be defined.

"Every job I've ever gotten, it's come at the last minute," Jaffe said. "In Atlanta I completed my deal in early October and the season started about three or four days later. The same thing happened when I got a deal to work for the New York Islanders. I reached agreement while vacationing on the beaches of Spain, and left for training camp the day after I got home."

Billy is cognizant of the fact that he breaks a trend for Bruins analysts, but he tries to place some of that on luck. He had worked with Eric Haugen at NHL Network, and when Haugen went to work at NESN in 2011, he recommended Jaffe as an analyst.

"From 2008 to 2011, I had done a lot of work for the NHL Network. That gave me some national recognition, but the in at NESN was through Eric. The lucky part is that [Mike] Milbury was leaving at the same time Kathryn Tappen was leaving. That left an opening for you as host and for me as an analyst."

Billy loves to talk hockey. Okay; he just loves to talk, period. But he acknowledges that talking hockey in Boston is different than other places he has worked. He understands full well that the hockey fan of New England doesn't need to have things explained at the same level the fan of Atlanta did.

With the great Bobby Orr and Billy Jaffe in the booth at TD Garden.

"Sometimes the fan in Atlanta didn't know a blue line from a clothes line. They might not know if the puck is puffed or stuffed. In Boston, you don't have to worry about offending the hard-core hockey fan. You kind of assume that most of them already are real fans. Fans here know the game. My job is to point out more the subtle nuances of the game."

He also says the biggest adjustment he had to make was moving from the Thrashers to the New York Islanders. That was the first time he dealt with fans who knew something about the game, given the spectacular successes of the Islanders franchise.

"Coming to Boston, I assumed that the knowledge base was already there, but I also assumed that the Bruins fan was just that much more passionate."

The Islanders moved on from Billy, and while many feel it was because of his direct and frank way of analyzing, he says he doesn't really know to this day what happened.

"I was honest. I was fair. But they never held a meeting with me, and they never told me why they were making a change. I was told the classic, 'We're going in a different direction. We're going to make a change.' They just never told me why."

In Boston, the Bruins own 20 percent of NESN and the Red Sox own the other 80 percent. That leads to the assumption by many that the telecast becomes the "house organ" and that the broadcasters are instructed to go easy on the locals. When I mentioned to Billy that I've never been told how to approach the telecasts, and never been told to "go easy," he agreed completely.

"Not only have I never been spoken to about the telecasts, I've never been spoken to at all. If they're saying something behind our backs, I haven't been told about it. I've never been told by

NESN, 'Oh, you can't say that.' I'm at practice all the time. I'm at the rink. There is ample opportunity if anyone has any problem with anything we say, and no one ever has. Ever." Billy says he's had two examples of players who spoke to him critically about something he said, but never while working at NESN for the Bruins telecasts.

"I'm sure there's been a player or two who hasn't loved what I've said, because they're human. I'm at 80 percent of the Bruins practices. My philosophy is that if they don't like what I've said, they should have the opportunity to tell me. I actually love that. Talk with me, tell me what's bothering you. Tell me I'm wrong. Tell me why I'm wrong. Teach me."

Billy is my "insider." He talks to everyone, and he has better connections than almost anyone in the game, at the professional, college, and junior levels. He doesn't consider himself a "scoop breaker," although he does seem to get more than his fair share. Rather than talk about an injury a player has, he prefers to tell you how that injury impacts his team. Every single day he talks to people around the NHL—from a goalie coach for a Western Conference team to a player for an Eastern Conference team to an assistant general manager.

But Billy also realizes that the other analysts—former Bruins players—have an element he doesn't.

"Those guys have earned the reputation they have around here. They've been great players, at the highest levels of the game, and Bruins fans know and love them. I will never have that. It probably gives me a chip on my shoulder that I've got to be that much more educated and that much more prepared. I wasn't a pro. I wasn't a Bruin, and there is equity in that."

Andy Brickley

Andy Brickley is one of us. He grew up in Melrose, Massachusetts, and always dreamed of putting on the Bruins sweater.

"I was 8 and 10 when they won the Cups in 1970 and 1972," Andy recalls. "At that time, with Bobby Orr and the Big Bad Bruins, and what the hockey culture was like, everyone wanted to play the game. The MDC rinks were going up everywhere, and if you didn't play hockey then you weren't an athlete. Every day in my driveway I dreamed of being Orr, Esposito, Hodge, Cashman, Sanderson—all of those guys."

Andy was a little different than other youngsters with a dream. He always said when it was baseball season, he dreamed of being a member of the Red Sox; when it was hockey season, he dreamed of being a member of the Bruins. The difference between him and some of his friends is that he might have been able to do either one.

Andy attended the University of New Hampshire because he said he would have missed hockey. He was probably a better baseball player (first baseman) than he was hockey player at that point in his life, but UNH gave him a chance to do both. He wanted to stay in the Northeast because he felt that's where the best college hockey was being played, and he wanted to prove the naysayers, who said he wasn't good enough to play Division I hockey, wrong. He did.

Andy jokes (only half-heartedly) that when his uncle called to tell him he had been drafted, he thought it was to go into the Army. In fact, he was selected No. 210 overall by the Philadelphia Flyers in 1980, the last pick in the draft. That meant that when Andy was finished at UNH he was going to turn pro with the Maine Mariners of the American Hockey League.

I was there, broadcasting the games. To this day, I don't refer to Andy as "Brick" like everyone else does. I call him "Whip" because Bob Froese, who was in charge of inventing nicknames for everyone with the Mariners, decided that Andy looked like famous Canadian professional wrestler "Whipper Billy" Watson. Everyone on the Mariners called him "Whip," and most of us still do.

It was clear very early on that Andy thought the game better than anyone else playing at that level. As he told me, he had to.

"I wasn't the fastest guy and I wasn't the most skilled guy, so I felt I had to be the smartest guy. Sometimes it was frustrating, because I wasn't always sure that other teammates were thinking the game along with me. But I learned very quickly that, at the pro level, that frustration was unacceptable. And I had teammates who made that very clear. You can't go up to a 10-year vet when you're a rookie and say that. Even if you're right, you're wrong. I couldn't tell you the first thing about physics, but I could tell you about the physics of hockey," Andy laughed.

Andy had 83 points (29 goals, 54 assists) in his first pro season with the Maine Mariners in 76 games. He even earned a three-game cup of coffee in the NHL with the Flyers. I don't want to make it sound like everything was great all the time. I think Andy would admit he was a bit of a handful back then (and only slightly less of a handful now). He was outspoken and blunt, but he loved the game, and only wanted the best from himself, his teammates, and his team. I don't care what level you play at; if you are a point-per-game player, you've got skills, and Andy had incredible skills.

Andy bounced around after his first season in Maine but returned to the Mariners in the 1985–86 season. In 60 games, he had 60 points (26 goals, 34 assists). Andy and I continued the parallel paths of our careers, and we both moved from the Mariners to the New Jersey Devils the next season. And Andy spent the whole year in the NHL, picking up 23 points (11 goals, 12 assists) in 51 games.

Among my duties with the Devils was the position of traveling secretary, meaning I was responsible for things like airplane boarding passes (this was the days before full-time charter flights), buses, and game tickets. When the Devils played in Washington, I always arranged tickets for Andy's girlfriend, Diane, who worked in the hotel industry in that area. She was always so appreciative, and would bring me something like a small cake from the hotel when she arrived at the arena. She went on to become Andy's wife.

We were both there when the Devils made the playoffs for the first time ever, in 1988. They got an incredible boost from goaltender Sean Burke after the Olympics and lost to the Bruins in seven games in the Eastern Conference finals. We were both influenced, to an incredible degree, by Tom McVie, who coached with the Mariners and later the Devils.

After that playoff year, the Devils had a decision to make. They wanted to keep Jim Korn, Perry Anderson, David Maley, and Andy, but they had to expose someone to waivers. Behind the scenes, they wanted to keep Andy, but general manager Lou Lamoriello took a calculated risk that he would pass through waivers. Lamoriello didn't know that Brickley had an advocate in Boston.

John Cunniff was a South Boston native who played collegiately at Boston College and professionally as well in the WHA. He joined Terry O'Reilly's Bruins coaching staff in 1987–88, but

61

he had also been instrumental in Andy's career from the time Andy was 17 years old. When the Devils exposed Brickley to waivers, Cunniff urged the Bruins to pick him up.

Brick played 177 games for the Bruins, his hometown team. He had 113 points (37 goals, 76 assists) and 40 points in 43 games in 1989–90 for a Bruins team that went to the Stanley Cup Final. That season injuries began to catch up to Andy. His only appearance in that spring's playoff run was two games in the Final, and he wasn't able to do much.

Andy left the Bruins in 1992 and played briefly for Winnipeg, as well as making different stops in the American Hockey League and International Hockey League. With the Dallas/Utah Grizzlies of the IHL he won back-to-back championships.

About to turn 39 years old, Andy returned to Boston after his season in Salt Lake City, expecting to train and continue his professional career. WBZ Radio called Andy because there was an opening doing the color analysis for Bob Neumeier. This was the job that Barry Pederson had held, but was forced to give up. Andy was asked to audition for the job, which he told me he had no interest in accepting. But he was a father to a young daughter, and his wife, Diane, pointed out that he was not going to be able to play forever. He went to the audition and was offered the job before he left the building.

His body was, by his own admission, beat up. He had undergone 10 major operations over the course of his 14-year professional career, including a back operation the previous January.

"Here was an opportunity to start a new career, in hockey with the Bruins, and a chance to continue to make my living around the game I had grown up loving. It also gave me a chance to be home, and be a dad, so that kind of made up my mind for me," Andy reflected.

After one season on radio, Andy moved to the television side with Channel 38 and NESN. He briefly had his dream post-playing job taken away long before he ever expected.

"I did what a great percentage of the workforce would love to do. I told my bosses I didn't appreciate them. They thanked me for that opinion, and wished me luck in my next endeavor."

Soon Andy was given an opportunity to return to the Bruins, and he thanks the fans for that. After he was fired, NESN hired Phil Esposito and Gerry Cheevers to split the 41 telecasts the network was splitting with WSBK TV.

"Those guys are wonderful guys. Great to have a beer with and talk hockey with, great to reminisce with, and great senses of humor. Those guys were my idols, and great guys, but the fans kept asking, 'Where's Brick? We want Brick. Bring back Brick.' That was big. It made my bosses reconsider. I had to eat crow, and let them know that I really wanted to keep doing this. And I thought I was pretty good at it. We found some common ground, and they gave me another chance."

Andy has done both TV and radio, but he says doing TV is much more fun. As he puts it, radio is mono and TV is stereo. And he knows that doing hockey on TV in Boston is the best of all.

"The beauty of hockey in this town is that if you go out and give it your all, you're going to be accepted, no matter what the results are in terms on wins and losses. If the effort is there, and there is nothing phony about it, you're always going to be okay in this town."

Andy's hockey hero from growing up here might surprise people. Everyone, including me, automatically says Bobby Orr, and Andy speaks reverently of Orr as well. But for him, right up there with Orr is Derek Sanderson.

"When Derek retired [from the color analyst position], I was the guy who followed him, the next guy in line. I have a personal connection with him. But I just loved his swashbuckler attitude and the cockiness. I just loved Derek's personality, and he was a great player.

"The greatest player was Bobby, but the best guy I ever played with was Ray Bourque. Patrice Bergeron is pretty similar—how humble they are, how giving they are, always thinking of others first, very family based. When the best player on your team has that work ethic and that value system, how do you not fall in line?"

Jack Edwards

Trust me when I say I know the pressure that goes with calling play-by-play for the Bruins. There is always the knowledge that you are following in the footsteps of legends. Bob Wilson and Fred Cusick were as good as anyone who has ever called a game, so Bruins fans are used to hearing the best, and you never want to be felt wanting.

Jack Edwards took a unique path to his present position as TV play-by-play voice of the Bruins. He began as a sports announcer on local TV in Boston at a time when that position meant more than it does today. When you did sports on TV back in Jack's time, you had five full minutes, a lifetime by today's standards. And Jack knew things were pretty good, from a sports perspective too.

"I was in Boston during a golden age in local sports history. Certainly not the golden age that we've experienced since the turn of the century, but it was pretty good. The Red Sox came within a strike of a World Series championship. The Bruins got to two Stanley Cup Finals but had the misfortune of running into the big Edmonton machine. The Celtics won the championship three times. And the Patriots even made it to the Super Bowl, although they got smoked by the Bears. We even had Marvin Hagler as the undisputed middleweight champion of the world."

Jack used that experience to earn an opportunity to move to the giant machine known as ESPN. But Jack told me it was a case of being careful what you wish for.

"Instead of going from a situation where your sports knowledge was 10 yards wide and a mile deep, I went to a situation where it had to be a mile wide and an inch deep," Jack recalled. "It wasn't the thing that made me happiest. Then when ESPN decided they didn't care about hockey anymore, I really wanted to leave. But I also figured I wouldn't have a chance at the Bruins job until Fred Cusick became an old man, and I was just about right. I did a year for HDNet, then I was given a chance at Dave Shea's job to do play-by-play for the Bruins. Then I was really fortunate that you weren't able to take the full-time gig. Everything sort of fell into place."

Jack was talking about the meeting I had when NESN wanted to go with a single play-by-play announcer, and they wanted me to take the job. As I described, I didn't feel I could accept in good conscience, and Jack was offered the position. I had given up my dream job, with the team I always wanted to work for, but Jack was given the opportunity of a lifetime for him, too.

If I had to try and describe Jack's style of play-by-play, I would probably say excited and emotional. He is a hockey fan, through and through, and as a native New Englander, a Bruins fan to his core. That means from time to time he might go over the top—check that. He *absolutely* goes over the top, and he even knows it.

"I usually get a little feeling as I do it like, 'Wow, that was really over the top!' I have a sense for it, and if I could stop myself from doing it proactively I would, but...sometimes I wish I had a filter in place, and sometimes I'm glad that I don't."

As is always the case with local announcers, Bruins fans are far more accepting of Jack's emotions than fans of the opposing teams. He has angered fans, and even team personnel, of the opposition, but feels it kind of goes with the territory.

Just as I do, Jack takes great pride in the overall product of Boston Bruins hockey on NESN. He and I are in complete agreement with Kathryn Tappen that the local product is on a par with any in the National Hockey League.

"I'm really, really proud of it, and I'm proud that we're independent. I'm proud that we're not part of a national package that says, 'This is your format. This is your style.' I honestly think any objective eye would be challenged to find more substance and more real learning to be had. I honestly think part of that is your role. You've done NHL play-by-play for a number of years, but you also have an extensive background in sports talk radio and interviewing. I listen to you talk to Bill Belichick every Monday, and I think, 'Is this the same guy who stands at the podium each week and gives six-word answers?' You are a unique person to be in that pivot position to go from the play-by-play to the intermission or the postgame. If you compare our intermission numbers, we hold more of our audience than almost any other telecast in the league."

Jack had the opportunity that I never had—he was the play-by-play voice for a Stanley Cup championship team. He has also had the chance to call some of the biggest Bruins games in recent memory. But when I talked to him about what that biggest game might be, he surprised me. I might have guessed the Game 7 playoff win over Toronto in 2013, coming back from three goals down in the third period. Or I might have guessed the Game 7 overtime playoff victory over the Montreal Canadiens in 2011. But Jack hit me with another that made a lot of sense.

"The three-goal comeback against Toronto was incredible, but the game for me was Game 6 against Montreal in 2008. A lot of preseason prognostications had the Bruins not only being in the lottery, but had them as candidates for the first overall pick. They get into the playoffs on like the third to last night and they end up going against Montreal, who is a prohibitive favorite. They go down two games to none right away. They find their way back into the series. In the third period of Game 6, you could actually feel Boston becoming a hockey town again."

The Bruins were down three games to two heading into that game but staved off elimination. The Bruins trailed by one goal twice before taking their first lead late in the third period. The Canadiens tied it up but then Marco Sturm scored with 2:37 remaining in regulation. The Bruins hung on to win and force Game 7, which they lost 5–0. But Boston hockey was re-energized.

"You could feel the passion of the fans who had never left the Bruins, but they had been skeptical for a long time. From Game 6 of that series until now, you can feel that passion back for the fans. Sure, the team has had some down times, but Bruins fans never stop believing."

Jack certainly engenders a lot of opinions—positive and negative—but I think Bruins fans know he's one of them, and they love him for that. It made me wonder, if Jack could redo anything from his time with the Bruins, would he?

"I've thought about that over the years, and I'm one who regrets nothing. I've learned so much from my mistakes. They've made me a better person, and they've made me a better announcer. I even hope they've made me easier to work with. If I hadn't made those mistakes I probably wouldn't have the perspective I've been able to gain over the past few years. It's not that I enjoyed making those mistakes, and it's not to say I've profited from those mistakes, but I wouldn't change a thing."

Bob Beers

Bob Beers was drafted by the Boston Bruins in the 1985 NHL draft. By his own admission, he was not necessarily planning on an NHL career.

"Out of high school I went to Northern Arizona University before transferring to the University of Maine. Then I was a 10th-round draft pick, No. 210 overall, so I wouldn't say I was overly confident I was going to play in the NHL. I was kind of a late bloomer, I'll put it that way. Coming out of high school, it was just about getting a scholarship and getting the chance to play college hockey."

He played professional hockey for nine seasons, playing 258 games for the Bruins, Tampa Bay Lightning, Edmonton Oilers, and New York Islanders. Then he made the transition to the broadcast booth. But he told me he wasn't sure if he was ready to retire at the age of 30, and found the shift from player to broadcaster difficult.

"Barry Pederson did the games on radio for a year, then Andy Brickley did it for a year before moving on to NESN. So for

1997–98 radio had an opening. I really had no desire to do that because I wanted to keep playing."

The Bruins producer is a guy named Rick Radzik, but everyone calls him Schmautzie. That probably gives you an idea of Rick's hockey heritage. But he also has an ear for talent. It was Radzik who talked Brickley into auditioning for the Bruins radio job, and after Brick moved on to NESN, Radzik set his sights on Beers. He had always been impressed with Bob's intelligence and interview ability, so he asked him to audition. It was a unique audition at that.

"I went to WBZ and did a period in an empty room off a monitor with Bob Neumeier. Actually it was funny, because we were doing a game that I had been playing in only a couple of months prior. It was a Bruins and Rangers game that I played in. Neumie said don't worry about any names or anything, and that's not what they were concerned with. Let's just say we ended up with some very interesting names—but not mine—and I was offered the job."

Despite his misgivings about retirement, like Brick before him, he decided he couldn't pass up the opportunity. He worked the 1997–98 season entirely on the radio, but the urge to play never quite left him. Suddenly, the creative Beers came up with an idea that would combine his new career with his old.

"So my second year of doing the games, I called Peter Laviolette, who I knew and was coaching the Providence Bruins. I asked if I could play some games for them. He was all for it. So I practiced for a couple of weeks, and started playing when my Bruins broadcast schedule would allow it. The Boston Bruins games always took priority, but when the schedule worked out, I would play for Providence, too. I did that for two seasons."

You may have heard of player/coaches in sports, but I don't know of too many player/broadcasters. Beers was able to squeeze two more seasons out of his playing career.

He ended up working with Bob Neumeier for three seasons before Neumie made the decision to leave the play-by-play booth and go to work in talk radio (as my cohost on WEEI) and on television. Neumie, among his other skills, is considered one of the top horse racing analysts and handicappers in the game, and is still a staple on network coverage of Triple Crown races and the Breeders' Cup. Suddenly, Beers added another job to his résumé—talent recruiter.

"After my three years with Neumie, he told me he wasn't going to be coming back. I remembered from my time when I was playing in Providence, and the announcer there was Dave Goucher. So I told Gouch to keep an eye on the situation in Boston, and put his name in. He was hired to replace Neumie, and we ended up working together for 17 years until Dave left to talk over the TV job for the Vegas Golden Knights."

Like everyone who calls games for a team for a number of years (and Bob has now been at it for more than 21 seasons), there are games that are impossible to forget.

"There are three games I will remember forever. The first, of course, was the Cup-clinching game in Vancouver, and what that meant for everyone back in New England. The second was the seventh game of the Toronto series, when the Bruins were down three goals in the third. Everyone thought the Bruins were done—people started leaving the building and they couldn't get back in! And the third was the Game 7 against Tampa Bay in 2011. That was a great game. No penalties, 5-on-5, up and down, action and intensity. Then Nathan Horton gets set up by David Krejci for the game winner. The team that wins goes on to the Final."

When you've been doing games on the radio for more than 20 years, you get a chance to know a variety of coaches. So I asked Bob a simple question—who was the best coach over that time?

"Claude Julien was here for 10 years and won a Cup, so you would have to say he's the best coach during my time here. But I really enjoyed Pat Burns. My first year on radio was Pat's first year as Bruins coach, in '97 –98. He was a lot of fun to be around. I got to know Claude pretty well during his time here too. I wish Mike Sullivan had been here longer. I thought Peter Laviolette should have gotten a job here, but Mike O'Connell gave the job to Robbie Ftorek instead of Peter after Mike Keenan left."

Just like Brickley on the TV side, Beers has the unique experience of being both a former Bruins player and a broadcaster. He is perfectly able to compare the game he played to the game as it's played today.

"I think I liked the era that I played in a little more. I like certain aspects of the way the game is played today, but there are other things that I do not like. I like the speed, but I feel there is less physical play and there is a lot less accountability. In the era I played you were accountable, and if you weren't then you didn't play. If you get knocked down in front of the net, now it's a penalty against the guy who knocks you down. Back then, you got yelled at when you came back to the bench because you should have been stronger. There are certain things you see in the game today that I just have trouble digesting. I was raised a certain way, and was told to play the game a certain way."

For a kid who went to Northern Arizona just for the scholarship and the chance to play college hockey, Bob Beers has turned his considerable talents into a superb broadcasting career.

Dave Goucher

If there's anyone else who has covered the Bruins whose career path most resembles my own, it's former radio play-by-play voice Dave Goucher. Gouch grew up in Pawtucket, Rhode Island, and I grew up in Brunswick, Maine, but we both had a passion for hockey and a fervent hope we could someday broadcast games for our favorite team, the Bruins. I'm happy to say, we both pulled that off.

"I remember vividly playing youth hockey in Rhode Island when I was a kid. We had a lot of 7:00 games on a Sunday night over at Brown University or Providence College. I would be with my parents driving home from the game and hanging on every word that was coming out of the radio from Bob Wilson. And I never heard him fail to deliver on a big call or a big moment in a game. Like you, I listened to Bob and I listened to Fred Cusick. I can still hear those guys. You know what this is like, but to just be a part of that lineage is just beyond belief."

Dave graduated from Boston University and knew he wanted to continue broadcasting hockey games, but had little idea how to accomplish that wish. He was sharing a beverage with longtime college broadcaster Bernie Corbett at the Eliot Lounge (just ask any of your Boston Marathon friends) when Bernie dropped the nugget that he had heard the Wheeling Nailers of the ECHL were looking for a broadcaster.

"If you had forced me to point it out on a map, I probably couldn't have found it. But I was fortunate, because Larry Kish was the GM of the team down there, and had played at Providence College, so when I applied we had some common ground. When he offered me the job, I remember thinking, 'Someone is actually going to pay me to broadcast hockey games!' And I was in Wheeling for two years."

Dave honed his skills, and took advantage of another opportunity when the time came. He was flying back to Rhode Island to visit with his dad, when a friend from BU told him that the Providence Bruins were in the market for a new play-by-play announcer.

"So I contacted them, and gave them the elevator speech, and told them I was coming home the next week, so they wouldn't even have to fly me up there. I went in on a Friday and interviewed, and two or three weeks later, I was moving home to Rhode Island. The fact I had grown up in Pawtucket, and still had a lot of ties to the area, probably helped my candidacy as well."

Interestingly, the man who hired Dave to broadcast the Providence Bruins games was Ed Anderson—the same man who hired me to broadcast the Maine Mariners games back in 1979.

I had spent eight years with the Mariners, seven of them broadcasting the games, so I understood completely what Dave was telling me.

"I was in the minor leagues for five years and six years and seven years, and you start to wonder if you're ever going to be able to make it," Dave said. "Then when Neumie [Bob Neumeier] left the Bruins job, I threw my hat in the ring at WBZ-AM. I think there were 60 or 65 candidates in the mix. They narrowed it down to 10, then five, and I was still in the running. Then I got the call I will never forget. They said, 'If you're agreeable, we would like to make you the next radio announcer for the Boston Bruins.' I thought, if I'm *agreeable*?! Do you want me to walk up there backward?!"

Dave and Bob Beers ended up doing the Bruins games on radio for the next 17 years. In my opinion, they were a perfect broadcast team, almost never stepping on each other and always complementing each other's style on the broadcast. I've talked about the people who helped teach me the game—names like Sid Watson, Mike Emrick, and Tom McVie. Dave also took the time to learn, and he had a couple of willing teachers.

"I learned a lot about the game from Bob [Beers] and Andy [Brickley], to be honest. After Bob and I worked together for so many years, I think we had a real feel for where each other was going to go. I developed a pretty good sense for how Bob saw and thought the game, and we just learned kind of a sixth sense for what each of us were going to do. I've said this before, but if Bob and Brick aren't the two smartest hockey people I know, they're in the top five."

You simply can't spend 17 years calling the Bruins games on the radio and not think about some of the players who stood out over that time. So I simply asked Dave who some of those guys were.

"Early on, you think of a guy like Joe Thornton. He's just a unique human being. I never really saw him in a bad mood, and he always seemed to be just a happy-go-lucky guy. His kind of carefree, love-of-life attitude was something I always admired.

"Then there was Billy Guerin. He and I went to prep school together for a year. When he came to the Bruins, it was kind of cool to see him playing for the team and I was broadcasting the games. We were two guys who used to fall asleep in math class together. It was pretty awesome to spend time with him at that stage in our lives.

"And somebody like Bergie [Patrice Bergeron]—he's just my favorite. I watched him come into the league as an 18-year-old, and then saw him continue to grow. Someone once made the comparison to him and Jean Ratelle. He's just the classiest guy you would ever want to meet.

"Zdeno Chara is probably on that short list too. He's a unique person—the incredible physical condition that he keeps himself in. To be able to play at his size, and with his physical condition, and to play at a really high level is just unbelievable."

Doing games on TV is fun, and the pay is a little better than doing the games on the radio. I've done both, and I enjoy doing the games on TV. But there is one area that the radio announcers have the complete advantage of the television broadcasters. After the first round of the playoffs, network TV takes over the broadcast rights. That means that Mike Emrick is the only TV play-by-play announcer who gets to call the Cup-clinching game. But the radio team is there for every game, right through the final horn of the championship game. And it's something the TV guys envy the radio guys for.

Dave got to make the final call when the Bruins won the Stanley Cup in 2011.

"It's the pinnacle of my career," Dave said. "I thought of guys who had been in the league two and three times as long as me, and never had the chance to do it. I've always thought, to this day, how grateful I am that I had the chance at least that one chance to call a Cup-clinching game. That's kind of a short list for Bruins announcers. I don't know what they did in 1941, but you think of 1970, 1972, and 2011, and I think those are the three Cups when the Bruins announcers were able to call it. You know, no one ever hears Fred Cusick's call of Bobby Orr's Cup-clinching goal against St. Louis. They only hear Dan Kelley's call. But I've heard Fred's call, and it's unbelievable. And of course Bob Wilson. I never, ever think of myself in the category with those guys, but just from an opportunity standpoint, I'm so grateful."

And you can't talk to a guy who has broadcast Bruins games for 17 years and not ask the obvious question: Other than the Cup clincher in 2011, what is the game that will live forever in the highlight reel in your head?

"I would say the comeback against Toronto in Game 7 in 2013. Bergie scores to tie the game with 50 seconds left, and then he scores the clincher in overtime. Here's what I remember. They were down 4–1 halfway through the third period, and I start getting text messages on my phone from my buddies. Things like, 'This sucks! Do you want to play golf tomorrow? What are you doing next week?' And I literally pushed my phone about 10 feet away because I didn't want to read anymore. Then it gets to 4–2 and then 4–3, and I grabbed my phone and the tone of the texts had all changed!"

Dave left the Bruins job after the 2016–17 season, but it really took the opportunity of a lifetime to get him to leave Boston.

"I had spent seven years in the minors and 17 years with the Bruins doing the games on radio, and I probably thought this was going to be my last job. But after doing radio for 24 years, I get offered the chance to be the first ever TV voice, for the first ever pro sports team in Las Vegas. And, well, it was the only kind of unique opportunity that would get me to leave Boston."

There have been some remarkable talents working radio and television for the Bruins over the years. I hope this gives you some insight into a select group of the professionals I've had the pleasure to work with.

CHAPTER 3
MIKE MILBURY

There might not be a more polarizing figure in the history of the Boston Bruins than Mike Milbury. And he's been that way from virtually every position within the organization and out, from his days as a player, to his coaching and general manager stints, to his current role as a national broadcaster.

Mike was born in Brighton, Massachusetts, but grew up in Walpole. He played college hockey at Colgate University, where he had very good offensive numbers for a defenseman but even better penalty-minute statistics. As a junior, Mike was the team's co-leader in assists with 19, but he also led the team with 68 penalty minutes. He followed that up with a senior season with four goals and 26 assists for 30 points and a team-leading 85 penalty minutes.

After graduation, Milbury got a chance to play five games with the Bruins' top minor league affiliate, the Boston Braves. The Bruins had one of those truly unique situations where their minor league affiliate played in the same city they did. He then signed with the Bruins as a free agent before the following season.

Mike spent 12 seasons playing for the Bruins and his team was in the playoffs for 11 of those seasons. He was known as a hard-nosed, stay-at-home defenseman who played every shift like it was going to be his last.

"You respected Mike because you knew his path to the NHL wasn't an easy one," teammate Peter McNab once said. "He worked so hard and just fought for everything he got out of his career."

Milbury did what he was told, as far as moving the puck out of the defensive zone to the forwards as simply as he could. But sometimes he'd do something to help the Bruins without being instructed, like start a fight or throw a big hit to turn the momentum of a game. *Boston Magazine* once named him the city's worst pro athlete, mostly because it didn't take into account Milbury's intangibles.

"It certainly must be to my credit...that I was able to survive in the NHL for 12 years," Milbury once said about the magazine's insult.

On a team that was coached by the irascible Don Cherry and featured rough-and-tumble players such as Terry O'Reilly, John Wensink, and Stan Jonathan, Milbury fit right in. He says that Cherry was the perfect coach for him.

"The coach I had the most fun ever playing for was Grapes [Cherry].... It just wasn't for long enough. He was terrific at what he did, and brought an intense, business-like approach to what he did. Grapes could be intense, but we always had fun too."

If you ask almost any fan, they'll tell you Milbury is best known for an incident as a player in 1979. The Bruins were playing the Rangers at Madison Square Garden during the pinnacle of the Big Bad Bruins. A fan grabbed Jonathan's hockey stick and that set everything off. To the surprise of no one, O'Reilly climbed over the short Plexiglas and set off in pursuit of the stick-stealing fan. He was quickly followed by gentle giant Peter McNab and a few other players. Milbury actually came back from the team's dressing room and joined his teammates. Milbury caught the fan and proceeded to remove the fan's shoe and beat him with it. O'Reilly was suspended for eight games and McNab and Milbury for six each. All were fined. The television image of Milbury beating the Rangers fan with his own shoe lives to this day and is a staple of almost every Bruins-Rangers telecast—on NESN or on the national affiliate.

When you watch the Madison Square Garden incident with the benefit of hindsight, it seems kind of funny. But then you think of what could have happened and shudder. Fans should never enter into the field of play, and I always kind of root for a player to beat the crap out of the idiots who venture there. The same should also hold true for players, though, and nothing should draw the player into the stands, no matter how loathsome the act from the fans. We've seen fans end up in penalty boxes and even scale the glass to get on the ice, and it almost never ends well. I can appreciate the spirit of sticking up for a teammate, and I know all too well how Rangers fans can be in New York. I know if a player did today what Mike and his teammates did in 1979 he would likely miss a quarter of the season. But it's hard not to laugh at the sight of Milbury swinging and hitting a guy with his own shoe.

Milbury's NHL career finished after 754 regular-season games and 86 postseason contests. In the regular season he had 49 goals and 189 assists and was plus-175. He had four goals and 24 assists and was plus-15 in the postseason.

As Mike's playing career started to wind down, he began to think about what was coming next. Bruins general manager Harry Sinden, whom Milbury says was the best coach he ever played for when Sinden briefly got behind the bench, wanted Milbury to keep playing.

"But I wanted to get started on phase two. I was more interested in managing a team, but Harry said if I wanted to be a manager I should coach first. He gave me a four-year deal—two years as manager and coach of the team up in Portland, Maine, and two years in Boston with some unnamed position."

Milbury began his career as coach of the Bruins American Hockey League affiliate in Portland, Maine (the same franchise with which I began my career back in 1979).

Mike Milbury had a long history with the Bruins that went back to his playing days. *(AP Photos)*

When Milbury was coaching in Portland he again made news by leaving the arena of play. Again, he did so in support of a member of his team.

One of the most popular players in the history of the Mariners was a Western Canadian by the name of Steve Tsujiura. Steve was Japanese-Canadian and stood 5'6" and weighed about 165 pounds. He was a skilled player who was held back from his NHL dreams primarily because of his size. He still lives in Portland and remains immensely popular to this day.

Mike was coaching Steve and the Mariners in Sherbrooke, Quebec, and the arena organist played a Japanese ditty every time Tsujiura stepped onto the ice. It was racist, inappropriate, and degrading, and every time he played it, Milbury seethed.

Finally, Mike had heard enough. He left the bench, went through the stands, climbed into the organ loft, and threatened to throw the musician over the railing. Needless to say, the organist didn't play the tune again.

Steve felt like his coach had his back, and his Mariners teammates were impressed that their coach went to such lengths to support his player.

"As much as a like to say I had Stevie's back—and I did—we were also down by three and I was trying to get an emotional lift out of it. I was legitimately pissed about it though. They were being disrespectful to one of my players and it was offensive. I like to think I was straight-up with people, and I think if you asked guys on those Bruins teams they'll tell you I was."

If he didn't already know it, he learned quickly that a coach is at the mercy of his GM, leading Milbury to wonder which position was better.

"My first year of coaching we had a great year going, until Harry traded away all of my key players at the trading deadline to get Andy Moog for the Bruins. I spent the two years coaching in Maine, and it just so happened that Terry O'Reilly decided he had enough of coaching. I had been in frequent contact with Harry over my time in Maine, but I also took advantage of the opportunity to grow a lot on my own. It was a great way to get started. And it led to me going back to Boston for the 1989–90 season."

Mike's two seasons with Maine weren't great. He had a 44–25–7–4 record in 1987–88 and lost in the second round of the playoffs. The next season he went 32–40–8–0 and missed the playoffs.

But the plan between Sinden and Milbury was that Mike was going to eventually be back in Boston in some capacity. O'Reilly's unexpected decision to stop coaching opened up a spot. Mike told me he always thought he was a better coach than he was a player or general manager. He also said every coach takes bits and pieces from every coach he has ever had.

"I think every good coach tries to use his own personal history as a bit of a guideline. Everyone eventually faces something he has never faced before, and you seek advice from people who helped mold you. Then you had to decide if you would take the advice or not. Sometimes it was a little thing you would take from a previous coach. For instance, Harry had a habit where he would come over and touch you on the shoulder. With other coaches, they would treat you like you were a leper or something. But I always remembered that Harry made a point of putting his hand on your shoulder while he was talking to you. It was something about the gesture that I thought was important as a player. You just sensed that he cared about you, even if he was giving you a hard time. Both coaches [Sinden and Cherry] were conditioning sticklers, both knew there was a time to put down the hammer. I definitely learned things from both of those guys."

Milbury only coached the Bruins for two seasons, finishing with more than 100 points each time and winning the division title both times. The Bruins lost in the Stanley Cup Final in 1990 and the conference finals in 1991. But even as a successful coach, controversy followed Milbury. He was the coach of the Wales Conference team in the 1991 All-Star Game, but named checker Brian Skrudland of the Montreal Canadiens to his team, plus tough guy Chris Nilan of the Bruins. Neither deserved All-Star consideration, especially when you consider that Milbury passed on players like Guy Lafleur and Kirk Muller. As it turned out, both Skrudland and Nilan were injured (Nilan sprained his ankle while shooting baskets on the Celtics court at the Garden) and didn't play in the game. But it was classically a case of Milbury being his own man.

Mike also said he learned a lesson that Tom McVie repeated to me many times during our time together: a player never cares as much about the coach as the coach cares about the player.

"If you're going to do something, and try to do something as best you can, then you have to be emotionally invested in it. I put a lot of time into trying to be as good a player as I could, so when the time came to play I was going to be completely invested emotionally in trying to play. I put in a lot of time as coach preparing for the game, and preparing the players for the game, so why wouldn't I be emotionally invested? Different guys have different ways of showing it, but I think every coach is very invested in what his team is doing. But Harry always taught me that the players will never care as much as the coach or manager. Players work hard for, what, an hour or two each day, and they go home. The manager and the coach are there all day; it's a completely different level of commitment on their part. Of course, they can't get physically hurt, and they can't make as much of a difference in success or failure as a player."

After two seasons behind the bench, Mike wanted to start a career in the front office. Milbury was bumped up to assistant general manager to Sinden, who was in the market for an eventual successor. Mike could see Sinden wasn't going anywhere any time soon, so Mike left in 1994 for a short-lived and ill-advised foray into college hockey. In March 1994, Boston College announced that Milbury would follow Steve Cedorchuk as head coach of the

Eagles. Mike never coached a game at Boston College, resigning June 2, 1994, saying he had philosophical differences with the athletic director. Things worked out just fine for Boston College, as they hired Jerry York away from Bowling Green University, who has become one of the finest coaches in the history of the game.

Mike was named the head coach of the New York Islanders in 1995 and added GM duties three months later. Coaching the Islanders wasn't like coaching the Bruins, as the Islanders' dynasty of the '80s was quickly fading into history. Mike's Islanders missed the playoffs in 1996 after a 22–50–10 season. The next season the Islanders were 13–23–9 when Mike decided to focus on just his GM duties and hired former Bruins coach Rick Bowness as the new coach of the Islanders in January 1997.

To say that Milbury, who coached 64 more games with the Islanders after being an in-season replacement in the 1997–98 season and coaching into the next campaign, was hamstrung by Islanders ownership would be an understatement. Mike made his fair share of bad decisions, but Islanders owner Charles Wang also mandated some of those. We are talking about an ownership that decided to sign goaltender Rick DiPietro to a 15-year, $67.5 million contract. I guess 10 or 12 years wouldn't have gotten the job done.

By Mike's own admission, operating within the constraints of the Islanders ownership ultimately became too much to bear.

"I remember telling Charles Wang, 'Look, I just can't do this anymore.' And he said, 'Yeah, yeah, I know. I make all the decisions and you take all the blame.' So I tried to help sort out the business side of the Islanders, and straighten out that mess, but after a year I found that I didn't love it. Charles asked if I could see myself doing that same job in five years, and when I said that I couldn't, he said, 'Okay, I'm going to bring in my son-in-law for the job.' We had no contract but we had an agreement that when it ended, I would get a year's pay. I had a year coming to me when we parted company, but he actually paid me for two years, which was really nice."

Longtime Bruins radio analyst Bob Beers got his first taste of Milbury as a head coach when he was recalled from the Maine Mariners of the American Hockey League during the 1989–90 season. Beers says there were some similarities between Mike and Bob's AHL coach, Rick Bowness, who went on to later coach the Bruins.

Both were old-school hockey guys with high expectations.

"When I got called up, Mike Milbury was my coach. Now, Mike as my first NHL coach was definitely an eye opener. He did some very unique things," Beers said. "He was unconventional in terms of motivating guys and motivating the team. But he was also lucky that he had guys like Ray [Bourque] and Cam [Neely] that were the leaders. When you play for the Bruins, you better fall into place when guys like that are the hardest workers."

Beers then played for Milbury with the Islanders. Needless to say, Milbury's unique coaching methods hadn't changed much.

"We had a very poor showing one night, and he had us at practice the next morning at 8:00 AM. He wouldn't let the Zamboni driver redo the ice, and we weren't allowed to wear jerseys because he said we didn't deserve to wear the Islanders emblem. We practiced with no pucks, and bad ice, for an hour-plus. Then we went in and did video, and that was a complete rip session. Then we did a weight circuit after that, and then we went back out onto the ice.

Pat Flatley was our captain, and he gathered up our jerseys and just told Mike, 'We're wearing our jerseys.' Then we did another hour or so of one-on-one, two-on-two battle drills. And then after practice, he sent me and [goalie] Tommy Salo down to the minors.

"I wish he had done that before the practice," Beers recalled with a laugh.

When Milbury's stint with the Islanders ended, the broadcast world beckoned. Sam Flood offered Mike a job on NHL Network, and *Hockey Night in Canada* also stepped to the plate. He was finally able to reach agreement with NESN for a package of Bruins telecasts, and suddenly Mike Milbury was a member of the hockey media. He decided early on he was going to tell it like it was...or at least how he saw it.

"For 35 years I had worked under scrutiny, and some of it blistering. When I became a broadcaster I just said, 'Now it's my turn.' I always had only one rule—if you see it, say it. When I hear a broadcast I want to hear someone give me a strong opinion, right or wrong, and give me a good observation. Look, we all make mistakes on the ice, but it's my job to point out those mistakes."

It's safe to say the league office, teams, and players don't always appreciate Mike's honesty. But he remains unafraid to stir the pot.

"I've gone after Alex Ovechkin and at times the people in Washington have gone apoplectic about it, but I still feel I was right. It doesn't mean I don't think he's one of the greatest goal scorers of all time. He can be that and still have flaws in other phases of his game. Sometimes people have trouble with criticism, but I have no trouble delivering on that. I don't need to sugarcoat. It sometimes gets me in trouble in the office in Manhattan, because things have gotten so polite and I don't need to be polite."

And don't think it was just the Caps who had issues with Milbury's rhetoric. He heard from the Nashville Predators because he called rambunctious defenseman P.K. Subban a clown, and he hears from the Pittsburgh Penguins from time to time when he sets his sights on arguably the best player in the world.

"The Penguins used to call all the time if I had any kind of a tweak on Sidney Crosby. He was a petulant child for a while, and they would always call if I had any kind of criticism at all. Sam [Flood] would get the complaints and give them to me, or sometimes he wouldn't give them to me. Bettman would call about this, that, or the other thing."

More than 19,000 people signed a change.org petition to have Milbury removed from the NBC analyst's desk in 2015. Now that tells you how well he can stir the pot.

Part of me is envious of Mike, because there are certainly times when I wish I could be as fearless and blunt as he is. But I also think of Mike as the classic "ready, shoot, aim" kind of guy. I'm not sure he always thinks of the consequences of his words or actions. He will tell you, as he has me, that he thinks of them and just doesn't care. But I feel at times he has some regrets, even if he'll never admit them.

I do not think the host of the broadcast necessarily gets painted with the same brush when the analyst goes off the rails, but as a loyal teammate you sometimes feel the need to defend him. And the Mike Milbury I know is worthy of defense—most of the time.

The thing I've come to learn is that Mike is an incredibly intelligent individual and able to converse on almost any subject. But he also wears his heart on his sleeve and is emotional. The same emotions that brought him into the stands at Madison

Square Garden or the organ loft in Sherbrooke, Quebec, can also lead him to speak "off the cuff" from the studio or the broadcast booth. When he criticizes Sidney Crosby, for instance, it is usually because he wants and expects so much from one of the biggest stars in the game.

I've loved dealing with Mike professionally and knowing him personally. He is blunt and honest, and actually has a better sense of humor than he gets credit for. I love watching his work on NBC and NHL Network. Like every other fan, I can't wait to see what he says next. As long as I'm not the one in the crosshairs, it's fine.

But there is another side to Milbury—one he probably prefers that most never see. For all his bluster and bite, he is fiercely loyal and never, ever forgets a friend. His broadcast partner, Kathryn Tappen, says he was always there for her.

"Mike was one of my biggest allies and he was the guy pushing for me to get into NBC," Kathryn recalls. "I've joked with Mike that I'm probably the longest-tenured colleague he's ever had, and he admits that's true, without question. To me, he's the greatest guy in the world. He's been so supportive, and helped me with stuff I've gone through personally. He's been a father figure to me."

As a player, coach, general manager, and broadcaster, Mike Milbury has been a mentor to some and a thorn in the side of others, but his career has always been entertaining.

CHAPTER 4
BOSTON GARDEN

I never attended a Boston Bruins game at Boston Garden as a fan. As I mentioned earlier, I was the oldest of five children growing up in limited circumstances in Maine, and we simply didn't have the money to make that happen. I was a basketball player in school, not a hockey player, and the only time I ever set foot in the building was on April 14, 1973, when my friend's father included me on a trip to see the Celtics. It was the same night the team retired "Loscy" in honor of Jim Luscutoff.

As the radio voice of the New Jersey Devils in 1986, I finally got to set foot in the Garden for a hockey game. It was November 15, 1986, and I remember walking around the building for more than an hour after the morning skate and long before the game started, to see if it matched the vision and memory I had in my mind about *the Garden*. I felt like I knew every inch just from what I'd heard on the radio and later on television. I walked and walked. I especially remember walking the inner concourse and thinking of Larry Bird running laps in that same spot.

Now, if you're looking for a sentimental remembrance of the Garden, you're probably not going to be very happy. I wouldn't say I had a love-hate relationship with the old building, just that I loved it enough to know it was time to move on. Sometimes, at home, there have been disagreements about what needs to be saved and what needs to be thrown away. I've often said to my wife, "Not everything old is a valuable antique; sometimes it's just old and needs to be replaced." I'm so happy I had the chance to work in that venerable old arena, but I was also happy when it was replaced.

I know how sentimental we are in Boston about history. There are people who hope that Fenway Park lasts another 106 years, and they never want to see a baseball game in any other venue.

Many people felt the same way about the original Boston Garden. But I also saw rats the size of small house cats, and I had my feet stick to the floor in the press box. In its day, the Garden was a sports mecca in America, but those days were long past.

Remember, when I first starting visiting the Garden as a professional, it was nearly 70 years old. The Garden opened in 1927 when the Bruins outgrew the Boston Arena down on Huntington Avenue (still in use by Northeastern University and known as Matthews Arena). The ice surface measured 191 feet by 83 feet, and the Bruins built their teams to thrive in those close quarters. It was intimidating to play there, and not simply because the Bruins were bigger and badder than most. Opposing players felt like the fans were right over their shoulders, and the building would literally shake when the team began to impose their will on the opponents.

All of the first five Stanley Cup championship teams used the Garden to their advantage, and from Eddie Shore through Bobby Orr and Phil Esposito, the greats of the game added to the mystique of the place.

From a broadcaster's point of view, there was never a better place on God's green earth to call a game, that's for sure. The radio booth was a little higher than the television booth, but it was still terrific. You kind of had to contort yourself to crawl through the tunnel at the top of the stairs and into the press box. But that TV booth was the best place I had ever seen for calling a game. It was a little gondola hanging over the ice, and you felt like you weren't just in the middle of the action, but actually on the ice. You could hear everything, and it was the closest to an actual game I've ever been. I've always wanted to watch a preseason game from the bench to just get a feel for the speed and noise of an NHL game, but the TV booth at the Garden was pretty close.

Fans were also basically right in the thick of the action, too. The stands were designed nearly straight up, so fans were practically parallel with the rink. Hanging over the boards and screaming at the top of one's lungs was both possible and encouraged. It was intimidating to make your way to the upper reaches of the Garden as a fan, and it was intimidating to play a game as a visitor on Garden ice.

The Garden's last season was the 1994–95 lockout-shortened season, my first year calling the games on radio. I shifted to television the next season and the Garden officially closed in September 1995 with the Last Hurrah ceremonies, including a skate by nearly every living legend of Bruins lore. You can read more about the biggest, most emotional moment of the Last Hurrah in our chapter on Raymond Bourque. But I was sitting in the building as a fan that night, and to see Milt Schmidt, Johnny Bucyk, Bobby Orr, Phil Esposito, and so many other legendary Bruins skating on the Garden ice was emotional for every Bruins fan. No player wanted to stop skating, and no fan wanted the night to end.

Those closing ceremonies and all the history and great memories aside, the Garden had lost its charm for me. By the end it was like, 'Okay, let's close it down and get out of here." The sticky floors and rats were never charming. It was time for a new building. There were remarkable, historic moments in the old Boston Garden. It just felt like it was time for a new venue, in a new era, and new memories.

Bobby Orr takes the ice at the old Boston Garden for one last time on September 26, 1995. *(AP Photos)*

CHAPTER 5

TD GARDEN

Bruins owner Jeremy Jacobs and Delaware North had plans to replace the old Boston Garden with a new, state-of-the-art facility. The team announced they had secured funding for a new arena, but the Massachusetts state government had to get involved. Senate president William "Billy" Bulger and the Massachusetts Senate killed the bill in a disagreement over what was called "linkage payments."

Initially, Jacobs backed out of the project. Among the issues were both the linkage payments and what was called the air rights—the space above the North Station and the train tracks, where the new Boston Garden was supposed to sit. Another round of negotiations resulted in a bill passed on February 26, 1993, that allowed for construction of the new arena.

Construction began in April, and the original name of the new building was the Shawmut Center, for the bank that had purchased the naming rights. Shawmut Bank was purchased by FleetBoston, and the FleetCenter opened on September 30, 1995. That name was ultimately changed in 2005, when the building was renamed the TD Banknorth Garden, and eventually officially became known as TD Garden. Most fans were more than happy to shorten that name to simply "The Garden," which likely wasn't what the naming sponsor had in mind.

The new Garden was built mere inches from the old Boston Garden, and it posed its own set of problems when it came to demolition. The old Garden sat vacant until 1998, when it was finally demolished. Because of the proximity to the new building, it was impossible to just implode or knock the building down with normal methods. The old Garden had to be taken down brick-by-brick, and the site was ultimately turned into the players' parking lot.

That parking lot will eventually be turned into a multi-use facility of restaurants, clubs, theaters, and office space. Not many people realize that when they finally get the chance to eat a meal or bowl a game in the new building, they will be doing it in the exact same space where Bobby Orr once made magic on the ice.

There are other facilities in the National Hockey League more grandiose and ornate than the TD Garden, but there are also significant differences with the facility in Boston. Public funding of private athletic facilities is simply not an option for lawmakers or tax payers in Massachusetts. In the same way that Robert Kraft had to privately fund the current home of the New England Patriots, Gillette Stadium, Jeremy Jacobs had to privately fund TD Garden.

I actually understand and endorse the state's reluctance to fund private facilities, but team owners, like Kraft and Jacobs, have had to pay the price. Jacobs owns the facility and rents space to the Boston Celtics, who are the secondary tenant of the building. There has been talk over the years of the Celtics constructing their own building, but they also would have to fund the project privately, and they continue to find financial benefit from renting.

The current TD Garden is still a work in progress. Delaware North has privately funded continued renovations of the facility, and plans are in place for even more renovation as the outside project continues. Ultimately, there will be completely new office space for the Bruins, and even more changes within the building proper. There is already a new and expanded Pro Shop that overlooks the train tracks of North Station, and other improvements continue.

CHAPTER 6
COACHES

If you live or grew up in New England, there is a sports truth: the hardest job in sports is manager of the Boston Red Sox.

Heck, Terry Francona won *two* World Series titles, including the first in 86 years, and got fired. John Farrell won back-to-back American League East Division titles and got fired. The easiest job is coach of the New England Patriots (I kid, I kid!). Bill Belichick seldom gets criticized and always wins. Of course, being the greatest coach in the history of the sport makes it a little easier. Somewhere in between are the coaches of the Boston Celtics and the Boston Bruins.

In my time with the Boston Bruins, the coaches have been Steve Kasper, Pat Burns, Mike Keenan, Robbie Ftorek, Mike O'Connell, Mike Sullivan, Dave Lewis, Claude Julien, and Bruce Cassidy. Some of them were great; some were abysmal.

Terry O'Reilly

I know Terry O'Reilly, but he was not a coach during my tenure with the team. I know and love the guy, who's known as Taz for the whirling-dervish style of play that had him hitting everything and endearing himself to fans as he bridged the gap from the Big Bad Bruins of the early '70s to the Lunch Pail AC group of the late '70s.

O'Reilly's playing career spanned from the 1971–72 season through the 1984–85 season, during which he played 891 regular-season games—all for the Bruins. He finished with 204 goals and 606 points, with his career-high in points (90) coming in 1977–78. (He finished eighth in voting for the Hart Trophy that season.)

Some consider O'Reilly Hall–of–Fame-worthy, but he hasn't been enshrined. However, the ultimate sign of respect and appreciation for O'Reilly's efforts with the Bruins came on October 24, 2002, when his No. 24 was retired and raised to the rafters with the rest of the legends of the franchise. By his own admission, O'Reilly did not possess the skills to have his number retired, but he is also arguably one of the most popular personalities in the history of the organization. As Bruins tough guy Shawn Thornton once told me about O'Reilly, "He worked harder than anyone and never backed down from anyone. He led by example. He deserves to have his number retired. You don't always have to be the flashiest."

O'Reilly coached the Bruins for three seasons, starting in 1986 and including a trip to the Stanley Cup Final in 1988. He compiled a 115–86–26 record. His tenure behind the Bruins' bench preceded my time with the team, so I rely on the opinions of those who played here when O'Reilly was running the team to assess his coaching tenure.

Ray Bourque doesn't even try to hide his admiration for the man.

"The best coach I ever played for was Terry O'Reilly. He is, in my eyes, the ultimate Bruin. Taz never asked for anything he wasn't willing to give, and he was always willing to give everything he had. I loved playing for Terry O'Reilly."

O'Reilly told me a wild story about one portion of his coaching tenure with the Bruins:

> We were playing in Hartford—it was April 2, 1988—and we had been beaten and just wanted to get out of the building. Someone had parked their car on the exit ramp from the building, and we

couldn't get the bus out of the building. My son Evan was not well, and I really needed to get home.

I didn't think it was such a big deal. We looked for over 30 minutes for the driver of that car, and we just couldn't find him. I said to the security guard, "Listen, we have to get out of here. I'm gonna just pop this vent window on the driver's side, slip the car into drive, and move it out of the way. I'm gonna give you my name and phone number, and have the owner send me a bill, and I'll see that it gets paid." I thought that was a real simple solution and would solve the problem.

But it didn't really work. We popped the window—okay, I popped the window—and I reached in, but it was one of those cars with the locking ignition, so we couldn't put it into drive. So I got everybody off the bus, and 20 of us physically pushed the car out of the way. The team got on the bus, and we left town. I didn't think there was any issue.

I got home to help with my son Evan. He was having a tough night. Evan had kidney issues, and was quite ill at the time. One of the symptoms was that he scratched all the time. I went into his room, and I lay down beside him and held his hands. He would wrap his fingers around my two index fingers. And whenever he would let go of my fingers and start to scratch, I would speak to him, and he would put his hands back and hold my fingers. That's how he fell asleep.

I want you to think about that scene for just a minute. Terry O'Reilly was one of the baddest of the Big Bad Bruins. He was feared because he was fearless, and he would take on anyone in the National Hockey League. And here he is lying in a bed with his son, calming him, and allowing him to get some semblance of rest. O'Reilly continued:

In the booth with Terry O'Reilly and Peter McNab.

So I woke up in the morning, and he's lying there beside me holding onto my fingers. The sun is filtering through the bedroom window, and I was thinking how beautiful life was. Then all of a sudden it was like someone turned on a neon sign in my brain that said, "You lost 4–2!" I jumped out of bed—it was like somebody had put a spring under me. There was so much work to do. I had to cut some video, plan some practices, and get ready for the playoffs that started in just a few days.

It wasn't until a few days later that I found out that a warrant had been issued for my arrest. I had been charged with third-degree criminal mischief and tampering with a motor vehicle. (Arturo Torres of Hartford told police he didn't want to press charges, but that he felt he had to.)

A few weeks later, we were playing Buffalo in the playoffs, and we had a chartered flight back to Boston. The pilot came on the P.A. and said the weather had closed in on Logan Airport and we may have to land in Hartford. I went charging up to Harry Sinden's seat, and said, "We can't land in Hartford; they're gonna pull me off the plane." The weather cleared and we managed to land in Boston, but I had a few nervous moments.

That should give you an idea of why Bruins players loved Terry O'Reilly as much as they did.

Steve Kasper

Steve Kasper was the first Bruins coach I covered. It was a forgettable time in the franchise's history and a rocky way to start another stretch of my broadcasting career. With Kasper at the helm the Bruins went 40–31–11 in his first season, 1995–96, but then sank to 26–47–9 in his second campaign. The Bruins finished last in the overall standings, had their streak of consecutive playoff appearances ended at 29 years, and earned the No. 1 pick in the NHL draft (which became Joe Thornton).

A sign that Kasper's tenure wouldn't finish well actually came in his first season, when he may have made the single biggest gaffe I've ever seen from a Bruins coach. The Bruins were playing in Toronto on January 3, 1996, and the game was on *Hockey Night in Canada*. Kasper dressed both Cam Neely and Kevin Stevens, but neither player ever touched the ice. Not a single shift for either player. Imagine, it's *Hockey Night in Canada*, and Neely and Stevens sit on the bench for the entire game.

Kasper said after the game that he felt the decision gave his team the best chance to win, and he wasn't trying to embarrass either player. It's safe to say neither Neely nor Stevens agreed with him. After the game, Neely said, "If [Kasper] thinks I'm not good enough to play on this team, to help the team win a hockey game, that's his decision and his opinion. But I know that my opinion doesn't mean much to him.... I've been here nine and a half years. I've been through a lot. I've played through a lot and, to be treated like that, it's tough."

I was flabbergasted. Remember, this was Cam Neely—the biggest, baddest Bruin of his era, who led the Bruins to two Stanley Cup Finals and two other Eastern Conference finals. He had fought back from a career-threatening injury. If there were a tougher or more popular player in the history of the Bruins, I can't remember him, and the list is really small. Neely is in the Hockey Hall of Fame, and his No. 8 hangs in the Garden rafters.

Thinking back, it was May 3, 1991, when Neely was injured on a hit by Pittsburgh defenseman Ulf Samuelsson. Neely developed a condition called myositis ossificans and played just 22 games over the next two seasons. In fact, Neely was only able to play 162 games over the remainder of his career. In 1994, Neely had the tip of his right pinky finger cut off, through his glove. It took 10–15 stitches to repair the injury, and Neely came back to finish the game, adding an assist in a 2–1 loss to the New Jersey Devils.

In the 1993–94 season, Neely was able to score 50 goals in only his 44th game of the season. I was in the building to see Neely's feat, and the emotion was palpable. Bruins fans knew how much Neely had been through physically and how much it meant to him to accomplish the feat. For many fans, Neely was the ultimate Bruin. He was big and could fight, but he could also score. He was the blueprint for the power forward in the NHL.

After that historic 1994 season, Neely was honored by the National Hockey League with the Masterton Trophy, which is given to the NHL player who best exemplifies the qualities of perseverance, sportsmanship, and dedication to ice hockey. It almost always goes to a player who overcomes career-threatening illness or injury.

Back to Kasper and that night in Toronto, no one was quite sure what Kasper was trying to accomplish with his head-scratching decision. But the move failed and caused a permanent rift between Kasper and Neely, and between Kasper and the fans. Kasper ended up being fired after that second season. I don't think Steve likes me a lot, because I had to say what I thought of the move on my radio show. Ironically, Steve and I had the same agent at the time, Steve Freyer, and I'm sure my words put Freyer in a tough position with Kasper as well. I didn't understand what he did then, and I don't understand it now.

Pat Burns

Pat Burns, a former Gatineau, Quebec, policeman who held his law enforcement position for 16 years, was next among coaches in my Bruins years. Like Neely, Burns is now in the Hockey Hall of Fame, although he received the honor posthumously in 2014.

Pat was always quick to admit he only became a coach because of Wayne Gretzky. Wayne was part owner of the Hull Olympiques, and he told Burns he would pay him more than he was making as a cop, and give him a longer deal, if he would coach the junior team. But he also said he didn't expect Burns would be there very long—he was too good.

Burns won the Jack Adams Award as NHL Coach of the Year with the Montreal Canadiens, the Toronto Maple Leafs, and the Bruins—all Original Six franchises.

Despite Burns' popularity and success, he and general manager Harry Sinden seemed at loggerheads throughout Burns' tenure. Elsewhere in this book, we tell you stories about the conflicts between Burns and Sinden (see "Tales from the Room"), but it was probably a case of two Type A personalities who saw too much of themselves in the disposition of the other.

Pat was the classic "don't ask the question if you don't want to hear the answer" kind of guy. He had a hard-edged, take-no-prisoners (no pun intended) attitude. We watched in amusement during a press conference when he was convinced a questioner may have had an ulterior motive. First, he asked who the person was, and then he asked who he worked for. Seemingly unsatisfied with the rather timid answer, Burns proceeded to ask (in French) if the reporter was from Edmonton (that night's opponent).

Burns was very popular with Bruins fans, who always appreciated hard-nosed, blue-collar players and sensed those same qualities in their coach. It may have stemmed from his prior profession, but Burns just seemed gruff, tough, and totally in-your-face. He himself said, "I'm a cop and a coach. That's all I am."

For all his popularity with the fans, I think players found him overbearing after a while. In every place he coached, he seemed to wear out his welcome with his players. He said it very simply, "Lead, follow, or get the hell out of the way." It usually didn't take too long before players wanted to get out of the way.

Pat went 105–97–46–6 with the Bruins from 1997 through his firing eight games into the 2000–01 season. He led the Bruins to the playoffs in his first two seasons, helping the organization turn the page on the Kasper era (or error?). But the Bruins missed the postseason in Pat's third and final full season with the team. Eventually Pat won the Stanley Cup with New Jersey, in 2003.

My relationship with Pat was always fine, but totally professional. I'm not sure he trusted many members of the media, even those who were part of the team's broadcasts. He wasn't ever unpleasant; he just maintained an "at arm's length" relationship. Ironically, I think we had better discussions after he left the Bruins. He would be a semi-regular guest on my radio show, and I think he came to learn how much I admired him and his abilities.

You can add Peter Laviolette to the list of coaches the Bruins cut loose only to have them win Stanley Cup championships elsewhere. In 1998–99, Laviolette, a native of Franklin, Massachusetts, was the head coach for the Providence Bruins of the American Hockey League, and his team was a wagon. They rolled through the regular season with a record of 56–15–4, followed by a 15–4 playoff record and a Calder Cup championship. At the end of the season, Laviolette was named the AHL Coach of the Year.

Peter was promoted to assistant coach of the Boston Bruins on Pat Burns' staff. The Bruins made a coaching change at the end of the season, and instead of considering Laviolette, the team handed the reins to Mike Keenan. Seeing the writing on the wall, and undoubtedly disappointed at being overlooked in favor of Keenan, Laviolette left to become head coach of the New York Islanders. After the team had missed the playoffs for seven consecutive seasons, Peter led them back to the postseason in his first year on the job.

He ultimately ended up with the Carolina Hurricanes and led that team to a Stanley Cup title. You can add stints as head coach of the U.S. Olympic hockey team and Philadelphia Flyers before he was hired as head coach of the Nashville Predators, leading that team to the Stanley Cup Final in 2017, bowing to the Pittsburgh Penguins.

It's easy to imagine that he would have had great success for the Bruins had he been hired here, as he has had everywhere else he has coached.

Mike Keenan

Mike Keenan's hiring was arguably the most regrettable coaching decision in the history of the Bruins, at least in the modern era. Keenan had a Stanley Cup championship on his résumé, with the New York Rangers, yet he could never hold a coaching job for very long in the NHL. There was probably a reason for that.

"Iron Mike" didn't just think he was smarter than everyone else in the league—he *knew* it. He alienated almost every player he ever coached. There were stories about his 1994 Stanley Cup title team, and how captain Mark Messier was the only person who kept that ship afloat. There were stories about the 1987 Canada Cup team that Keenan coached, and the near-mutiny on the part of the greatest players in the game. They reportedly balked at Keenan's iron hand, despite the pedigree of his Hall of Fame roster. Imagine coaching a team that included Wayne Gretzky, Mario Lemieux, Ray Bourque, Mark Messier, Paul Coffey, Glenn Anderson, Mike Gartner, Doug Gilmour, Grant Fuhr, and Michel Goulet, and imagine those players not wanting to play for you. That team, by the way, was the one Ray Bourque said was the greatest team he ever played on.

Consider Keenan's résumé: he was fired by the Philadelphia Flyers one year after leading them to two Stanley Cup Finals in three seasons. After leading the Chicago Blackhawks to the 1992 Stanley Cup Final he was forced to yield his coaching duties and focus solely on the position of general manager for a season. He coached the Rangers to a Stanley Cup championship in his only season there, then bolted for the St. Louis Blues almost before the championship parade was over. He left coaching positions in St. Louis and Vancouver after he couldn't coexist with star players Brett Hull and Trevor Linden, respectively. In September 2006 he abruptly resigned as general manager of the Florida Panthers after dealing franchise goaltender Robert Luongo (among others) to the Vancouver Canucks and losing a power struggle with his longtime friend, head coach Jacques Martin, who succeeded him as general manager.

Bob Beers remembers vividly the day Keenan was introduced to the media.

"He said, 'players play, coaches coach, and managers manage.' Then within about two weeks he was trying to get players off his roster and bring other players in. I guess he felt that coaches should manage too."

As it turned out, I had my own day of reckoning with "Iron Mike." That was the day he decided he wanted me—the Bruins' play-by-play man—fired.

Gord Kluzak and I were doing a game around Thanksgiving in 2000. The team was flat and uninspired. They were flat and uninspired a lot early that season. It became clear as we watched that Keenan had benched defenseman Don Sweeney, a frequent target of Keenan's ire. In the third period, we showed a shot of

Sweeney sitting at the end of the Bruins bench, and I said something along the lines of, "It's hard to believe Sweeney has done anything any worse than what the entire team has been doing tonight."

The next day Keenan and the team were watching video. As it turns out they did that with the sound turned up. When he heard my statement, he began ranting and raving in the dressing room, "I want that f—g guy fired! I want his f—g head!" He didn't know my name, but he wanted my job.

Equipment manager Peter Henderson called to give me the heads up that Keenan was attempting to get me fired. So I called my contact person at the Bruins, media relations magnate Nate Greenberg, to ask if I was in trouble. Nate sighed. Then he said, "Yes, Dale, I've heard from Mike. Let me just say this: you'll be here longer than he will." It turned out Nate was right.

The next game, I made a point of standing outside the press room, just down the hall from the entrance to the Bruins dressing room. If Mike had something to say to me, I wanted to give him the chance to say it. I watched as Sweeney walked down the hall toward the dressing room. He saw me standing at the end of the hall, and instead of turning right into the room, he kept walking straight toward me. He never said a word, but simply stuck out his right hand, shook my hand, winked, and walked back into the dressing room.

Remember the story of the equipment guys having to put the exercise bikes in the middle of the dressing room after games? Goaltender Andrew Raycroft says those bikes were mainly meant for him.

"He would make me ride the bike for 60 minutes after games that I didn't play. I'm sitting in the middle of the dressing room, because Mike wanted the media to see the guys peddling away after the game, and the trainers and equipment guys couldn't go home until I was done. It was like 10:30 at night, and he would have me on the bike, and they would have to stay and basically watch me ride the bike. If we were lucky we finally got to leave around 11:30 or so."

Keenan's tenure as head coach of the Bruins lasted just one season, and it was tumultuous. He alienated most of the players on the team, and Sinden made the change at the end of the 2000–2001 season after the Bruins had missed the playoffs with a 33–26–7–8 record.

Keenan's tactics were unorthodox, to say the least. Raycroft was playing for the team because John Grahame had hurt himself stepping off a curb, and Byron Dafoe was also injured. Raycroft was recalled from Providence, while Pat Burns was coaching, and Keenan more or less had to play him because there were no other options. Andrew says he was a 20-year-old kid, just trying to keep his mouth shut and do his job, but Keenan made that difficult.

"We were in Detroit, and things weren't going great, so he had this team meeting in the hotel conference room. I'm just a kid, and I'm sitting in the back minding my own business and not saying a word. All of a sudden Mike calls me up to the front of the room, in the middle of this meeting, and asks me if I thought Joe Thornton was one of our good leaders. Obviously, I wasn't going there at all, even if it was Mike Keenan. So I basically stammered for about 30 to 40 seconds, and the guys cut in and took me off the hook."

I can honestly say that I don't think Keenan's tactics ever worked—at least not for more than a single season. Players have told me that they rolled their eyes at much of what he said, and they always knew Mike was only concerned about Mike. As Peter Henderson said, Mike always had his favorites on every team, but he seemed to neglect the other players on the roster.

Keenan's constant game-playing eventually wore players out. He felt that a player had to be uncomfortable and "on edge." That may work for some, but for many, if not most, of Mike's players, his style prevented them from performing at their peak. They felt they were the victims of Mike's "games" and eventually they tuned him out completely.

There are people who swear by his abilities as a coach. There are people who sincerely like Mike Keenan, and who say he is a warm and accessible person. I know Mike married a woman from Maine. Unfortunately, those people never seem to outnumber the people who don't want to have anything to do with him.

Robbie Ftorek

Robbie Ftorek, a local hockey legend, replaced Keenan. Ftorek went to high school in the Boston suburb of Needham and played two seasons with the Needham Hilltoppers. In 1968–69 he had 38 goals and 36 assists for 74 points in just 18 games for Needham. He followed that up the next season with 54 goals and 64 assists for 118 points in just 23 games. Robbie had limited success in the American Hockey League and the NHL, but in the World Hockey Association he exploded. Ftorek had 216 goals and 307 assists for 523 points in 373 WHA games. He was selected for the WHA Hall of Fame in 2010.

He embarked on a career as a coach with the AHL New Haven Nighthawks in 1985. Like Keenan, who preceded him, Ftorek's coaching career was marred by controversy. In 2000 he was coaching the New Jersey Devils, and he scratched defenseman Ken Daneyko, who was two games shy of 1,000 in his career at the time, ensuring Daneyko would not achieve the milestone on home ice. General manager Lou Lamoriello fired Ftorek with just eight games left in the regular season, and Larry Robinson led the team to a Stanley Cup championship that spring.

Ftorek had an abbreviated career as coach of the Bruins, named in 2001 and fired by general manager Mike O'Connell near the end of his second season. He had led the Bruins to a first-place finish with a 43–24–6–9 record in his first season, but the Bruins were 33–28–8–4 when he was fired with just nine games left in his second season. Ftorek became the first coach to ever be fired in the closing days of a regular season with a winning and playoff-bound team—by *two* different franchises. O'Connell finished the season as interim coach.

Some players had issues with Ftorek, but Raycroft enjoyed his tenure with the coach. Andrew was playing in Providence, and he said Ftorek was a regular visitor to see the minor league affiliate play. He developed a relationship with young players before they ever got a chance with the NHL team. Sometimes those relationships paid off.

"Robbie was amazing for the younger players. He loved the young guys. I'll give you an example...It's the end of the Olympic break, and I think Byron Dafoe's wife was having a baby. So I get the call the day of the game, and I show up to Long Island and he just says, 'You're playing tonight.' Meanwhile, Johnny

Grahame has been putting work in all year, and Robbie throws me the start."

Mike Sullivan

Another local legend, Mike Sullivan of Marshfield, Massachusetts, and Boston University, took over for the next two seasons. With Providence in the AHL, before he ascended to Boston, Sullivan's team posted a remarkable record of 41–17–9–4 in his only season there.

In 2003–04, Sullivan's Bruins rolled to a record of 41–19–15–7 for 104 points and first place in the Northeast Division. The team had added Sergei Gonchar and Michael Nylander at the trade deadline, and appeared to be loading up for a strong playoff run. The team was deep, although without a standout offensive player. Thornton was the top scorer with 73 points, and Glen Murray was the leading goal scorer with 32. But they were also the only two players to top the 50-point plateau. Andrew Raycroft was the No. 1 goaltender, finishing 29–18–9 in 57 games played with a 2.05 goals-against average and .926 save percentage.

The Bruins were eliminated by the Montreal Canadiens in the first round of the playoffs. You will remember these were the playoffs in which captain Joe Thornton played with broken ribs. He played in all seven games, but didn't have a point and was minus-6.

The loss was especially galling after the Bruins took 2–0 and 3–1 leads in the series before dropping three in a row. They really weren't in any of the last three games, losing 5–1, 5–2, and 2–0.

The ensuing NHL lockout led to the league historically cancelling the 2004–05 season. The Bruins, who had let most of their free agents leave after the season (believing the new collective bargaining agreement would provide an opportunity to sign star players from other teams at affordable prices), greatly misjudged what the post-lockout landscape would be. Instead of Rolston, Nylander, and Gonchar, the Bruins instead signed lesser-lights like Alexei Zhamnov and David Scatchard, and brought in an over-the-hill Brian Leetch on defense.

Sullivan's team finished with a record of 29–37–16 and finished in fifth place in the division. O'Connell was fired as general manager near the end of the season, and then after the Bruins turned to Peter Chiarelli as their new GM in the summer of 2006, he didn't renew Sullivan's contract.

It took a while but Sullivan eventually worked his way back to being an NHL head coach. His Pittsburgh Penguins team won back-to-back Stanley Cup championships in 2015–16 and 2016–17.

If the Bruins had stuck with Sullivan, who knows what the outcome would have been. The coaching talent was clearly there; Sullivan just didn't have the players, and maybe he just wasn't ready to be a champion in Boston. Regardless, things worked out for him.

Unfortunately, things didn't work out for the Bruins or Chiarelli after the new GM made his first coaching hire. They struck out with yet another coaching decision. Fans might remember Dave Lewis' unflattering record of 35–41–6 and a last-place finish in the division in 2006–07, his only season behind the Boston bench. I remember Lewis as the most open coach I ever dealt with. I would meet with him in his office before every game, and he would tell me everything—even things that he asked me to keep to myself. He would tell me bluntly and plainly why certain players were playing and why others weren't. He would give me pregame strategy and explain what he was thinking for each decision. It made it much easier to broadcast the games, because Lewis let me inside the coaching office and the dressing room. It was ironic that one of the villains of Bruins lore was actually an affable guy I got to know well. After all, more than 20 years earlier, Lewis had been the antagonist in one of the uglier moments in Bruins history.

I was working for the Maine Mariners of the AHL when the parent New Jersey Devils hosted the Bruins in a preseason game at the Cumberland County Civic Center. The Devils always played a preseason game in Portland, but bringing the Bruins to town made it extra special on October 7, 1984.

There was a sellout crowd and the loyalties probably swung in favor of the Bruins, especially after a play by Lewis. He went low at center ice and took out promising Bruins defenseman (and my future broadcast partner) Gord Kluzak, who tore ligaments in his left knee, leading to major reconstructive surgery and his missing the entire 1984–85 season. Gordie reinjured his knee in September 1986 and missed another whole season. Kluzak was never the same player, and he never forgave Lewis for the low hit that began the downfall.

While Lewis was always accessible and easy for me to deal with as a play-by-play announcer, I'm pretty sure Gordie never had a conversation with him. He never forgave Lewis for what he saw as a premature end to his stellar playing career. He didn't have a lot of opportunities to make conversation, as Lewis didn't last beyond that first season.

Claude Julien

Lewis' firing resulted in Chiarelli making up for his mistake by hiring the greatest coach of my Bruins lifetime, and possibly in the entire history of the franchise. Fans may not have known much about Claude Julien when he was hired, but I did.

I first knew Claude as a player for the Fredericton Express of the American Hockey League. Julien shuttled between the AHL and the Quebec Nordiques of the National Hockey League, but the Maine Mariners played against the Express a lot and I knew Julien as a stay-at-home defenseman.

Julien held the position of head coach for the Bruins for 10 seasons. Although Chiarelli had struck out with his first coaching hire, the Bruins had begun to spend money in free agency much more freely than ever before. In summer 2006, the team had lured free agents Marc Savard and Zdeno Chara to the franchise. Patrice Bergeron was a blossoming young star and Tim Thomas had been brought back from Europe to man the net. The assembled talent, combined with Julien's defense-first philosophy, helped the Bruins make a remarkable turnaround.

As the team began its climb back to league superiority, it had to suffer through one of the worst playoff defeats ever. In 2010 the Bruins had a 3–0 series lead over the Philadelphia Flyers, then led Game 7 by a 3–0 score before falling 4–3 and being eliminated. Astute fans knew that the Bruins were playing without David Krejci, Marco Sturm, and Dennis Seidenberg; that Marc Savard was barely himself after coming back from a concussion; and that Thomas was battling a hip injury. Bandwagon fans didn't care and saw only a gut-wrenching playoff loss that should not have happened.

I can tell you that the reaction of Bruins fans to my talk show was almost unanimously against returning Julien to the position. In fact, he never seemed to resonate with Bruins fans, even in the aftermath of winning a Stanley Cup championship.

Claude had a reputation, which he didn't earn, of being hard on young players, and was accused of trying to "win games 0–0." He had a defensive mindset, and he required players to play all 200 feet of the rink. That wasn't a problem for most of the players, but some younger players (Phil Kessel, Tyler Seguin, Dougie Hamilton) chafed at Julien's style of play. When those younger players left the organization, fans had a tendency to blame Julien for the defections.

Julien didn't let the failure derail his plan, however, and in 2010–11 the franchise was right back in the playoff picture. In the first series, the Bruins battled back from losing the first two games at home and eliminated the Montreal Canadiens in overtime of Game 7. I am convinced that if Nathan Horton had not scored the game-winning goal in overtime of Game 7, the Bruins would have fired Julien, following what would have been back-to-back first-round departures.

The Bruins then gained some measure of revenge by sweeping the Flyers from the Eastern Conference semifinals four games to none.

Then the Bruins had a great playoff series against the Tampa Bay Lightning for the Eastern Conference title. The Bruins won their second Game 7, 1–0, at the Garden in a game that I still say is the greatest I ever saw. I was sitting in the Garden as a fan that night, or I should say I was standing, because almost no one sat the entire game. Start to finish, I've never seen a better-played game, a better-coached game, or a better-officiated game. There were no penalties called, to either team, and the score certainly didn't indicate the passion and intensity of the game. The Bruins were on to the Stanley Cup Final against the Vancouver Canucks.

In the Final the Bruins had more adversity to overcome. Boston lost the first two games of the series in Vancouver, and then lost star forward Nathan Horton in the first period of Game 3 in Boston. Horton, who scored the overtime game winner in Game 7 of the Montreal series, was felled by a concussive (and flagrant) hit by Aaron Rome, and was knocked out for the remainder of the series. The Bruins rode the remarkable goaltending of Thomas to a third Game 7 victory of the postseason and won their first Stanley Cup since 1972.

Claude Julien hoists the Stanley Cup after the Bruins defeated the Canucks in Game 7 of the Final in 2011. *(AP Photos)*

Julien propelled the team back into the Final two years later, but the Bruins fell to the Chicago Blackhawks in six games. Despite the defeat, that series will always be remembered in Bruins history for the heroic performance of Bergeron.

I remember walking out of the Garden with broadcast partner Billy Jaffe when we ran into Julien on our way into the player parking lot after the Bruins lost Game 6. We congratulated and commiserated with Julien for a few minutes when Claude had to take a call on his cell phone. It was trainer Don DelNegro, telling Julien that Bergeron was on his way to the hospital with broken ribs and a punctured lung. He'd suffered the punctured lung while getting a shot for the pain from the rib injury he'd suffered in Game 4. He was so numb in Game 6, he dislocated his shoulder. I always wondered if Patrice kept the extent of his injuries from both DelNegro and Julien until the game and series were over.

Julien's Bruins won the Presidents' Trophy in 2014 to add to his résumé, which already included the aforementioned Stanley Cup championship and Stanley Cup Final loss. Julien broke the team record for lifetime career victories and finished his decade with the Bruins 419–246–94. He was fired February 7, 2017, with the Bruins struggling and coming off two straight years of missing the playoffs on the last weekend of the season.

Perhaps in a stroke of psychic karma, Julien was named head coach of the Montreal Canadiens just seven days after being fired by the Bruins. It was also the second time that Julien had replaced Michel Therrien as head coach of Montreal. It was back to the other side of the Bruins/Canadiens rivalry for Julien.

Bruce Cassidy

General manager Don Sweeney named longtime minor league head coach and NHL assistant coach Bruce Cassidy as the interim to replace Julien. He guided the team to a record of 18–8–1, good enough to put the Bruins back into the playoffs, where they lost to the Ottawa Senators four games to two. Cassidy was getting his second chance as an NHL head coach after booting away his opportunity with the Washington Capitals, which ended in 2004.

He began the long road back serving first as an assistant coach with the Chicago Blackhawks and then as head coach of the Kingston Frontenacs and the Providence Bruins.

Cassidy was once a rocket ship, sailing through the lower coaching ranks and arriving as a head coach in the NHL at the youthful age of 37. That was after his playing career ended earlier than expected.

Cassidy was a first-round draft pick of the Chicago Blackhawks in the 1983 NHL draft and made his NHL debut at the age of 19 in March 1984. But as is often the case with players, he was done in by a series of physical issues. Between 1984 and 1988 he had three knee surgeries and had to have his ACL reconstructed. As a result, Cassidy spent much of his career in the minor leagues playing for the Nova Scotia Oilers, the Saginaw Generals, the Saginaw Hawks, and the Indianapolis Ice. He also played several seasons in Italy and Germany.

After Cassidy retired as a player, he began his coaching career with the Jacksonville Lizard Kings of the East Coast Hockey League. He followed with stints as head coach of the Indianapolis Ice (IHL), the Trenton Titans (ECHL), and the Grand Rapids Griffins (IHL). Those efforts led to his promotion to head coach of the Washington Capitals in 2002. Almost from the beginning, there were issues between Cassidy and his players.

Several players felt that the young Cassidy was unprepared for his position. They chafed at the leadership he provided and they feuded with him almost from the beginning. Some of the blame was probably his, but much also rested with the players who never seemed to give Cassidy the chance he deserved. Bruce, for his part, tries not to think too much of his brief 15-month tenure as an NHL head coach.

"I don't talk about my first go-round a lot, because first of all it was 15 years ago, and I think I forget most of it. I don't think I had a true appreciation for how difficult it really was. I had only been coaching for five years, and I kind of rose up quick."

His firing from the Capitals led to a 12-year journey back to the NHL. He was an assistant coach for the Blackhawks, head coach for the Kingston Frontenacs in the Quebec Major Junior Hockey League, assistant coach for the Boston Bruins' Providence farm club, and ultimately head coach for Providence, trying to work his way back to the NHL.

"I always wanted a second chance because the first one didn't go as well as I would have liked. There were some good parts, and there were some parts that you would want to be better. But I always realized that there are only 31 jobs. But I couldn't let it consume me. If my calling was to coach younger guys, and if I didn't get back to the NHL and coached in the American League, then I was okay with that. I almost preferred that to being an assistant coach in the NHL. I had my own ideas, and I always felt I was geared to be a head coach. Some people would say, 'Well, if you're an assistant coach in the NHL you've got a better chance to get that second chance.' Other people would tell me, 'If you want to be a head coach, then be a head coach.' You want to be as prepared as you can if you get that second chance."

Bruce was promoted from Providence and named an assistant coach for Claude Julien's staff in Boston before the 2016–17 season. Cassidy replaced Julien on an interim basis on February 7, 2017. The team went 18–8–1 over the final 27 games and returned to the playoffs for the first time in three seasons. The interim tag was taken from his title by Sweeney in the offseason, and he was named the head coach on April 26, 2017. For Cassidy, it was a dream come true.

"So, this time, I absolutely appreciate it more. I do believe, as I always have, that it's a privilege to coach in the National Hockey League, and I think it even more so now. I've been a Bruins fan my whole life, not just since I started working for the Bruins. I would go head-to-head with almost anyone on Bruins trivia, and I think I know more than most. Hell, I was at the game the lights went out here against Edmonton. So for me, an Original Six franchise *and* the Boston Bruins—it's a dream come true for me. I wanted to play for them, so I guess the next best thing is being able to coach for them."

As a guy who spent eight seasons trying to work my way out of the American Hockey League, I think I have a real appreciation for people who also pay their dues. When I told Bruce there were times that I wondered if I would ever get my chance to go the NHL, he admitted there were times when he wondered, as well.

"Yes and no. It didn't consume me. I always wanted a second chance because the first one didn't go as well as I would have liked. There were some good parts, and there were some parts that you would want to be better. But I always realized that there are only 31 jobs. But I couldn't let it consume me."

Bruins fans tell me all the time that they really enjoy watching Cassidy's team play. The criticism under Julien was that it was always a defense-first mentality and the game wasn't always fun to watch. Bruins president Cam Neely once said that Julien coached like he was trying to win every game 0–0. Cassidy tries to remember what it was like to play, and pass that feeling on to his players.

"I was told after I had been coaching for a few years, and someone said to me, 'Butch, don't forget what it was like to play.' And it made me think, you know what, you still have to have some fun playing the game. They can't be robots, and they can't be too structured either. You've got to let the guys play and be creative. That always stuck with me, for practices and for games. You want to get your work done, and have some rules, but you still want to enjoy playing. I think our guys do enjoy playing the game."

Don't mistake that overall philosophy with not having a certain style that Bruce prefers his team play. Ask him, and he rattles off a list of characteristics he wants his team to exhibit.

"I want our team to be hard to play against, fast, defensive, resilient, never give up, play 65 minutes if that's what it takes," Cassidy told me. "I would like us to have some pace, and make some plays without being reckless. Generally speaking, I think the teams I've coached transition well and are hard to play against in terms of structure, both with the puck and without the puck. I wouldn't say every team I've had has been fast, and not every team has been physical, and not every team has been the best defensive team or offensive team. In the American Hockey League you get a different hand every year, and you just play the hand you're dealt. You mold your style to the players

Bruce Cassidy took over for Claude Julien behind the bench in 2017. *(AP Photos)*

you have, and that's something I've learned over time. I would like an attacking style. I want an attack mentality, with and without the puck."

When you talk about molding your style to the players you have available, Bruce admits it's still a work in progress. It means getting the most from the players who have been here for a while and utilizing the skills of the players who have recently joined the organization. There are a couple of those younger players who likely represent the future of the Bruins franchise.

I asked Bruce if he felt the added pressure of trying to get franchise-altering play out of a couple of these very young, but very talented players.

"I assume you're talking, first, about Charlie McAvoy. And it's not necessarily about helping him get it out; it might be more about staying the hell out of his way. Maybe other coaches would have made him pay his dues more, and wouldn't have given him so much so quick. But it began in the playoffs in 2017. If the guy is better than what you have and he's that good early on, then God bless him. Let's use that talent and tap into it. Talent like that helps build the franchise, and that trickles down to coaches and management and others."

Bruins fans also know they have another young and supremely talented player among the forward lines, but Bruce has known about David Pastrnak even longer than Bruins fans have.

"I've coached David [Pastrnak] since he was 18 years old. I love his personality, and I love his passion for the game. It's a little more work in terms of balancing creativity and making the right play at the right time."

For those of us who have been around the team for a number of years, Bruce also represents a sea change in style and philosophy. Under Julien—an incredibly successful Stanley Cup–winning coach— the team seemed to be replicating what was being done in Foxboro by the New England Patriots. I co-host Bill Belichick's radio appearance every Monday after Patriots games, and there's no one better at telling you nothing than the taciturn head football coach. He's also arguably the greatest coach in the history of the NFL, so no one can complain about his abrasive style. Julien was a little more approachable than Belichick, but information was just as hard to come by as with the Patriots.

For his part, Bruce seems to be more open and more informative. He is also more willing to be honest about a player's performance. He is willing to say, "We need more from Player X," or "Player Y didn't give us what we needed tonight." That honesty is different, and thus far he doesn't feel it has been a detriment.

"I would prefer that you can be honest. I think it's the easiest way to deal with people. That's been said of me, but I also think I'm direct with players behind closed doors. I tell them what I think and what I think needs to be done. I think the players respond to it, because they know I care about them. It's not just a lot of hot air, and I never talk to them. Everything I ever say to the press has generally been told to them already. It's been talked about on the bench or in the office or at practice. Most of these players believe that I have their back, and I do. I will work with them, and give them second, third, or fourth chances. I never think, 'Oh, this guy can't play, and I don't want to work with them.' It was ingrained in me in the American League, that my job was to make the players better, and you have to have patience.

"I just have a tough time, if someone asks me a question, to skirt around the real answer. I would rather just deal with it. 'We weren't good enough. We're going to be better, and this is how we're going to be better.' I guess I'm not good with vanilla. It's just not me. And you know what? It can work for or against you. I guess I've caught a break here because no one has excoriated me for it. It seems like people appreciate my honesty. I'm not killing guys; I'm just telling it like it is. Maybe this market just responds better to that, and my players do. They know that I never absolve myself from blame either. If we aren't ready, it's my job to get them ready."

While much of the excitement around the Bruins after Cassidy took over involved the young stars, Bruce knew full well he still had at least a couple of players who might be as good as anyone in their generation.

First there's Zdeno Chara.

"For a guy his size, and his ability to move around the ice, to contribute offensively and still be one of the best shutdown guys in the league, it's really something," Cassidy said. "He's one of the best penalty killers in the league, but he's also a great power-play force. Look, I'm six feet, and it's just hard for a person my size to imagine what it's like for a guy 6'9" to do what he does. He's even bigger on skates, and the hand-eye coordination involved is truly amazing."

What Chara provides on the Bruins blue line, Patrice Bergeron provides up front. But Bruce also freely admits that even he might not have had a proper appreciation for Bergeron's game...at least not until he joined the Bruins' coaching staff in 2016.

"Patrice is a guy you just can't appreciate until you coach him. Until you've coached this guy, the outside world just can't realize what he brings—his details, his preparation, his work ethic, his desire to get better—people don't even appreciate the half of it. Look, he's not the physical specimen, he's not the fastest guy on the ice, he's not the biggest guy, he doesn't have the hardest shot, he doesn't have the best hands. But when you talk about the overall, the complete tool box, the respect for the game, the structure and the detail, that's what separates him."

Players such as Chara, Bergeron, David Backes, Adam McQuaid, and others provide so much to the Bruins on the ice, but perhaps even more off the ice. Coaches coach and players play, but leaders lead, and that leadership is much more effective when coming from the players within the dressing room.

"Leadership from within the dressing room is way more important than what we coaches say or do. You see guys like Jake DeBrusk, Anders Bjork, Charlie McAvoy—all those guys—the guys in the room have much more to do with making them better players and better people than from guys in suits. Those are the guys who play together and practice together, and it's a totally different form of leadership."

Bruce is still feeling parts of the new NHL out as he goes along. Like other coaches in the league, he is still not sure he has a complete grasp of the 3-on-3 overtime format, and how to best attack and take advantage of it.

"I think the overtime is exciting and I think the fans like it. I'm not sure that everyone has figured it out yet, in terms of the strategy involved. You don't see it all that often, and it's hard to replicate in practice. There's plenty of room for the coaches to mess it up. We're still trying to figure out what is the best way to win in overtime. I've never seen anyone use three defensemen out there, but I've seen coaches use three forwards. Are you better off counter-punching, or attacking? Because it's sudden death, should you just go all out to get that win right away? Goalies get involved a little more and move the puck instead of freezing it. I like it because it's exciting, and I'm a fan of exciting hockey."

If there were a criticism of Bruce in early stages of his Bruins coaching career, it was that he seemed too serious, even after wins. I had to just ask him, directly, if he was enjoying his time as the Bruins' coach—if he was having fun.

"My wife says that to me," he laughed. "Guys ask me a question and I want go give them the best answer. I *am* having fun. I guess I should smile more. I always thought I was kind of an easygoing guy, especially away from the rink. But when the puck drops, it's a little different. You kind of get dialed in, and you're getting judged on a lot of different things, and you want to make sure you've got all your ducks in a row."

As I've said, I've dealt with a number of Bruins coaches over the years, and I really enjoy dealing with a guy as direct and honest as Bruce Cassidy. I have the feeling his players are enjoying their time with him as well.

CHAPTER 7
HARRY SINDEN

Harry Sinden began his career in the Bruins organization as the player/coach of the Minneapolis Bruins and the Oklahoma City Blazers of the Central Hockey League. As proof that timing is everything, Harry was promoted to head coach of the Boston Bruins for the 1966–67 season. The 33-year-old Sinden was the youngest coach in the NHL, and his arrival coincided with the arrival of the greatest player in the history of the team—Bobby Orr. Harry told me he didn't necessarily know, at that stage of his career, that a team needed a top defenseman to succeed. But he soon learned that to be true.

"I came to realize that you had to have that cornerstone defenseman to be successful. I'm not sure I knew it at the beginning, but I came to learn it. Bobby [Orr] and I arrived in the same year, and I became the beneficiary. One of the problems with people judging teams, coaches, or management is that they really don't understand how much the players mean to the success of the team. When you get a player like Orr, like I did, that is a gift. No matter what you think you can do as a coach or manager, if you don't have a guy like Bobby Orr things are going to be a lot different. The franchise was just languishing, and Bobby saved the franchise. There is no doubt in my mind, I was the lucky beneficiary of that."

Harry told me it didn't take long to figure out what he and the Bruins had in the 18-year-old Orr.

"Dale, you might say I'm full of crap to say this, but it only took one look at him," Sinden said. "This was such a special player, one of the most special players in the history of this league. I watched him play in the junior championships in Canada, and he was injured with a pulled groin, and he was still sensational.

138

I really came to realize what he was at our first training camp, when he was a dominant figure. Our first preseason game was against Toronto, the defending Stanley Cup champions, and he was the best player on the ice at the age of 18. He wasn't the best player because he scored three goals, or anything like that, he was just easily the best player. You would have to be blind to not realize what was there."

Despite the thrill of working with a planet player like Bobby Orr, Sinden had issues with team ownership and announced his retirement from the team in 1970, just days after the Bruins clinched their first Stanley Cup championship in 29 years. Harry left the game and actually accepted a position with a home construction company, Stirling Homex, in Rochester, New York.

After two years away from the game, Harry accepted the job as head coach and manager of the Canadian team in the Summit Series in 1972. Sinden's team was the winner of a thrilling come-from-behind win over the Russian team, the final game decided by Paul Henderson with just 34 seconds left in the game, one of the most famous goals scored in Canadian hockey history. Just days after the series, Harry signed a five-year contract to return to the Bruins, replacing Milt Schmidt as general manager after Schmidt moved to the position of executive director.

Sinden served as the Bruins GM for the next 28 years. He helped the Bruins establish the North American professional sports record of 29 consecutive playoff appearances. His teams won two regular-season titles and reached the Stanley Cup Final five times. He retired as the president of the Bruins in 2006, but had no idea when he returned to the Bruins that his tenure would last so long.

"Oh, absolutely not. I wanted to come back in a situation that gave me some control of what was going on. When they agreed to that, I certainly didn't know how long it was going to last, but I also knew that most of these jobs in professional hockey were based on winning and losing, so my future was going to hang on that."

Despite all the team's successes, it takes Harry almost no time to recall the most painful period. He doesn't want to talk much about it, but the departure of Bobby Orr to the Chicago Blackhawks in 1976 was the low point of his time in Boston.

"We did everything we could from a management standpoint to keep him," Sinden said. "I don't really want to rehash it. He was injured, and we knew his time was limited, but we had to keep him. He made the franchise what it was. It's history, and it's kind of painful to go back over it. But as far as Bobby and I are concerned, it's all been resolved."

As Harry watched Orr battle through one knee injury after another he began to think of that next No. 1 defenseman who could follow in his footsteps. It led Harry to make one of the most unpopular trades in the history of the Bruins.

"I lived by the principal that when you come to the decision that you can do something to help your team, and you refuse to do it because you're worried about what the media or fans will think, then you need to get out. Sometimes it doesn't work, and sometimes it does. I knew, especially when we traded Phil [Esposito], that we were going to get blasted like never before. With Bobby's physical situation being what it was, I knew this was the only chance we had to get that next cornerstone defenseman [Brad Park]. When you know, in your own mind, that the move will help your team then you have to do it. If you're wrong, then you're fired."

While Brad Park was the current cornerstone defenseman, Harry knew that physical limitations were catching up to the incomparable Park. It meant he had to seek the next great Boston defenseman, and he was able to draft Raymond Bourque with the No. 8 pick in the first round of the 1979 NHL draft. The choice was not met with unanimous approval even among his own scouting staff.

"I was not conflicted, because I saw Raymond play. Our scouts were conflicted between Raymond and Keith Brown, who was ultimately chosen by the Chicago Blackhawks the pick before we selected. But I had seen Raymond play, and he caught my eye. Our scouts were really high on Brown, and I didn't know him, but I really knew Ray, so I told the scouts, 'If you think he is better than Bourque, then you are telling me he'll be an All-Star player and he'll be one of the most outstanding players to ever play in the league.'"

Chicago made it easy by selecting Brown, and Bourque became a Bruin. Harry had his successor in the lineage of Orr and Park. Raymond Bourque was that bedrock blue-liner until the 1999–2000 season, when Raymond asked Harry to trade him, hopefully to a Stanley Cup contender. It was a request that Sinden completely understood.

"Raymond and I had always had that kind of relationship, and I understood at that time how he felt. You were doing the games, and you know, we were heading nowhere. We weren't going to make the playoffs, and he was in the final year of his contract. He was reluctant to ask me, and he was reluctant to leave, because he didn't want to look like he was deserting Boston, which he loved so dearly.

"I think he would have preferred someplace closer to home, like Philadelphia, the Rangers, or the Islanders, but Colorado was a very strong team, and Raymond had a relationship with their goaltender, Patrick Roy. When I called him to tell him we had made a deal with Colorado, he was surprised, but I don't think disappointed. And he did win the Stanley Cup. For Raymond's sake, and all he did for us here in Boston, I felt that if there was one Cup we didn't win that I was happy for, it was that one."

Harry pulled off another franchise-altering trade prior to the 1986–87 season. He dealt one of my current broadcast partners, Barry Pederson, to the Vancouver Canucks. In exchange, he received a young right wing named Cam Neely and the third pick in the 1987 draft, which he used to select Glen Wesley. But even Harry admits he had no idea what he was getting in Neely.

"I certainly can't say I thought I was trading for a Hall of Fame right winger. But I had watched the Memorial Cup finals that he played in a couple of years before that, even though I knew we had no chance to draft him where we were picking, but I certainly noticed him. Then when the opportunity came up, our chief scout happened to live in Vancouver, and he watched Cam play a lot. He told me that Cam was a player Vancouver was underutilizing and that they didn't realize how good he was. He was young, and he was big, and he said, 'Harry, you've got to think about him.' I relied on my scout's final evaluation, and we traded Barry Pederson for him."

While Harry was at the helm of the Bruins, the team suffered through some horrific times and injuries. Normand Leveille suffered a life-threatening and career-ending stroke, Gord Kluzak had his career cut woefully short by knee injuries, and Craig MacTavish served time in prison for DUI and vehicular homicide after killing a young Maine woman in an auto accident in Peabody, Massachusetts. Harry admits he often thinks about what might have been.

Harry Sinden, one of the most important figures in Bruins history. *(AP Photos)*

"I think about it all the time. The Celtics lost Reggie Lewis and Len Bias, and it was horrible for their franchise, but I honestly think us losing Gord Kluzak to his knee injury and Normand Leveille to the stroke was every bit as dramatic to the talent level on our franchise. I remember we traded for Ken Linseman from Philadelphia, and he said, 'Harry, your franchise is under a black cloud.' He was talking about Kluzak and Leveille and Craig MacTavish. I'm only talking about the talent of the players here, but things like that really hurt our franchise."

Harry was also one of the people trying to convince others in the NHL that it was a league in financial peril. He was correct, but few would listen. I remember, vividly, when the Pittsburgh Penguins signed Mario Lemieux to a huge new contract. Harry told me, simply, "Dale, Pittsburgh can't pay that contract." Ultimately, the Penguins were forced to declare bankruptcy, in November 1998, and the largest creditor was Mario Lemieux, who was owed more than $32 million in deferred salaries. Lemieux ultimately gained controlling interest in the team and still owns it to this day.

"In those years—the late '80s and early '90s—it was a battle to get the economics of the NHL across to anybody. So many of these owners, over the years, have so much money that it's not a factor in their minds when they try to win or lose.

"I can tell you I never had any financial restrictions from Mr. Jacobs. He did nothing to stop me from spending whatever I wanted. If I thought a player would guarantee we would win the Cup, I could go out and get that player, and I would have. I was trying to win the championship with a team that wasn't going to go out and break the bank. The league had a lot of teams that might not have broken the bank for them, but it might for other teams in the league. There were about six teams in the NHL that forced the league to shut down for an entire season because of them. Whatever you might think of Gary Bettman, he's an incredibly strong person to have done that."

The lockout was one of two that the NHL endured to achieve financial stability, and ultimately the tool that likely saved the league—the salary cap. That 2004–05 lockout caused cancellation of the entire season. In the 2012–13 season, another lockout shortened the season to 48 games. Many of us worried that fans would not endure losing the 2004–05 season and the league would not survive at all.

"I thought the league would survive, but I didn't know how many teams would survive. As it turned out, the lockout was the

144

thing that saved so many teams. When we shut down we had teams that had a way higher payroll than our salary cap is today, 12 years later. Think about that, we had teams spending more 12 years ago than the cap is today. The money wasn't necessarily out of the range of the Bruins, but we really felt that if we were going to keep a 30-team league, we had to help the league come to its senses."

Another area in which Harry was likely ahead of his time concerned fighting in the league. Hockey is the only professional sport that allows two combatants to drop their sticks and gloves, punch each other in the head, serve a five-minute penalty, and return to the game. Fighting in football, basketball, and baseball means immediate ejection.

But Harry presided over a team known all across New England as the Big Bad Bruins and tough guys are as popular as goal scorers in Boston. But Harry felt that the game had to expand its fan base, and he also felt one way to do that was to curtail fighting.

"Glen Sather once said to me, 'Harry, fighting is unnecessary. It's a waste of time.' I felt, at the time, it probably couldn't be avoided. We have players with sticks in their hands, and it's played on a surface that makes it hard to control yourself. But what fighting has turned out to be is a waste of time, and we just don't see much of it anymore."

Harry's way of thinking coincided with my partner Gord Kluzak's, but they approached it from different perspectives. Gordie was concerned about the long-term medical issues—and he was ahead of his time in that regard—while Harry felt that fighting was somewhat limiting to many peripheral fans. Harry knew that hockey fans would never abandon their sport, but that some potential fans were kept away by the fighting. He was probably right, and there is much less today.

Harry watches almost every Bruins game, either in person or on television from his winter home in Florida. He has some strong opinions about several of the current players, and it's not surprising that one of his favorites is center Patrice Bergeron.

"I've been around here for a long time, and Patrice Bergeron ranks among the very best players we've ever had here. He came out of the Junior League in Nova Scotia, and we had a scout named Daniel Dore, who was pining for this guy. No one was really paying attention to Bergeron, but Daniel was so adamant that we ended up taking him based on his constant whining about the guy. Patrice ended up being one of the best players we've ever drafted, in the second round. Sometimes when a guy scores 30 goals, he might not do anything in the other 50 games. A guy like Patrice might only score 20 goals, but in the other 60 he is still one of the best players on the ice and he wins games for you. He is one of the real crowns of my time with the Bruins."

I've talked about Harry always wanting that cornerstone defenseman, and he thinks Captain Zdeno Chara falls perfectly into that progression from Orr to Park to Bourque.

"I'm watching Zdeno Chara at the age of 41 and he's having a sensational year. He's among the top defensemen we've ever had here, no question about it. He might not look sensational, he might not be a great skater, but he's a great, great player. I love Zdeno. He also has to be one of the best captains we've ever had. He's such a nice man, he gets his teammates to believe in him, and he loves working with young players. He's just perfect."

And make no mistake, Harry doesn't mince words when he talks about Chara's pedigree. He thinks it will ultimately lead to a spot in the Hockey Hall of Fame.

"Rod Langway went into the Hall of Fame, and I think he had three goals in his last season. I was on the Hall of Fame [Selection] Committee at the time and spoke on his behalf. I said that when you played against Rod Langway, chances were you weren't going to get a good scoring chance. He got into the Hall without any statistics to speak about. Zdeno is every bit as good, and every bit in the same class."

Harry was once asked by general manager Don Sweeney to head over to the Agganis Arena and scout a Boston University player who Sweeney was very interested in. He headed over and watched the game with a man he hoped would coach the Bruins. Jack Parker was offered the job by Sinden, but ultimately decided to stay on Causeway Street.

"Jackie Parker is a sensational man, and he would have been a sensational NHL coach. He has such a hockey mind and a hockey sense. I was so impressed with him, and I was terribly disappointed when he decided not to take the job when [Sweeney] offered it to him. I understood, and Jackie and I are still good friends. The last time I saw him, I was scouting Charlie McAvoy for Donnie Sweeney, and Jackie and I sat together and watched him play."

Harry knows a thing or two about scouting young hockey talent, and he knew what he was seeing in McAvoy. He also had an idea, when the Bruins selected McAvoy No. 14 overall in the 2016 draft, where he might fit in.

"Charlie is not like Zdeno Chara or Raymond Bourque—and I never compare anyone to Bobby Orr—but the guy he reminds me most of is Brad Park. He has that brilliant pass out of his own end, some really good, hard hits. He makes some of the same mistakes defensively that Brad used to make. He's a much better skater than Brad, mainly because Brad was so injured by the time he got here. But what Charlie has accomplished so early in his career is just remarkable. It usually takes a while for defensemen to understand the game, and he's not all the way there yet, but he's on his way."

It's ironic that Harry was scouting a young college defenseman on behalf Sweeney. Harry drafted Sweeney No. 166 overall in the 1984 draft, and despite his diminutive stature, he went on to play more than 1,100 games in the NHL. But Harry admits he didn't think Sweeney was limited to just a possible career in hockey management.

"I certainly understood what a bright young man he was. After his career was over he was in the running for a job in the admissions department at Harvard University, and I got a call to ask me about Donnie. I told them he was a brilliant young man who had his life in order. I thought this about him before he ever went to work for us. The only other guy I thought might end up in hockey management was Mike Milbury, which is what he did."

Harry has made many, many more successful moves than bad ones, but when I asked him if there was a move he wish he could have back he didn't hesitate.

"Yeah, and like everyone else in management, there is more than one," he laughed. "The hiring of Mike Keenan is on that list. I really liked Mike, and I think he's a good hockey man, but we couldn't get any ideas across to Mike except his own. I'm not talking about me; I'm talking about our doctors, our trainers, our players, from anybody. We couldn't get him to listen to anyone except himself. I learned later—and it's a good line—that if you interview Mike Keenan, you hire Mike Keenan, and that's what happened to us."

Harry was emotional, both as a coach and GM. There are legendary stories about him racing over to the booth in the press box where the NHL officials supervisor would be sitting and making his point about what he viewed as a botched call. Sometimes, he could take that argument to the officials' room downstairs between periods to make that point. And occasionally he made a decision as GM based on emotion. Sometimes it was a mistake.

"Remember a player named Tom Fergus? We went to arbitration with Tom on a clause in his contract. The hearing was held in Boston the day before we played the Toronto Maple Leafs at the Garden, and his representative didn't win the argument on his behalf. Tom said in the paper that he never wanted to wear a Bruins sweater again. Well, we were playing Toronto the next night so I traded him to the Maple Leafs for Bill Derlago, who I didn't even know. Derlago was a terrible Bruin, and he didn't work out at all. Tommy went to Toronto and was a much, much better player than the guy I got for him. I let my heart lead my brain, and it was a huge mistake. It was a bad deal."

Like every other hockey fan, Harry was excited to finally see his team recapture the Stanley Cup in 2011. Harry knew how loyal Bruins fans were, and he certainly knew what it would mean to his fan base to win the Cup again.

"The Red Sox and Bruins own NESN. When John Henry bought the Red Sox, I was in a lot of meetings with him. I told him that there was a time in Boston when the only two teams that mattered to fans were the Red Sox and the Bruins. After the Sox won the World Series in 2004, I told him that he would see someday, when the Bruins won the Stanley Cup, exactly what I meant. In 2011 I think he got what I was saying. There may be parts of the region that ignore the Bruins, but the real fans never go away. I just know what the Bruins mean to their fans. Even when we don't have success, that feeling is just lying in wait...waiting to come back out.

"Our fans don't desert us, good or bad."

As I said, Harry still watches every game and still loves the sport. But for all the advances made, he sounds like a lot of Bruins fans when he admits the game is great but still missing something for him.

"Physical play is almost nonexistent. The skill play is good, the speed is good, and the goaltending is exceptional. I'm happy to see fighting is almost gone from the game. For the mass audience, I would say the game is better today. But I really miss the physical aspect of the game. You watch all the games, and there is the odd good check, but it is certainly not what we were used to 10 or 15 years ago. Overall, I think the game is terrific. It takes a lot more than the idiots like us who run the game to ruin the sport of hockey."

Harry Sinden turned 85 years old in 2017 and is as sharp as ever. He was a lightning rod for many hockey fans around New England at times, because he never hesitated to tell it like it was (like telling Joe Juneau, who was threatening to play in Switzerland during a contract dispute with Harry, that maybe he ought to "learn how to yodel"). But make no mistake—his imprint was all over this franchise for some of the greatest seasons in team history. And I've always loved talking hockey with him.

CHAPTER 8
NATE GREENBERG

The joke among all of us around the Bruins organization was that we didn't know exactly what Nate Greenberg did, but we were positive he knew where all the bodies were buried. But we also knew this: if there were a Hall of Fame for doing team business at Locke-Ober (a famous, but sadly closed Boston restaurant), Nate would be a first-ballot choice.

Nate began as a self-described "one person PR department" in 1973, the year after Bobby Orr's second Stanley Cup championship. He worked in that department until Harry Sinden was promoted to president in 1989 and Nate was named senior assistant to the president. He retired from the team in late June 2007, after 34 years with the organization.

His early years were spent riding herd on the wildly popular Bruins team of Orr, Esposito, Sanderson, and others.

"Hockey teams, as you know, have more good guys per square inch than any sport out there. In 34 years of dealing with players, I could count on one hand the number of jerks. For the 20 odd years I was a PR department of one, they made my job easy. For instance, my hardest job with Bobby [Orr] was that he never wanted to talk to the media. He wanted the media to talk to all of his teammates. We've been friends for almost 50 years, and my only problem was that he wanted his teammates to get the attention. The press wanted Orr, Orr, and more Orr, but he wanted them to talk to the rest of the team."

As far as the worst time in Nate's career? For him, it's not even a question. On the night of January 25, 1984, Bruins forward Craig MacTavish was involved in an automobile accident in the Boston suburb of Peabody. Kim Radley, who was 26 years old and from West Newfield, Maine, was in the car MacTavish hit, and she died from her injuries four days after the accident. MacTavish ultimately pleaded guilty to vehicular homicide and driving under the influence. He was sentenced to a year in prison and missed the 1984–85 season as a result.

"This was the toughest time in my entire career. I really like Craig, personally, and I felt so bad about the accident that had taken the life of this young lady from Maine. He was one of my favorite players."

Craig was serving his sentence in Lawrence and Nate wanted to visit him and show his support.

"I'm pretty sure it was Gord Kluzak who went with me to visit him in prison up in Lawrence. If you ever needed a reason to make sure you didn't do anything wrong, you only had to see this place. The conditions were absolutely horrible. I think after six months he got moved to Salem, which was somewhat better."

After serving his time in prison, Craig said he wanted to meet with Kim Radley's family. He wanted to try and make amends, as best he could, under the circumstances.

"Craig wanted to meet with the family, and express his regrets and profound sorrow for the accident that had cost this young woman her life. We had good friends in the State Police, and one of those friends helped us connect with the family and set it all up. They set it up, and the family drove down from Maine, and that was the start of a friendship. Every time Craig was in town, the family came down. They would come to the morning skate, and they would come to the game. I think it lasted until the day Craig stopped playing, but it wouldn't surprise me if they still do get together. Everyone always kept it very quiet."

The year I was doing Bruins games on the radio, Johnny "Chief" Bucyk was sitting with me in the press box, hours before the faceoff. Chief looked down into the stands, and said to me, "Do you see those people there?" Sitting in the stands at the old Boston Garden was Craig MacTavish and what appeared to be a family. Chief was the first one to tell me the story, and I watched MacTavish visiting with the Radley family before a game. I was dumbfounded by the idea that they visited with the man who was responsible for the death of their daughter, but apparently they had reconciled with Craig years before at his request. It was touching to see.

As you might expect, there was some controversy about MacTavish's return to the team. There were a number of fans who were not willing to forgive and forget, even though the Radley family apparently was. Many fans expressed their disgust at the actions of MacTavish on that January night in Peabody, and ultimately general manager Harry Sinden decided it would be best for all involved if MacTavish left the Bruins. According to Nate, all it took was a phone call.

"Harry called Glen Sather in Edmonton and basically gave Craig to the Oilers for nothing. He felt it was best for Craig, to get his life in order, to leave Boston and get as far away as possible. Harry saved Craig's career, and gave him away just to allow him to get his life back in order."

Craig went on to play eight seasons for the Oilers, helping them win Stanley Cup championships in 1987, 1988, and 1990. He was ultimately traded to the New York Rangers, and helped them win the Cup in 1994. All this was possible because Sinden made a deal with his best friend, Sather, to give a man a second chance in life.

Nate was also there, every step of the way, when Bobby Orr left the Bruins and signed with the Chicago Blackhawks. Bruins fans were apoplectic—and especially with Sinden for "letting" Orr get away. But Nate knew the true story.

"Obviously, Harry knew every bit of the deal we had offered Bobby. Harry knew that Bobby had been offered an ownership stake in the team, a much better deal than the one he took from the Blackhawks. He took bullets from every angle for a long time about that one. That was the worst time. Bobby was No. 1, and Ray was 1a during my time. Harry took the bullets from the fans for that one, and of course, his relationship with Bobby was strained for years and years too."

I've always wondered why Sinden didn't take his case public, although I'm not sure it would have mattered in the long run. At that time, Bobby still had ultimate trust in Alan Eagleson and would have believed his agent over the Bruins GM every time. Even if Harry had attempted to tell Bobby about the Bruins' real offer and its value, I just think Eagleson would have convinced Orr it was a lie. But to hear Nate tell it, the effect on the organization was profound and felt for a long time.

"You can't even imagine the setback that was to the franchise. I saw it firsthand. Back in the day, we had a waiting list for tickets that was something like 30,000. I always laughed when I would hear something like that, but then I actually saw it. You lose a guy like Bobby Orr and that waiting list dries up overnight."

As he said earlier, Nate rates the departure of Bobby and Ray Bourque as 1 and 1a on his list of all-time disappointments.

"There is no question the trade of Ray Bourque was one of the most disappointing moments of my time with the Bruins. I hated to see it happen. I was thrilled for Raymond to win it, but you wanted to see it happen here. Every team only has a few players at the very top of their profession and Ray was one of ours."

If you think about it, the Bruins lost three of their top five players ever. Bobby left to sign with Chicago, Phil was traded to the New York Rangers, and Raymond was traded to the Colorado Avalanche. It's tough to overcome the loss of any one of those players, let alone all three of them at various times.

Nate Greenberg was probably the perfect person for the perfect job at the perfect time. He was affable and accessible and knew everyone in the city of Boston.

CHAPTER 9
BOBBY ORR

It's kind of a staple in the sports talk radio business. When things get a little slow (like the day before or after the baseball All-Star Game), there are those stupid topics that some hosts (like me) trot out.

We'll ask about listeners' favorite sports movies, first sports memory, youth sports horror stories. Or there's the tried and true, "Who's on your Mt. Rushmore of Boston sports?"

There might be some slight disagreements on a player or two, but for the most part it's the same four names: Ted Williams, Bill Russell, Tom Brady, and Bobby Orr. No one ever has any disagreement about the hockey representative.

If you're a hockey fan and grew up in New England, you say the name Robert Gordon Orr with reverence. Sometimes you don't even have to use the name. You can simply say, "Number 4." And for those of us who grew up here, he is simply the greatest player to ever play the game.

I understand the statistical argument against Orr. Wayne Gretzky's numbers are simply staggering. My favorite stat ever is that if Gretzky had never scored a goal in the NHL (and with 894 goals, he scored more than any player in league history) he *still* would be the top point producer ever. That's right; Gretzky's 1,963 assists would place him first all-time in NHL scoring. But anyone who ever saw Orr play will agree with what Tom McVie once told me: "A team of five Bobby Orrs will always beat a team of five Wayne Gretzkys."

No player in the history of the NHL revolutionized the game more than Bobby Orr. He's still the only defenseman in history to lead the league in scoring—and he did it *twice*. He still holds the NHL record for assists and points in a single season by a defenseman. He won the Norris Trophy eight straight seasons (1967–68 through 1974–75), and captured the Hart Trophy three consecutive years (1969–70 through 1971–72).

The Bruins began scouting Bobby when he was 14 years old, and at that age he was dominating players who were three, four, and five years older. He began his NHL career with the Bruins for the 1966–67 season, when the team finished the year with a record of 17–43–10 and Bobby suffered the first of many knee injuries. Bobby still had 13 goals and 28 assists for 41 points, won the Calder Trophy as Rookie of the Year and was a second team NHL All-Star. It was only the beginning.

Bobby still holds the NHL record for points in a season by a defenseman (139) and plus/minus (a ridiculous plus-124). In 1969–70, he finally led the Bruins back to the promised land, helping them win the Stanley Cup. He became the only player in history to win four major awards (Art Ross Trophy, Norris Trophy, Hart Trophy, and Conn Smythe Award) in the same season. It's hard to even imagine that ever being challenged.

Bobby's overtime goal clinched that championship. The photo of Bobby flying through the air as he scored the Cup-clincher is one of the most iconic shots in sports history. To this day, if Bobby agrees to appear at your event, he brings a stack of those black-and-white photos and will sign one for anyone who asks. The joke is that if you don't own a copy of that photo, personally autographed to you, then you don't want one. Bobby might have singlehandedly ruined the sports collectibles market for that photo because he never lets anyone pay for one.

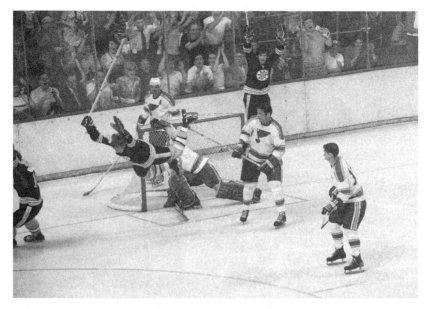

Bobby Orr scoring the most famous goal in NHL history. *(AP Photos)*

The Bruins won a second Stanley Cup during Bobby's era in 1972. The Bruins owned New England, and hockey grew at an enormous rate during those years, with new rinks popping up all over the region and a generation of American players taking to the sport like never before.

Bobby has an effect, to this day, on any hockey fan who runs into him. He has the same sort of effect on NHL players too. Ray Bourque just would not allow anyone to make the comparison to his Hall of Fame predecessor, no matter how hard they tried.

"My first year I had 17 goals and 65 points, and the press started asking me questions about Bobby Orr. I always answered the exact same way—if I could be half the player Bobby Orr was I would have a really good career."

Raymond also said that just meeting Bobby was a thrill.

"I met him a few times my first year, and I was just in awe. Then my second year, I break my jaw early in the season in a fight, and my jaw is all wired shut for six weeks. So, finally, the day comes when I'm getting my wires out and I'm practically yelling at the doctor, 'You've got to get me out of here! Bobby is coming to practice!'

It was the only time Ray could remember having the chance to practice with Bobby, and he was not going to let a broken jaw stand in the way.

Andy Brickley says, quite correctly, that all the MDC rinks in the Commonwealth of Massachusetts should simply be named "Bobby Orr Arena." There would not have been the explosion of youth hockey, or the broader interest in the sport, without Orr's time with the Bruins. And you see it even today. Occasionally Bobby will visit the Garden, meeting with clients (he heads up a player agency called the Orr Hockey Group, which represents some of the biggest stars in the league, including Connor McDavid). Trust me; Bobby has the same effect on people in the media too.

In 1996 the NHL All-Star Game came to Boston, and Bobby was kind of an obvious choice as goodwill ambassador for the game. I was hosting my radio show, and I asked Bobby if he could join me in studio to talk about the game.

On the January day the interview was scheduled, there was a full-fledged blizzard in Boston. They don't close radio stations, so rather than drive I took a commuter rail train into Boston, but naturally assumed Bobby would not be joining me for his scheduled appearance. Because of the weather, my engineer and I were the only people in the building. But for a native of Parry Sound, Ontario, the blizzard was simply not an issue, and Bobby came traipsing into the radio station with his snow boots and parka on. He had made a commitment to me, and he was going to keep it.

During a commercial break, Bobby was telling me that he was scheduled for a big media appearance at Fan Fest the day before the game. I casually mentioned that I would also be there that day with my son. Little did I realize what an experience that would wind up being for me and my son.

NESN had come up with an idea that they wanted to do a feature about the fan fest through the eyes of a child. Coincidentally, my son Taylor was 10 and NESN agreed he'd be the perfect subject for the feature. Bobby told me to look him up, and he would do an interview with my son.

The day of Fan Fest, I was nothing more than a chauffeur, taking Taylor to the event and then watching my son film his feature with the crew from NESN. We were all watching from the back of the room when Bobby held a huge press conference with the hockey media from around the world. The NHL media relations people announced ahead of time that there would be no one-on-one interviews, just the group session with Bobby.

Taylor and I watched the press conference as some of the biggest names in the hockey and sports media asked their questions of the greatest player ever. After the event broke up I went up to pay my respects and say hello. Bobby looked at me and before saying anything else, asked, "Dale, where's your son?"

I was taken aback. I said, "Bobby, they told everyone there are no one-on-one interviews."

Bobby repeated, "Dale, where is your son? Go get him, let's go. Get the cameraman. I told you I'd do an interview."

So Taylor and the NESN crew headed up to the dais with the great Bobby Orr while the entire NHL media contingent watched with envy. Cameras from the biggest media outlets were filming my son interviewing Bobby Orr. Taylor asked about three or four questions, and they were pretty much what you would expect a 10-year-old to ask. "What is it like to be Bobby Orr?" "How do you become a great player?"

After the fourth question Taylor stopped, more than a little flustered by the overwhelming attention, and Bobby, trying to help him out, asked, "Anything else?"

"No. That's it," Taylor said.

Bobby looked at Taylor and broke out laughing. "That's it? Now that's the best end to an interview I've ever had."

He gave my son a big hug. And Taylor got an exclusive interview with *the* Bobby Orr. Just another example of how Bobby is every bit as great a person as he was a player, and how he's touched my life and that of my family. We still have the tape to prove it.

As I mentioned earlier, there was a period of about four years when I was away from the Bruins. After NESN re-hired me to host the games, I was in the TD Garden studios extra early for my first game back. I will freely admit I was a little nervous about my first day back around the team and taking on a role as host, which was much different than I was used to as play-by-play announcer. I was alone in our Garden studio, my back to the door and working on my notes for the game that night.

Suddenly, these arms came around me from behind in a big hug, and a voice said, "Damn, it's good to have you back around the team!" It was Bobby Orr, and my day was made.

Bobby still stops by the set from time to time, just to say hello and check in. Not too long ago he stopped by on a day my daughter happened to be visiting for the weekend from college. We talked for a little bit before I asked if I could introduce him to her. He was happy to meet Brianna, and spent 10 or 15 minutes just talking with her about college and what she was studying. As far as Brianna was concerned, there was no one else on earth that Bobby Orr wanted to talk to. And now she has her own photo with the greatest player who ever lived.

Bobby's time with the Bruins ended in great controversy. He was represented by Alan Eagleson, and in 1975 Eagleson negotiated a free agent deal with the Chicago Blackhawks. The greatest player in Bruins history ended his career in another uniform. But Eagleson, according to Bobby, never informed his client that the Bruins had offered 18.6 percent ownership of the team in their final contract offer.

Let's try to put that in perspective. We don't know the actual numbers, but *Forbes* magazine, in its most recent valuation, said the Bruins were worth $800 million. That means 18.6 percent of the most recent valuation would equal approximately $148,800,000. Let's just let that number sit there for a minute. $148,800,800.

The great Russ Conway, former sports editor of the *Lawrence Eagle-Tribune*, began an investigation of Eagleson in 1990, and in 1991 he began a series of reports called "Cracking the Ice: Intrigue and Conflict in the World of Big-Time Hockey." The series of reports ran for much of the 1990s and earned Conway a well-deserved nomination for a Pulitzer Prize.

It was Conway who exposed much of what Eagleson did, including taking Bobby Orr away from the Bruins. Eagleson had a personal relationship with Blackhawks owner Bill Wirtz, and that led to him not telling Bobby about the incredible contract offer made by the Bruins. Eagleson ended up being disbarred, fined, and imprisoned. He's still the only person ever to be forced to resign from the Hockey Hall of Fame, as players such as Bobby, Brad Park, Bobby Hull, Gordie Howe, Jean Béliveau, Mike Bossy, Henri Richard, Darryl Sittler, Johnny Bucyk, Ted Lindsay, and others said they would withdraw from the Hall if Eagleson were allowed to remain.

Bobby signed with the Blackhawks, but because of the overwhelming nature of knee injuries, he was only able to play 26 games over three seasons. There is a telling story about his early days with Chicago. Bobby was on the ice and the Blackhawks were practicing the power play. Bobby was asked to kind of take over that part of the practice, and after talking about going here and doing that, a fellow Blackhawks player reportedly said, "Yeah, the only problem with that is—none of us are Bobby Orr."

I've talked to Bobby over the years about his knee injuries. We've talked about the advances in medical technology. All of Bobby's knee surgeries involved completely opening up his knee and trying to make repairs. If arthroscopic knee surgery existed when he was a player, it's hard to imagine the difference in recovery time and career length he would've enjoyed. It's also hard to imagine how much greater he might have been.

But for those of us in New England, he is still the greatest of all time.

CHAPTER 10
RAY BOURQUE

If you think about it, the chain of franchise defensemen in the history of the Boston Bruins is the envy of the National Hockey League.

Eddie Shore was a four-time Hart Trophy winner and a two-time Stanley Cup champion and a Hockey Hall of Famer, who was considered the best defenseman of his era in a career that spanned 14 seasons.

Robert Gordon Orr is universally considered the best defenseman in the history of the National Hockey League. In fact, the only argument is whether or not he is the greatest *player* in the history of the league. Over his 10-year Bruins career, Orr completely revolutionized the position of defenseman, and demolished the league record books. Orr won eight consecutive Norris Trophies, as the league's best defenseman. He also won three Hart Trophies as league MVP, and even led the league in scoring on two different occasions. Orr led the NHL in plus/minus six times, including a nearly mythical plus-124 in 1970–71. He led the Bruins to two Stanley Cup championships, and won the Conn Smythe Trophy as playoff MVP both times. Orr entered the Hall of Fame in 1979.

Brad Park was acquired, along with Jean Ratelle and Carol Vadnais, by the Bruins from the New York Rangers, for Phil Esposito and Carol Vadnais in November 1975. It was thought at the time that Park's best days on defense were behind him, but that proved totally incorrect. Park spent eight seasons on the Boston blue line, scoring 417 points and putting together a plus-233 rating. He played in four All-Star Games as a Bruin, and was inducted into the Hall of Fame in 1988.

And that lineage of blue line immortality led to Raymond Jean Bourque. Just to get the résumé out of the way first: Raymond played 21 seasons for the Bruins and was a captain from 1988 until 2000. He holds the NHL career records for goals (410), assists (1,169), and points (1,579) by a defenseman. He was a First or Second Team All-Star 19 times, and won the Norris Trophy as the league's best defenseman five times. He won a Stanley Cup championship as a member of the Colorado Avalanche, and was inducted into the Hall of Fame in 2004.

What Raymond brought to the Bruins on the ice is indisputable. Along the way, he also managed to be involved in a couple of the most iconic moments in the history of the franchise.

Phil Esposito was one the Boston Bruins' all-time great forwards after being acquired from the Chicago Blackhawks, along with Ken Hodge and Fred Stanfield. Espo, as he was called, became the first NHL player to top the 100-point plateau, in 1969, then he followed up with a 99-point season, then five consecutive years of triple digits. He won the Art Ross Trophy five times, and led the NHL in goals scored in six straight seasons, from 1969 to 1975. He was a member of both Bruins Stanley Cup championship teams in 1970 and 1972. Despite being traded to the New York Rangers in November 1975, when he retired from the game, the Bruins elected to retire his No. 7.

The problem with "retiring" Esposito's No. 7 was that it was in use, and had been since 1979, when the team gave it out to an 18-year-old first-round draft pick—Raymond Bourque. Obviously, Esposito had no issues with Bourque wearing No. 7, as he had been traded and had not retired with the Bruins. In the lead-up to Phil's special ceremony, he had told anyone who asked that he was proud to have Raymond continue to wear his No. 7. He admired Bourque both as a person and as a player. He didn't know that Raymond had other plans.

171

"I wear No. 29 to start the season, and I have a great camp. But I show up for the first game and No. 7 was hanging in my stall. Now, I know who wore No. 7, but I'm 18 years old, and I just put the sweater on. As I'm going out on the ice, Bobby Schmautz pulls me aside and says, 'If you hear any hecklers or anything like that, don't worry about it. Just play your game.' All I can think is, awesome, right?"

There had been some bad feelings between Harry Sinden and Espo after the trade to New York, but finally, on December 3, 1987, the team held a ceremony at Boston Garden to retire Phil's No. 7.

"Now no one had said anything to me, at any time, about what was going to happen when we retired No. 7. So it's 1:00 in the afternoon on December 3 and Taz [coach Terry O'Reilly] calls me from Harry's office. They had an idea."

The Bruins took warmups that night, and Raymond was wearing his usual No. 7. When the team went back to the dressing room, Ray went to a storage room and made an equipment adjustment.

After several speeches and gifts, it came time for Raymond to make a presentation on behalf of the current team. He skated over to Esposito and began to remove his game sweater, with the 7 on the back. Underneath that sweater, Bourque had a second sweater on, with No. 77 on the back. He told Esposito that 7 was his, and always would be. A visibly moved Esposito watched in disbelief as Bourque turned around to show Espo the number 77. To this day, Esposito claims it was one of the greatest honors of his career.

"The only people who knew what I was going to do were Harry, Taz, my wife, and the equipment guy. It was perfect."

Raymond seemed to be the master of secret plots and plans. The next one came on September 26, 1995, and, again, brought down the house at the Garden.

Bruins owner Jeremy Jacobs had built a brand-new arena in the city of Boston, known now as TD Garden. It was built just inches from Boston Garden. On the night of September 26, the team played the Montreal Canadiens in a preseason game, the last event ever to be held at the Garden. After the game, the team held what was known as the Last Hurrah. Scores of former Bruins players came back for one final skate on the Garden ice, in front of a sold-out and passionate crowd.

Almost no one knew about the plan Raymond had hatched, and it involved a former Bruins star named Normand Leveille, who was the 14th overall selection in the 1981 NHL draft and was such a dazzling prospect that he stepped immediately into the Bruins lineup. As an 18-year-old rookie, Leveille scored 14 goals and 33 points in 66 games before an ankle injury cut short his season.

Normand started the 1982–83 season with three goals and nine points in his first nine games. The ninth game came on October 23 in Vancouver. Normand scored both Bruins goals in a 3–2 loss at the Pacific Coliseum, but it was the last game of his career. In the first intermission Normand suffered a brain aneurysm caused by a defective blood vessel. After seven hours of surgery and three weeks in a coma, Leveille survived, but his career was over.

"I was injured, and wasn't in Vancouver," Ray recalls. "My wife and I were watching the game back home, and I didn't think anything of it when he left the ice. I just thought he got hurt. We go to bed after the game, but I get a call from Steve Kasper in the middle of the night. He says, 'They don't think Normand is going to make it through the night.'

"Normand was in a coma for a while, but they were finally able to get him back to the hospital in Montreal. We played in Montreal, and a whole bunch of us went to visit him in the hospital. He was in such bad shape. Jean Ratelle would have us record these tapes that they would play for him, so that even though he was in a coma, he could hear some familiar voices.

"Later in the year, we played in Montreal and Normand was able to come to the game. He was sitting in the first row, in the corner, right on the glass. We won the game and the whole team skated to the corner to tap on the glass. He had the biggest smile."

Normand couldn't speak English and Raymond had taken him under his wing. He roomed with him on the road, and took to ordering whatever Raymond ordered when they were out at a restaurant. Raymond took Normand's physical condition hard, and was always there to help Leveille. On the night of September 26, all Normand wanted was one last chance to skate in a Bruins sweater, and Raymond made sure to help make that possible.

In the bowels of the building, while player after player was being introduced to the Garden crowd, Leveille sat on a folding chair in a hallway outside the Bruins dressing room. Raymond Bourque patiently crouched, tying Leveille's skates like a father helping his pee-wee hockey player. Bourque helped Leveille make his way to the Bruins bench, and with the assistance of defense partner Don Sweeney, assisted Leveille as he inched his way onto the carpet.

"He wanted to skate one more time, and I wanted to make sure it happened," Bourque said. "There were very few people who knew he was going to do it, and it was very, very emotional for all of us. But he skated."

Leveille handed Bourque his cane, and Raymond turned it sideways, allowing Normand to grasp it and make his way slowly onto the ice. With former general manager Harry Sinden standing alongside with tears in his eyes, and an adoring Garden crowd cheering and crying as well, Leveille made the short skate to center ice, where he was engulfed by Bruins players from every era. Leveille sat on a folding chair provided by Sweeney, beaming, while being hugged and congratulated. For many, it was one of the finest moments in the history of the Boston Garden.

Believe it or not, I even have my own story that shows the type of person Raymond is. To make a long story short, I had broken my ankle leaving the Garden after a home game. Two days later we were going to Dallas for a game against the Stars, and I was struggling.

I made my way to Hanscom Air Force Base for the team charter to Dallas. With my overnight bag slung over my shoulder, and my game briefcase, the trip from the car to the plane on crutches I was not yet used to was a real chore. I made my way up the plane's rear stairway, threw my bag in an overhead compartment, and collapsed into my seat near the front of the plane.

After landing in Dallas, we deplaned to the rear again, meaning I was one of the last people off the plane. When I went to retrieve my bag, it was missing, and all I could think was, "Guys, please don't tease the announcer today of all days." I asked the flight attendant if she saw what happened to my bag, and she said, "Oh yeah, Raymond took it."

I got to the bus, waiting on the tarmac, and Raymond had carried my bag to the bus, and placed it in the luggage storage underneath. When the bus arrived at the team hotel, Raymond grabbed my bag again and placed it near the front desk for my check-in.

Now, Ray Bourque was the captain of the Boston Bruins, the most senior member of the team and the unquestioned best player. He could have simply asked any player on the team—and certainly any younger player—to grab my bag and put it on the bus. Instead, without being asked, he saw my physical struggles and took it upon himself to help out. No questions, and no big deal— to him. It was a very big deal to me.

While those Ray Bourque moments did not involve actual game action, so many other moments were pivotal in the success of the team. I was there when he scored the game-winning goal in the third period of the 1996 All-Star Game played in Boston, winning the MVP Award. I was there the night Ron Tugnutt of the Quebec Nordiques made 70 saves against the Bruins, and 19 shots came off the stick of Ray Bourque.

"Do you remember that last shot?" he asked me. "Randy Burridge was screening in front, and I ripped a perfect wrist shot, but Ron just flashed out that glove and robbed me. When the game ended, we all went over and congratulated him. It was unbelievable!"

Raymond's Bruins career came to a close on March 6, 2000. He was 38 years old, and the Bruins were no longer perennial playoff competitors. He worried that he wasn't going to have many more chances to win a championship, so he asked GM Harry Sinden to consider trading him to a playoff contender.

Ray Bourque, always a fan favorite. *(AP Photos)*

"We were building our dream house in Topsfield, and I didn't want to go too far from home. The Flyers were playing really well, plus Reggie Lemelin was working for the Flyers. We played Philly in a Saturday matinee at the Garden, and I was hearing before the game that it's a done deal. I thought I was to leave the building that day with the Flyers. You saw me pick up the puck after the game. So did Harry."

But the deal was not done. In fact, when Raymond finally reached Sinden on the phone after the game, he was told that there were several other teams involved. The recruiting of Raymond Bourque began.

"I get a call from Celine Dion's husband, Rene Angelil, who has since passed away. We had met through Celine, and had played golf a few times. He was best friends with [Colorado Avalanche GM] Pierre Lacroix. He says, in that husky voice of his, 'Hey Ray! It's Rene. Pierre doesn't know I'm calling you, but I'm telling you Colorado would be a really, really good place for you. You would love it there!' Yeah, Pierre didn't know he was calling, right?"

The Bruins played the Ottawa Senators on the following Monday, but Sinden had told Raymond to stay home, and away from the arena. As Ray and his wife, Christianne, got ready to watch the game, he got a call from Dave Andreychuk, who said, "They've just pulled me off the ice from warmup. We must be going somewhere together."

Sinden called Raymond in the third period of the game and told him he had been dealt to Colorado. Pierre Lacroix called from Patrick Roy's room—with a group of players including Joe Sakic, Adam Foote, Shjon Podein, and Dave Reid. They all celebrated his arrival with the Avalanche. I'll let Raymond tell the rest of the story:

"We played Game 6 of the Final in New Jersey, and most people didn't think we had much of a chance to win. All of my closest friends and family flew into New Jersey—my dad, my sisters, my brother, my wife's family—because I knew that if we lost it was my last game ever. We win the game 4–0, and the whole group flies to Denver.

"We're on the plane heading back to Denver, and [team captain] Joe Sakic stops by my seat. He says, 'Ray, how we gonna do this?' I ask, 'Do what?' and he replies, 'The Cup thing.' I just said, "F—k off, Joe! Let's win the damn thing first."

The Avalanche won the Cup with a 3–1 win in Game 7. Sakic handed the Cup directly to Ray after commissioner Gary Bettman handed it to him.

"We win the Cup and Pierre Lacroix says, 'Take it home with you tonight.' I have this big van because I have this big group that had flown to Denver to see the game. I have a big cooler in the van, and I bring everyone back to my house after the team party at The Chop House. We get to my house around 3 a.m., and I start beeping the horn. My neighbors all come out of their houses, and I put the Cup on the sidewalk and the cooler in the street. We were there with the whole crew and all my neighbors until around 6:00 AM. Then when you wake up the next morning, it's a little weird to see the Stanley Cup sitting on your kitchen table."

I was there, and served as emcee, on June 12, 2001, three days after the Colorado Avalanche won the Stanley Cup, and Raymond accepted the invitation of the mayor of Boston, Thomas M. Menino, to bring the Cup back to Boston. The rally at Boston's City Hall Plaza was attended by more than 20,000 fans, who would have preferred to see their beloved Bruins hoist the Cup but were so happy that Bourque finally got his chance. It took Raymond 1,612 regular-season games and 214 playoff games, but he finally got to see his name on the Cup.

"Mayor Menino called my agent, Steve Freyer, and said the city wanted to do something for me at City Hall Plaza. I really wasn't for it, and said I couldn't do that. Steve asked if I would do it if the Bruins signed off on it, and I said that was really the only way I could even consider it. [GM] Mike O'Connell said the team had no problem with it, so I agreed to do it, even though I wasn't sure if I should or not."

The honors kept coming after Raymond's retirement. His birthplace of Saint-Laurent named the Arena Raymond-Bourque in his honor. His No. 77 was retired by both the Bruins and the Avalanche, and he became just one of six players to have his number retired by more than one team.

Raymond also represented Canada in the 1981, 1984, and 1987 Canada Cup tournaments.

Standing with Ray Bourque after he won the Cup with Colorado in 2001.

"The '87 Canada Cup team was the greatest team I ever played on. Wayne Gretzky, Mario Lemieux, Mark Messier, Paul Coffey, Grant Fuhr—it was unbelievable. Line after line of All Stars coming over the boards."

He played for the NHL All Stars against the Soviet Union in Rendez-vous '87 and was able to wear the Canadian sweater in the 1988 Winter Olympics. Led by Bourque, the Bruins franchise made 29 consecutive playoff appearances, ending in 1997, and the Bruins played the powerhouse Edmonton Oilers (of Gretzky, Messier, Kurri, Coffey, and Fuhr) in the 1988 and 1990 Stanley Cup Finals.

With a franchise that benefitted from the career of Bobby Orr, being the second-best defenseman in team history is nothing to sneeze at. Raymond Bourque played every minute of his 21-year NHL career like a Hall of Famer. He is still a beloved member of the Bruins family and the Boston community.

CHAPTER 11
HAL GILL

Harold Priestly Gill III was born in Concord, Massachusetts, and the name certainly fit his hometown. But by the time he was playing star quarterback for Nashoba Regional High School in Bolton and for Providence College of Hockey East, he was known simply as Hal. His four years at Providence earned him a selection by the Bruins in the eighth round (No. 207 overall) of the 1993 draft.

There was only one thing that stuck out about Hal's game coming into the National Hockey League in 1997: he was huge! At 6'7", 250 pounds, he was the biggest player to wear a Bruins sweater until Zdeno Chara arrived a decade later. Hal's size was a double -edged sword during his Bruins career. Boston fans saw a player that big and wanted him to send opponents airborne on every hit.

"Playing for the Bruins, I always felt like fans would be upset because I didn't put every guy through the glass. Then, later, I would play in Montreal, and I would do a poke check and 20,000 fans would cheer. You're always afraid that you'll go play in Montreal and they'll hate you—and they can be a tough crowd to play for—but they were really good to me. I think they appreciated what I did, and how I played. I'm not sure Bruins fans ever did."

As a talk show host in Boston, I felt like I spent a fair amount of time defending Hal to irate and less-than-understanding Bruins fans. While hockey fans in Boston are notoriously loyal, they also seem to pick a player who draws their ire. Chara has been a player like that for a decade, and it's probably not a coincidence that they are the two biggest players in team history.

Despite all the efforts of the National Hockey League to make the league kinder and gentler, Boston will always be known as the home of the Big Bad Bruins. Fans love that nickname and that style of play. They have little patience for players they perceive to be the slightest bit "soft," and they certainly have high expectations for the biggest players.

I also think players of Gill's and Chara's sizes take certain precautions on the ice. Andrew Ference once told me that if Chara wasn't careful, he could actually kill someone on the ice. When you are 8, 10, or 12 inches taller than your opponents, and 20 to 40 pounds heavier, there may be some reluctance to take advantage of that advantage. It's always something I felt applied to both of the Bruins giants.

When Hal began playing for the Bruins, there were certain players he gravitated to. Some probably wouldn't surprise you, but some might.

"Ray Bourque was my idol growing up," Gill told me. "I always say he was kind of like a father figure to me. He would scold me and give me the business, and it was difficult, but it was kind of like having a father out there on the ice. Then my brothers were like Ted Donato, Steve Heinze, and Rob DiMaio. All of those guys were so supportive, and helped me so much, not just hockey-wise, but trying to handle myself off the ice.

"The other guys were P.J. Axelsson, Shawn Bates, Sergei Samsonov, and Joe Thornton. We came into the league together and learned a lot as we were going through it together. Andrew Raycroft was, and still is, one of my best friends. Don Sweeney was kind of like my uncle, I guess, because he was Ray Bourque's brother."

Hal's first coach for the Bruins was Pat Burns, and Hal told me he didn't mind Burns' direct approach. At their first meeting, when Burns told Gill he had made the team, he also said, "Jacques [Laperriere] seems to think you can help us and I trust him, so I guess you're on the team." Not exactly a resounding vote of confidence. But Hal also said Burns, while direct, was also honest and appreciated players who gave him an effort.

Then things turned dramatically for Hal, and the entire organization, when Burns was fired and replaced by Mike Keenan.

"I think my time with Mike Keenan made me appreciate Pat Burns even more. Pat was fair. Mike played the head games. He actually wanted you to confront him. At one point he was yelling at me, and I finally just said, 'Listen, if you want me to do something, just tell me what to do. I'm not going to yell back at you and I'm not going to confront you. That's not the way I was raised, so it's not going to happen.' So he told me to be stronger in front of the net and to move the puck up the ice faster.

"He would do anything to try to get more out of you. He would go at your parents, he would go at your kids, he would go at your wife. Everything was fair game to try and get you to play better hockey. I just didn't really appreciate it very much."

As I said previously in this book, Keenan had certain players that he liked (like Joe Thornton) and certain players that he hated (like Don Sweeney). Hal said the players on the team also knew who was on each Keenan list, and he also knew exactly where he was slotted.

"I was one of those guys that he hated. I lost 20 pounds because he wanted me to ride the bike all the time. I felt like I was completely weak the whole season because all I ever did was ride the bike. He destroyed me. I'm not a big believer in the bike. I think it's good for flushing out your legs, or getting a workout in if you needed it. You would see all those bikes lined up, and you just knew you were in for a 40-minute session of spinning. It was right after a game, and it was miserable. That next summer when I was going to train, I had no strength. It was a tough year for Donnie [Sweeney], and it was a tough year for me."

Keenan wanted everyone around him—players, trainers, equipment managers—to be on edge. What he really wanted was confrontation and for players to go right back at him.

"I remember Jason Allison and Joe Thornton just yelling at him, and I think he got excited about it. I was raised to have respect for my coach, and I wasn't going to yell at him."

Keenan considered himself an innovator, and wasn't afraid to think outside the box. But sometimes he asked players to think outside that box with him, and many weren't interested. Hal thought at least one of his ideas went too far.

"He played me at forward one game, and made me skate as a winger for a week in practice because he said my foot speed wasn't good enough. He made me do a lot of things that I didn't think helped. I didn't think playing forward was going to help me develop as a player, and have better foot speed as a defenseman."

And sometimes Keenan did things for no apparent reason, just because he could, I suppose.

"We were doing the team picture, and [team photographer] Steve Babineau had everyone all set up, and Keenan came in and decided to change where everyone was standing. It was just stupid things like that. It was just a complete gong show every day."

Keenan's run was just a single season, and few players were sorry to see him go. But the organization surprised many by passing up on assistant coach Peter Laviolette and giving the job to former local high school legend Robbie Ftorek. As far as Hal was concerned, Ftorek was at the opposite end of the coaching spectrum from Keenan.

"I thought Robbie [Ftorek] was really good. He was very individual. He would coach each individual's skills. He did some things I had never heard of. He would iso-cam you for an entire game, every single shift. Then he would go over it with you and ask, 'You jumped off the bench here. Where were you and where were you going? What was your first thought when you jumped over the boards?' And he would take an hour and go through the whole game like that. It was very detailed and trying to get you better as a player."

Hal certainly knew the next Bruins coach very well—he had played with Mike Sullivan earlier in his career. But he also felt that Mike Sullivan the coach was a lot different than Mike Sullivan the teammate.

"I played with Sully. When he was coaching here, it was hard for me because I noticed a big change from when he was a player to when he was eventually our coach. We had some down times as a team, and I think it weighed on him, being a Boston guy coaching for the Bruins. He wore it heavier than anyone else.

"I remember one time he came in and he said, 'You guys, this is miserable. This is tough. I've got guys at Dunkin Donuts saying, "Sully, what's wrong with the team?"' We all got kind of a laugh out of it, and we would say the rest of the season, 'Sully, what's wrong with the team?' But when you're the local guy, everyone maybe thinks that they know you. Look, when you win, everything is great, but when you lose, it becomes a difficult situation. And I think Mike wore it heavy."

It was a December night in 2005 during Sullivan's reign as coach that changed everything for the Bruins. On December 1, 2005, general manager Mike O'Connell traded star center Joe Thornton to the San Jose Sharks.

"The Joe Thornton trade was probably the most bizarre thing I was a part of here in Boston. I really respect Mike O'Connell because he came in the room, and he really faced the music. He made the tough decision, and he traded Joe, and I still don't know if it was OC's choice or it was handed down to him. He stood there in the locker room and said, 'Does anyone have anything to say?' That's when Nick Boynton stood up and just let him have it. But he faced the music, I guess."

In 2006, Hal signed as a free agent with the Toronto Maple Leafs. He had one of the best seasons of his career. Then in February 2008, Hal was traded from the Leafs to the Pittsburgh Penguins. The Penguins went on to the Stanley Cup Final, where they lost in six games to the Detroit Red Wings. They marched right back to the Final, and on June 12, 2009, Hal was able to hoist the Stanley Cup over his shoulder.

His two years in Pittsburgh also gave him an opportunity to play with more of the best players in the National Hockey League. He had played with Bourque and Thornton in Boston; now he got the chance to play with Sidney Crosby.

"I would probably say Sidney Crosby is the best player I've ever played with. You think of the guys you've played against—guys like Mario Lemieux, Jaromir Jagr, Wayne Gretzky, Mark Messier. Everyone has their particular role, and their strengths and weaknesses, but Sidney and Evgeni Malkin were both special. Some nights we would just sit back and say, 'These guys will find a way to win.'"

189

As a free agent in 2009, Gill had another unique opportunity. He became one of the few players to see the Bruins and Canadiens rivalry from both sides when he signed with Montreal.

"When I signed with Montreal, I was walking through the North End of Boston because I lived there, and some guy stuck his head out of a manhole and said, 'Dude, are you serious? Why? Why would you sign with the Habs?' I always laughed. I had been away from the Bruins for about five years, playing for other teams, and someone said to me, 'No shit! You're still playing hockey? Good for you.' If you weren't a Bruin, here in Boston it was like you were dead to the Bruins fans. That was loyal as you could get."

He arrived in Montreal more than a little nervous about the reception he would get from Canadiens fans. He says he shouldn't have worried.

"Growing up in Boston, everyone hated the Montreal Canadiens. It was deep in your bones. It was like the Yankees. Then when I signed with the Habs, I would say, 'I know you guys hate the Bruins,' and people surprised me. They would tell me, 'No, no...we love the Bruins! Those are the best games ever! We love playing against the Bruins.' It was just a completely different mentality than Bruins fans growing up around here. One side hates the other guys, and one side loves the other guys."

But he also got to see the rivalry, on the ice, in a totally different light. He was a member of the Canadiens when Chara knocked Max Pacioretty completely out with a vicious check into the side glass near the bench in March 2011. Fans wanted to have Chara arrested for assault when the Bruins made their next visit to Montreal. Gill wisely chose to remain apart from the controversy.

"That seven-game series the year the Bruins won the Cup was really interesting. It was surreal. We were that close to beating the Bruins, then Nathan Horton knocked the shot off of Michael Ryder, and that was it. It was always tough to play against that team, they were so big and strong. Then we had that whole deal with Zdeno Chara and Max Pacioretty. That was one of the best playoff series I think I've ever been a part of."

After stints with the Nashville Predators and Philadelphia Flyers, Gill wound up playing more than 1,100 games across 16 seasons in the NHL. He had a brief stint in the front office for the Florida Panthers and then a short stint as a Bruins analyst on NESN before he became the full-time color analyst for the Nashville Predators games on radio. He and his family moved to Nashville.

CHAPTER 12
JOE THORNTON

There was never a bad day on Planet Joe. That's what I always thought from the time the Bruins selected Joe Thornton first overall in the 1997 NHL draft through the day the Bruins traded him to San Jose. Heck, Joe hasn't changed much and anytime I catch him on TV or he's back in Boston to face the Bruins, I think the same thing.

They didn't come more laid-back than Joe, and that cost him here for sure. Bruins fans have been raised on Cam Neely and Terry O'Reilly; they're not usually satisfied with someone who appears to be relaxed out there on the ice. When he was with the Bruins, Joe was one of the many athletes cursed by his own great skill. He was able to make it look easy out there, and that can get translated to a lack of trying. I'm certain many people mistook Thornton's friendly nature and willingness to be a playmaker rather than a scorer for lack of competitiveness. I always felt they misread him.

After bottoming out with 61 points and finishing last in the overall NHL standings, the Bruins earned the No. 1 pick and right to draft Thornton, who was everyone's choice as the first pick in the draft in Pittsburgh. From draft day on, Joe had such a happy-go-lucky face.

I remember that draft night I hosted a party that the Bruins held at the Garden to show the festivities on the big screen at center ice. There was a lot of hooting and hollering because everyone knew they were going to pick Joe. The Bruins also had the eighth pick, and they selected speedy winger Sergei Samsonov. All Bruins fans knew and expected Thornton, but I felt like Samsonov surprised them. Suddenly, it felt like the Bruins had just rebuilt the entire hockey team in a less than an hour.

Sergei came in more polished and ready to play in the NHL. He was 19 and had already played a year of pro hockey for the Detroit Vipers in the International Hockey League. He had been playing against men and his demeanor was of a much older and more mature player. Joe came in at 18, straight out of the Sault Ste. Marie Greyhounds of the OHL. He had been a junior hockey star, and had 41 goals and 122 points in 1996–97, finishing second in OHL scoring that year. Ironically, the only player with more points that year was his future replacement as a playmaking center with the Bruins, Marc Savard, who had 43 goals and 130 points for the Oshawa Generals.

With Thornton and Samsonov in tow, the Bruins' public relations staff thought up the new slogan "The Future's So Bright, You've Gotta Wear Shades." Unfortunately, for the length of their stay with the Bruins, the future never got quite bright enough to even make you squint.

Right away you could see Thornton was big and strong and with the right coaching he could develop into the next cornerstone player for the Bruins. Coach Pat Burns had his own plan for developing Joe, and that included breaking him in slowly. I think Bruins fans were frustrated at Burns when Joe played just 55 games as a rookie and had seven points. By comparison, Samsonov had 22 goals and 47 points and was voted the Calder Trophy winner as Rookie of the Year. Bruins fans felt strongly they were going to have a rookie of the year candidate, they just always thought it would be Thornton, not Samsonov. Sergei had a fine NHL career, playing 888 games for six different teams. But his 571 career points fall far behind the 1,427 points Thornton had through the 2017–18 season.

A very young Joe Thornton after the Bruins drafted him in 1997. *(AP Photos)*

It wasn't just youth and inexperience, or Burns' plan, holding Joe back that season. I remember he used to have an awful habit of high-sticking people, a habit that continued beyond his rookie season. He was a tough player but he couldn't stay away from infractions that carried repercussions. That problem would be on full display in his Garden return in an enemy sweater, but more on that later.

Pat wanted to turn Joe into a three-zone player. He knew Joe could score, but Joe couldn't fulfill his potential without playing defense. I got the feeling they were butting heads stylistically, but what Pat had in mind is right, as evidenced by Joe's Hall of Fame credentials.

Joe began to come into his own in his second season. He had 41 points in 81 games and was plus-3 after being minus-6 as a rookie. Joe was as fine a playmaker as there ever was, but it drove you crazy sometimes because he refused to shoot. He could shoot and he could score, he just didn't have it in him sometimes to be that shooter. A lot of players have been like that over the years, some for the Bruins. Players like Adam Oates, for instance.

They gave Joe the captaincy in 2002, when he was 23. He probably wasn't ready for it. It's a rare guy that is ready for something like that at that age. Connor McDavid became the youngest captain in NHL history when the Edmonton Oilers put the "C" on him at the age of 19 years and 266 days, beating out Gabriel Landeskog of the Colorado Avalanche by 20 days. But I think those are rare cases in the NHL, and I don't think Joe was emotionally ready for it. So often teams think because a guy is the most talented on the team he's ready to be the captain. Sometimes teams think that the added responsibility will help the player grow and develop. I'm not sure that's true, but Joe still managed to play through it and have a heck of a Bruins career.

I always thought Joe was straight out of "Bruins Central Casting." He was a big, good-looking, happy-go-lucky kid who truly loved being a hockey player. Everyone on the Bruins always told me that Joe was the ultimate teammate. He was unselfish (sometimes to a fault) and quick to jump to a teammate's defense. He could play a dazzling skill game, with incredible soft hands and the ability to see passing lanes that others could not. When he wanted, he could shoot and score. Joe also could play a punishing physical game and was a very capable fighter. Bruins fans always love guys who are 6'4", 220 pounds and who can and will drop the gloves. But there was always that element of the fan base that thought "Jumbo Joe" was "Lazy Joe," even though he was anything but. His graceful strides and ability to thrive on the perimeter rather than crash the net worked against him.

Maybe the biggest indictment of Joe with the Bruins was that he wasn't able to get very far in the playoffs, regardless of the caliber of his supporting cast. In Thornton's last playoff series with the Bruins, the team lost a 3–1 series lead and dropped the best-of-seven series to Montreal, in 2004. Joe didn't have a single point in that series and controversy erupted when esteemed *Boston Globe* writer Kevin Paul Dupont penned a scathing column urging the Bruins to remove the captaincy from Joe. I told Kevin he was wrong to write that. It was apparent to most that Joe probably shouldn't have been playing. He was banged up. As it turned out, it was revealed after the series that Joe was playing with broken ribs.

Joe may have been hurt, but he was also ingenious. A teammate told me the following story about what happened after Game 7 at the Garden:

"After we lost Game 7, Joe really didn't want to talk to the press after the game. They had hammered him pretty good because he wasn't scoring any points, and the team didn't want to talk about his ribs. So Joe climbed into the laundry bin, and they covered him with towels. You know, 6'5" Jumbo Joe was all curled up in one of those laundry bins. Then they just wheeled him right through the dressing room, with all the media standing there, and down the hall. When they got to the end of the hall, Joe climbed out of the bin and the media started running after him through the players' parking lot. Joe just started running home. Stuff like that probably didn't help Joe's cause, but he really was hurt in that series."

Joe finished the Bruins portion of his career with 454 points in 532 games. His Bruins career ended abruptly on November 30, 2005, when general manager Mike O'Connell traded his star player to San Jose in a deal that shook everyone around the NHL, including me. At the time of the deal, Joe had 33 points in the team's first 24 games. Joe said he was at dinner in Boston with his parents when O'Connell called to tell him he was traded to the Sharks. Joe said, "I had no idea it was coming." Well, neither did anyone else. How did Thornton fare after the trade to San Jose? He had 92 points in 58 games with the Sharks and finished the year with 125 points to win the Art Ross Trophy as the league's leading scorer. He became the first player in league history to win the Ross Trophy while splitting the season between two teams, then became the first player in the history of the NHL to win the Hart Trophy as Most Valuable Player while playing for two different teams.

I know what O'Connell was trying to do. He was trying to save his job. He thought he could jumpstart the team (which was

8–13–5 at the time of the trade). I was home watching a game on television when the news broke that they traded Joe. Right away, I thought, "They sucked for a reason, so they could get the No. 1 pick and draft Joe, they took the right guy, and now they're going to trade him?"

The deal seemed crazier once you heard what they got for him. Marco Sturm was a good player, but not someone on the level of Joe Thornton. He had his moments for the Bruins, including the overtime goal in the 2010 Winter Classic victory against the Philadelphia Flyers at Fenway Park. Sturm had 106 goals in 302 regular-season games for the Bruins and scored a couple big goals for Boston in the 2007–08 first-round playoff series, which kicked off the Claude Julien coaching era. The Bruins pushed the top-seeded Montreal Canadiens to seven games that season. But Sturm's career was littered with injuries and he was working his way back from an injury when the Bruins traded him to the Los Angeles Kings during the 2010–11 season, literally for nothing. The Bruins needed to create some salary cap space.

Brad Stuart was probably the centerpiece of the trade. A defenseman who could move the puck and hit like a brick wall, Stuart had been drafted by the Sharks third overall in 1998. The Bruins saw Stuart as at least a No. 2 defenseman for the years ahead, but he was a bit nonchalant (ironic considering he was traded for Thornton) and never lived up to his potential. He played in 1,056 NHL games, including 103 for the Bruins, but was never the driving force for any of the six teams he played for.

And then there was Wayne Primeau, a spare part who had never been anything more than a bottom-six forward, and that's what he was until the day he retired. Primeau's brother, Keith, was a multi-time NHL All-Star, everything Wayne was not. Wayne Primeau was out of the league after the 2009–10 season.

The Bruins had this big, talented, good-looking kid who should have been a Bruin for life...and they traded him for three forgettable players.

If you're looking for a silver lining (and you may need a magnifying glass for your search), the Bruins did turn things around after shipping Joe out of town and getting little in return.

First, the Bruins cleared some salary cap room that enabled them to pursue unrestricted free agents Marc Savard and Zdeno Chara. New general manager Peter Chiarelli, with help from assistant GM Jeff Gorton, landed both marquee free agents on July 1, 2006.

Second, if you play the trade tree, so to speak, out even further, the seeds were planted for the Bruins to achieve the ultimate glory. In 2007 Chiarelli traded Stuart and Primeau to the Calgary Flames for Chuck Kobasew and Andrew Ference. In 2009 Chiarelli traded Kobasew to the Minnesota Wild as part of deal that included Craig Weller going to the Bruins. In 2010, Chiarelli dealt Weller, Byron Bitz, and a second-round draft pick to Florida for Dennis Seidenberg and Matt Bartkowski. Ference and Seidenberg ended up being critical parts of the Bruins defense corps during their Stanley Cup title run in 2011.

O'Connell didn't save his job; he was fired at the conclusion of the 2005–06 season, replaced by Chiarelli. But O'Connell's fingerprints were on the Bruins' 2011 Stanley Cup run, starting with the way he began a rebuild with the Thornton trade.

Oh, remember Joe's penchant for getting a little carried away with his physical play from when he was a rookie? Well, Joe returned to the Garden with the Sharks for the first time on

January 10, 2006. Boston was buzzing for the return of the former No. 1 pick who was putting together what would eventually be a Hart Trophy–winning campaign in teal and white.

I was calling the game with Andy Brickley and the sold-out Garden crowd was electric. Hopefully they didn't go out for an early beer run, because Thornton ran Bruins defenseman Hal Gill from behind just 5:13 into the first period. The two players had staged a spirited battle behind the Bruins net, and Thornton finished his check on Gill in the corner, but the hit was a little late and Gill was injured enough that he missed the remainder of the game. Joe received a five-minute major for intent to injure and a game misconduct. When Andy and I watched the replay, you could make the argument that the hit was from the side, but Joe was done.

"I was in shock," Thornton said after the game. "I was excited about coming back. It was unfortunate I couldn't play the whole game."

Always the affable fella, Joe went to the Bruins dressing room to check on Gill, his teammate since Gill broke into the NHL one year after Joe. The center told Gill, "Good hit." Joe then told the media, "We're still friends."

If Joe's early exit wasn't enough of a disappointment for Bruins fans, the Sharks pounded the Bruins 6–2. The Bruins fans missed seeing more of Joe that night, and they missed him for at least the rest of that season, as the Bruins failed to reach the playoffs and the Sharks made the playoffs nine straight seasons after the trade.

We have a tendency to point to the most talented guy on a team when it comes time to dish out blame for a team's failures, and Joe has dealt with that his whole career. He was likely the scapegoat for O'Connell when he traded him out of Boston, and you could make the same argument when then-Sharks head coach Todd McLellan stripped Thornton of his captaincy in 2014. Joe will always have a strange legacy for some fans. He didn't win here, and hasn't won the Cup with San Jose, but to put the blame for that on the shoulders of any one player is completely unfair. The Sharks have gone to the Stanley Cup Final once and the conference finals three times with Joe in their lineup. But Joe has regularly worn an alternate captain's "A" with the Sharks since then.

Like a lot of guys in this city who you don't appreciate until they're gone, Joe was a great player who could've owned this city if it hadn't been for the trade. He is a lock for first-ballot Hall of Famer, and is arguably the greatest player in the history of the Sharks—even if that "hair shovel" he began sporting on his face, along with teammate Brett Burns, might be the worst look ever. He takes as much joy from playing the game as anyone I've ever met, and is a tremendous ambassador for the game. If ever there was a Canadian hockey player meant to live the California lifestyle, it was Thornton, and he made the most of it.

The Bruins won the Cup after Joe's departure and were contenders for years before and after 2011. But you can't help but wonder what could have been.

CHAPTER 13

THE BOSTON BRUINS AND THE SPORTS TALK RADIO WARS

WFAN Radio became the first all-sports radio station in America in July 1987. That was the summer between my first and second seasons with the New Jersey Devils, and like every other red-blooded American sports fan in the metropolitan New York area, I thought I had died and gone to heaven.

A radio station where I could hear guys talking about sports 24 hours a day, 7 days a week? To be sure, they weren't very good at the beginning (remember Pete Franklin in afternoon drive?) but it was still a watershed moment in American radio.

If we fast-forward to September 3, 1991, WEEI became the first all-sports radio station in Boston. I had just completed my three seasons as the radio voice of the New England Patriots, and when I was offered the chance to host the midday show on the new format, I jumped at it. Much like our predecessor in New York, we weren't very good at the beginning, either.

WEEI was anchored by possibly the worst morning drive show I have ever heard. Boston radio veteran Andy Moes was joined by radio rookies Rob Buttery and Suzanne Lee, and with such radio staple bits as "Best Butt in Baseball," it's little wonder the show didn't last long. I followed in middays, and another Boston radio legend, Eddie Andelman, occupied afternoon drive. Even though WEEI was the flagship radio station for the Bruins radio network, the Bruins were clearly second-class citizens during the broadcast day. In fact, during Andelman's show, they were clearly the subject of ridicule and scorn. Eddie hated hockey and hated the Bruins, and if he mentioned the team at all it was to make fun of them. But it wasn't always that way.

Andelman was one of the inventors of sports talk radio, not only in Boston, but nationwide. He wasn't the only person doing it, but he was clearly one of the most successful. He and partners Mark Witkin and Jim McCarthy began a show called "The Sports Huddle" on WBZ Radio in 1969. The show ran on Sundays from 7:00 to 10:00 PM, and with the 50,000-watt signal of WBZ (which could be heard over much of the Eastern United States), it became appointment listening for sports fans in New England.

"The Sports Huddle" was irreverent, innovative, and funny as hell. They poked fun at everyone, and given the state of Boston sports for much of their lengthy run, there was much to poke fun at. Younger Boston fans may not believe it, but Eddie even liked hockey in the early days. Then came a trip to California.

Eddie and his partners organized a fan trip to the West Coast to see the Bruins play a couple of games in the California sunshine. With the cooperation of the Bruins, one of the selling points for fans making the financial commitment was a meet and greet with a couple of Bruins players. The story goes that general manager Harry Sinden pulled the plug on the meet and greet after a subpar performance in the game before the trip and the need for a "punishment practice." The players did not appear, and Andelman spent the rest of his radio career harpooning Sinden, the Bruins, and hockey in general.

Eddie was very influential in Boston radio for a long time, and years of him declaring hockey "boring" and "unlistenable" on the radio took hold for a large portion of the fan base. Loyal hockey fans didn't buy into Eddie's diatribe, but many others in Boston did. What Eddie said became the law of the land for a long, long time. Fans who didn't know if the puck was puffed or stuffed would call sports radio and declare that "hockey was boring" and "no one wants to talk about hockey." It became a self-fulfilling prophecy.

You can imagine my thoughts when WEEI decided to pair me with Eddie on a new midday program in 1995. He was even more bitter about it, having been "demoted" from his afternoon drive position. He didn't want to be working in middays, and he really didn't want to be working with me. The fact that I was the TV voice of the Bruins on NESN by that time made the professional relationship even rockier.

I had always felt that there was a loyal and passionate fan base for the Bruins in Boston. I also completely disagreed that hockey was "boring" to talk about on the radio. I also had a good professional relationship with Sinden, who had brought me on board with the team. Eddie made no secret of his antipathy toward Sinden and never missed an opportunity to say so.

I tried to talk hockey with Eddie, but it was always a battle. His default answer was always to just mock the sport and its fans. He coined the term "Hockey Krishna" to mock us, and the Bruins never gained much traction on our show unless there was a chance to denigrate them.

After six successful but largely unpleasant years (for both of us), Eddie left WEEI in 2001, and took his talents to another all-sports station trying to get its start in Boston, WWZN. Ironically, WEEI management selected Bob Neumeier as my new midday cohost— a former NHL play-by-play announcer for the Hartford Whalers and the Bruins, and a hockey lifer like me. Suddenly it was not only okay to talk hockey on the midday show, it was encouraged.

Despite some very unsuccessful attempts at competition by a couple of other stations, WEEI was unchallenged as the all-sports behemoth in Boston for a number of years. Then real and legitimate competition arrived in August 2009.

WBZ-FM, better known in Boston as 98.5 The Sports Hub, arrived. While WEEI continued to broadcast at 850AM, the Sports Hub had a powerhouse signal on the FM frequency. They had competent and aggressive station management and started to acquire play-by-play rights to three of the four major sports teams in Boston. Soon they had the New England Patriots, the Boston Celtics, and the Bruins to anchor their station.

They also put together some talented host teams, and suddenly WEEI had more competition than ever before. We had been challenged in the past, but those challenges had failed, and we assumed this one would too. We were wrong.

The Celtics won their 17th NBA championship in 2008, and the Bruins added a Stanley Cup championship in 2011. The Patriots were Super Bowl contenders virtually every year. The Red Sox won World Series titles in 2004, 2007, and 2013, which helped WEEI, but not enough.

I had been one of the few people on WEEI to talk about hockey in any significant way for many years. For a long time, none of the other hosts spent much time talking about hockey on WEEI, and when they did, it was with derision. I had a regular segment with Kevin Paul Dupont, a hockey writer for the *Boston Globe* who is in the media wing of the Hockey Hall of Fame, for a time. Eddie Andelman dubbed the segment "Dupey and Dopey." Some hosts pretended to talk about hockey, but it became clear it was just not a sport that many of them watched or understood.

Then when NESN made the change to a single play-by-play announcer in 2007, I talked less hockey for a time. I was hurt, and I acted like a petulant child. I felt the Bruins should have stuck up for me, after all the years I had spent being one of their lone voices in the wilderness. As I said, I was wounded by losing the play-by-play job that had meant so much to me, but I didn't handle things professionally. I ignored the team for a while, but couldn't keep it up. The game and the team meant too much to me.

Mark Hannon, who was the general manager for The Sports Hub, told me that he always felt Bruins fans were underserved in the market and that it was an area that his station could use to its advantage against WEEI. They had the games on their air, and the hosts on the station not only talked about hockey, but went out of their way to cultivate hockey fans. The message was, "You have a place to talk about your sport and your team here."

Then came the 2010–2011 season. Peter Chiarelli had been remaking the Bruins, and that construction job bore fruit that season. The Sports Hub had a hot hockey team to broadcast and hosts who had been telling fans that theirs was the only place that welcomed hockey fans. Then, in February 2011, I was fired by WEEI.

The show that I co-hosted with Michael Holley was called "Dale and Holley," and it was the only show on WEEI at the time that was beating our competition at The Sports Hub. But station management was feeling the heat from the competition, and I was told I was being fired so that the station roster could get a younger feel and appeal to a younger demographic. Michael Holley was moved into afternoon drive with Glenn Ordway, and a new show, with Mike Mutnanksy and Lou Merloni (the former Red Sox player), was installed in middays. Ironically, the biggest Bruins fan of that lot was Merloni, and he was a regular at the games.

The plan failed in the long run. Eventually, Ordway was fired from his position, and Mutnansky was reassigned to night-time work on the station. The station had a run with Tim Benz cohosting with Merloni, and Mike Salk teaming up with Holley. Those shows also failed, and eventually, three years later, I was rehired to co-host afternoon drive with Michael, and Glenn was brought back to co-host with Merloni and (former Patriot) Christian Fauria in middays.

But in the short term, at the time, WEEI jettisoned their only real hockey voice in the heat of a Bruins Stanley Cup run. I was reassigned to weekend and vacation fill-in work, in addition to filling in on Red Sox play-by-play once a week. The Sports Hub seized control of the top spot in the sports radio universe, a position they held on to for a while.

To be certain, the hosts on WEEI tried to jump on the Bruins bandwagon, and they tried to talk about the team on a daily basis. But after years of neglect and mockery, Bruins fans felt no allegiance to WEEI, even if they listened to certain day parts for other sports. Many Bruins fans had already made the switch to The Sports Hub, and the station and Bruins fans celebrated the Stanley Cup championship together.

I watched the Cup clincher on a TV in the broadcast booth at Tropicana Field in St. Petersburg, Florida, calling a Boston Red Sox–Tampa Bay Rays game with Joe Castiglione. Bittersweet doesn't even begin to describe my feelings that night.

Since the last lineup shakeup, the fortunes of WEEI turned around. The morning show, "Kirk and Callahan," became a monster in the ratings, winning the morning drive battle with The Sports Hub for the first time in years in 2017. But Kirk and Gerry have a unique show that is certainly not hosted by "Sporty McKenzie," as they like to say. They talk less sports than the other shows, anyway, and certainly don't talk about the Bruins very much.

The midday show on WEEI is known as "O.M.F.", or Ordway, Merloni, and Fauria. They have also been competitive with The Sports Hub in the ratings battle. Glenn spent a short time calling hockey a long time ago, but is still known as a basketball guy after years of calling Celtics games with the legendary Johnny Most. Christian is a two-time Super Bowl champion with an unquestioned pedigree when it comes to football, but a bit more limited for hockey. Merloni is the former Red Sox infielder with an encyclopedic ability to break down baseball, but he is known primarily for that. He certainly knows the game of hockey, as a big fan, but probably doesn't get the credit he deserves for hockey knowledge.

Our afternoon drive show became "Dale and Holley with Keefe," adding former Sports Hub staffer Rich Keefe to the lineup. When Michael left, we became "Dale & Keefe." We often finish second to "Felger and Mazz" on The Sports Hub, but we've been known to close the gap and give them a strong run for their ratings. Both Michael and Rich are incredible basketball minds, and along with football, that's likely their area of greatest interest. They certainly watch hockey, and talk about it from time to time. I feel Michael gets a bad rap from hockey fans because of his so-called "Holley Hockey Minute." It began as a funny bit, and was always very creative, but I think some Bruins fans felt like he was making fun of them. I understand their feelings, based on the station's history; I can also tell them that wasn't the intent.

There has been a lot of upheaval in the sports talk radio business in Boston of late. Our corporate owner, Entercom, purchased all of CBS Radio, and The Sports Hub was sold by Entercom to

Beasley Communications. By the time this book hits the shelves, who knows what the landscape will look like.

What that means for hockey fans going forward remains to be seen, but part of those changes involved station management. Mark Hannon, the man who identified the need for a safe space for hockey and Bruins fans, left The Sports Hub. He is now the market manager for Entercom/Boston, including WEEI. What's guaranteed is that with the competition between the stations so stiff, there's no way either one can ignore any sport. Both stations will continue to fight for the hearts and minds of hockey fans in Boston.

CHAPTER 14

TALES FROM
THE ROOM

There's a truth in hockey: If you want to know what's going on with a team, don't ask the general manager, the head coach, or even the players. If you really want to know what's going on with a team, and within a dressing room, go to the men who spend the most time there. You have to talk to the trainers and the equipment managers.

Peter Henderson was the equipment manager for the Bruins from 1998 until 2006, when general manager Peter Chiarelli brought in his own people. I knew Peter from our days with the Maine Mariners, where he began his professional career just as I did. He was always diligent, hardworking, and very funny—all qualities that made him popular with coaches and players wherever he worked.

To get an idea of the work load, Peter described his normal schedule to me:

"On a normal day I would get to the rink around 7:00 AM. If the Celtics were playing at home, I would watch the first quarter of their game, then go home, meaning I would leave around 8:00 PM. On a Bruins game day, I would get there around 7:00 AM, and if we were home, I could leave around 11:00 PM or midnight. If we were on the road, we would get on a plane, go somewhere, set up the dressing room, and hopefully get to bed around 2:00 AM. Then we would be back to work the next day at 7:00 AM. That would be seven days a week from the start of training camp until the end of the playoffs. We couldn't even take all of Christmas Day off because we were either practicing or traveling the next day."

Are you sure you want to be in show business?

One of the hardest jobs for the equipment manager is learning the idiosyncrasies of every player. Every player knows exactly how he wants things, and some players were a lot harder to please than others.

Paul Coffey is considered one of the great skaters in the history of the NHL. But you might not know just how particular he was about his skates.

"There was a game on Long Island where Coffey wore a brand-new pair of skates for warmup, another brand-new pair for the first period, a new pair for the second, and another brand-new pair for the third period," Henderson recalled. "And it's not like he wore four new pair of Bauers, or something. He wore a pair of Grafs, then a pair of Bauers, and then a pair of CCMs. He was all over the place. Sometimes companies would tell me they wouldn't send me new skates because they knew they were for Coffey and that I would just end up returning them.

"But he was very particular about the sharpening. If I made three or four passes on the sharpener he would start yelling at me, 'Stop!' His skates were also a size-and-a-half to two sizes too small so his toes were all curled into the front of the skate."

What Paul Coffey was to skates, Ray Bourque was to hockey sticks. Ray used normal, wooden Sher-Wood sticks, but when it came to which sticks, he was *very* particular.

"At the end of his time in Boston, we were getting eight dozen sticks a game for him," Henderson said. "He would go through every stick and mark them—some he would reject, some he would mark as good, and others he would mark with 9-1-1, meaning only to be used in an emergency. The guy from Sher-Wood would drive down from Drummondville, Quebec, with his car loaded with sticks. The ones Ray rejected went back into the car. But his stick was so popular with youth and adult league players that the

Sher-Wood guy would just bring them to retail stores on his way home and sell every one. He never had to leave the state with a single stick."

Peter worked with several coaching staffs during his time in Boston. He started with Pat Burns, followed by Mike Keenan, Robbie Ftorek, and Mike Sullivan. It seems everyone has stories about Keenan, and almost none are positive. But say this about Keenan: he had a way of convincing team ownership and management that he knew what he was doing.

Defenseman Bob Beers, who went on to be the Bruins' radio color analyst after his playing days, told me Bruins coaches had been trying to get new exercise bikes for the workout area for years, and on the day Keenan took over as head coach, he also had $25,000 worth of new bikes installed in the room.

It seems Keenan had a reputation of loving the equipment manager and hating the trainer. Guys who worked for previous Keenan teams told Peter he was going to be just fine, but that trainer Don DelNegro was going to have to be careful. It turns out they were right, and DelNegro grew sick and tired of Keenan's treatment and quit the team. He was driving to his home in Lake Placid, New York, when he was talked into returning to the team.

Peter has a number of stories from the Mike Keenan era, such as the time Keenan called the entire team back to the arena one night and made them sit in their stalls and take a written test. They had to wait while he graded all the tests and gave them back.

As the team approached Thanksgiving, the players asked Keenan when practice would be, so their families could plan the holiday dinner. Keenan told them practice would be at 11:00 AM, and the families planned their Thanksgiving dinners for 6:00 PM.

A week later he decided to change practice to 4:00 PM, so dinner plans were changed. Then he switched it again...just because he could and probably to make the players angry. He liked people to be on edge.

The team was flying to Denver, and Keenan decided mid-flight to change the arrival airport to Colorado Springs. The pilot radioed ahead and the equipment truck and bus drivers were diverted to Colorado Springs. Then he changed his mind and decided to go to Denver, causing the drivers to divert again. The plane finally landed in Colorado Springs with no buses to pick up the team. Hall of Famer Johnny Bucyk traveled with the team and was in charge of all logistical plans. Keenan wanted Bucyk to suddenly come up with hotel rooms at the famous Broadmoor Hotel in Colorado Springs, with no prior reservations, and to cancel the rooms in Denver. He was finally convinced that his plan simply could not be accomplished, and the team ended up going back to Denver. Keenan's constant changing of plans drove Bucyk crazy.

Keenan had another little trick he thought would motivate a team. He wanted the team's exercise bikes in the middle of the dressing room after games, so that when the media came in they saw Keenan's team hard at work riding the bikes in the middle of the room. Peter picks up the story:

"One game, [assistant equipment manager] Keith Robinson and I moved all the bikes into the room. The Bruins won the game, and Keenan comes in and says, 'Hendu, what are the bikes doing in the middle of the room?' I felt like just saying, 'Bleep off, and leave us alone!'"

For all the problems with Mike Keenan, Peter said working for Pat Burns was just the opposite. He recalled that Burns was always concerned with the support staff, and tried his hardest to make life as easy for them as he could. He also wasn't opposed to using Peter as camouflage when needed.

Burns had his disagreements, at times, with general manager Harry Sinden. Their relationship was often up-and-down. One time, when the team was boarding the charter, Harry went to sit beside Burns, and Pat told Sinden that Peter was sitting in that seat. Harry went to another seat, and Burns called out to Peter, "Hendu, you're sitting here with me."

On another flight, after a difficult loss, Burns again used Henderson as his "Sinden buffer." Harry sat across the aisle from Henderson and Burns and before the plane took off, Harry started a cell phone conversation with Mike O'Connell that included lines such as, "Mike, I'm not even sure they practice their breakouts!" There were other criticisms about Burns' coaching and the team's play. Henderson nudged Burns and said, "Do you hear what he's saying about you?" Burns just smiled and began whistling.

Like every other human being, equipment managers can have favorites, too. In Henderson's case, one of those favorites was Joe Thornton.

"Joe got such a bad rap in this town. He played in the playoffs against Montreal with broken ribs, and Kevin Paul Dupont wrote [in the *Boston Globe*] that the Bruins should strip the captain's 'C' off his chest. Joe plays with broken ribs and gets ripped for it, while Patrice [Bergeron] plays with broken ribs and is a hero. Not that Patrice wasn't heroic, just that Joe was unfairly criticized."

Henderson's appreciation for Thornton even extends to the personal. When Peter's mom passed away in Camden, Maine,

Thornton paid for all of her funeral and burial expenses. That's something only Peter and Joe knew—until now.

After leaving the Boston Bruins, Peter went to work for the Providence Bruins for several seasons. Then he moved on to the New England Sports Center, one of the largest hockey facilities in New England. In his position there, he stills sees people from his professional hockey days. Some former players are now scouts and look for talent during events at the facility. The Bruins alumni team also plays there several times a year, and Peter says Ray Bourque goes out of his way to find Peter and say hello.

"I'm not gonna lie. It's pretty cool when Ray stops into the Pro Shop, gives me a hug, and catches up for a while," Henderson said. "It sure makes me look good to the other guys there."

CHAPTER 15
MARC SAVARD

*D*azzling. That's the one word I would use to describe center Marc Savard. He joined the Bruins as part of general manager Peter Chiarelli's reworking of the Bruins on July 1, 2006—the same day the Bruins signed Zdeno Chara as an unrestricted free agent.

Savard had bounced around from the New York Rangers to the Calgary Flames to the Atlanta Thrashers, garnering a reputation as a guy with a bit of a selfish streak who wasn't committed to being a two-way player. He picked up nearly 100 points in his last season with the Thrashers before he hit the open market and the Bruins lured him to Boston.

Bruins fans soon found out what an amazing offensive force Savard could be. He had 96 points in his first season with the Bruins despite the team's horrible performance under Dave Lewis. When Claude Julien came in to coach, he continued the project coach Bob Hartley had started in Atlanta to help Savard round out his game. It worked, and Savard became the Bruins' unquestioned No. 1 center.

Savard had 78 and 88 points the next two seasons, respectively, but the decrease in production wasn't because of a drop-off in effort. It was all about becoming more of a team player and fitting into Julien's system that stressed defensive responsibility and generating offense from that defensive play.

With Savard, Patrice Bergeron, and David Krejci on the center depth chart, the Bruins looked set at that position for generations—that is, until the afternoon of March 7, 2010. With a cheap shot that's been watched a million times by hockey people across the world and inspired the NHL to begin to crack down on blindside hits and hits to the head, Savard's career was knocked off the rails by Pittsburgh forward Matt Cooke.

Now, it should be remembered that Cooke wasn't an innocent player who did something dumb. This was a guy who'd thrown other cheap hits, injured other players, and had his share of run-ins with the league office. Unfortunately, he was still in the league and on the ice when Savard crossed the attacking blue line and made a pass. Savard never saw Cooke crash into his head, as Savard explained in an article for The Players' Tribune:

> The only memory I have is of being taken off the ice on a stretcher and then realizing that my kids were at home watching the game. So I put my hand up to let them know that dad was OK. I wasn't OK.

The minute Savard hit the ice, my first thought was about Bergeron, and what he went through after a cheap shot in October 2008. It was a long road back that season for Bergeron, and it took him a couple years to be himself again. I wondered if he'd ever play again.

Savard left the ice on a stretcher. He described in the above-mentioned article a feeling of exhaustion every day when he woke up for two months. Nonetheless, like most hockey players who've been bred to battle back from injury, Savard returned to the ice. He returned at possibly the worst time for a player who hadn't played for three months: the playoffs. Against the Philadelphia Flyers no less.

No one was thinking that Savard was anything less than 100 percent in his first game back. He scored the overtime game winner in Game 1 of the series against the Flyers. He skated to the side wall and threw himself against the glass and was mobbed by his teammates the way every kid imagines in a scene of jubilation that hadn't occurred at the Garden in years.

Savard wasn't all right, though, and he's admitted that he rushed back and probably made his condition worse. The Bruins famously lost that series in seven games to the Flyers after leading it 3–0. Chiarelli went about recharging the Bruins' roster, a process that soon became more difficult when he found out about Savard's condition. On the eve of training camp, we learned that Savard was not physically able to participate.

Savard made one more comeback and played 25 games for the 2010–11 Bruins. His decision to come back made me queasy. It was obvious he wasn't the same guy and I thought back to Patriots quarterback Steve Grogan, who played with a neck roll. Every time he scrambled, you just wanted him to go down rather than take another hit. These athletes are often too brave for their own good.

A routine hit by Colorado defenseman Matt Hunwick on January 22, 2011, knocked Savard out for good; he never played again.

Although he was unable to travel to Vancouver for Game 7 of the 2011 Stanley Cup Final, Savard watched them on television and joined his teammates for the "rolling rally" to celebrate the victory a few days later. The Bruins petitioned to have Savard's name engraved on the Cup although he didn't meet the specifications for inclusion, and he made it. I was so glad he was able to get his name on the Cup. I'm sure it was bittersweet seeing as how he had so little to do with the win but the Bruins wanted to honor him for everything he accomplished in helping them regain relevance, and for being a great teammate, and he was able to get that rare honor.

Marc was one of the players I really wanted to talk to while working on this book. I knew Bruins fans hadn't heard from him in some time, and I also knew he was an immensely popular player.

Marc Savard had a star-crossed career in Boston. *(AP Images)*

I reached out on several occasions, but I had been told by people who knew him better than I that he had been hard to connect with.

Steve Simmons of the *Toronto Sun* had written about Marc during the 2017–18 season, and what he said stung Savard. Simmons wrote, "Media called. Nobody answered. Now suddenly Savard is a media guy. My advice: If he calls, don't answer."

Marc took to Twitter, which he had used more and more to reconnect with his fans, and lay his heart bare to Simmons:

"I spent many years dealing with some serious mental health issues and post-concussion symptoms. I did not withdraw myself from hockey or the hockey world by choice. I was not in a good place! I needed those years to heal."

Simmons, to his credit, acknowledged in a follow-up column the hurt his words may have caused:

"What I wrote about Savard had nothing to do with concussions or his personal battles. But what I wrote about him was improperly worded and far too harsh. For that, I apologize."

The fact is many of us in the hockey media had been attempting to make contact with Marc, but none of us knew exactly where he was in his recovery. And none of us knew how long the recovery process had taken. When I was finally able to talk with Marc, I asked how long it had taken him to feel "normal" again.

"Oh, you know, two to three years," he said. "It was a really, really tough time. Luckily, I had a great family around me, including my wife and my kids. The whole Bruins organization was really great with me, starting with GM Peter Chiarelli, right down to Donnie DelNegro and the training staff. Everyone was phenomenal with me and I can't say enough good things about them. The doctors in Boston were incredible, and everyone helped me get to where I am today. I'm feeling the best I've ever felt, and that's why you're finally seeing more of me, and hearing more from me. Now I want to give back to the game that's given so much to me."

While Marc always considered himself a Bruin, the collective bargaining agreement and salary cap meant that Marc and his contract were actually traded a couple of times, even though everyone knew his playing days were over. That situation caused Marc some frustration as well.

"It was probably the most irritating thing," he said. "After all I had been through, I was still required to fly into town for every training camp, and at the end of the season, to be examined by the team doctors and told I still couldn't play. Even when my contract got traded, I had to still fly into those cities."

I'm happy to say, Marc Savard is back. He's made a couple of appearances on my radio show in Boston, and Bruins fans are always thrilled to hear from him. He's also begun appearing for Sportsnet in Toronto, and his wealth of hockey knowledge makes him a joy to listen to.

I often think about the career he could have had. Imagine the Bruins with Savard, Bergeron, and Krejci down the middle taking on that Chicago Blackhawks team in the 2013 Stanley Cup Final. The outcome probably would've been different. Who knows what else the Bruins would've been able to accomplish with probably the best trio of centers in the league?

The Savard injury was one we've seen far too many times with the Bruins and around the NHL. In addition to drawing a spotlight to hits to the head and head injuries, it also inspired an interesting story about payback.

For all intents and purposes, Cooke was a goon with no accountability. He never would've had the guts to do that to a Shawn Thornton or Gregory Campbell. He targeted Marc Savard, who never hit anyone in his life. What Cooke did was embarrassing. And I'm not just saying that because Cooke was on another team. I always thought that what Marty McSorley did to Donald Brashear in February 2000 was embarrassing as well. You wonder what clicks or what lock gets turned in a guy's head that he could do something so foolish and dangerous to another player.

Anyway, Cooke didn't have to answer for his actions that day in Pittsburgh. Most of the Bruins players on the ice said they didn't see the play and among the ones that saw it from the bench...well, one in particular wasn't able to do anything.

"I couldn't do anything. However much time was left on the clock, I never got back on the ice," Bruins tough guy Shawn Thornton told me. "Marc got decked, and I didn't play another shift that game. I've heard the argument, 'Well, if he was really a deterrent that wouldn't have happened.' It was a close game and he got hit. Listen; if I was on the ice I would have killed the guy."

Cooke remained alive, but eventually had to answer to Thornton. For days after, the Bruins' fan base was livid about the hit and the lack of a response from their team. The Penguins were scheduled to visit Boston for a game on March 18. What unfolded before that game involved Thornton, retired Bruins and Penguins forward Glen Murray, and Penguins forward (and ex-Bruin) Billy Guerin in a tale I'll let Shawn tell you:

"We went to Billy Guerin before the game and said, 'This can go one of two ways. Either we're going out there and it's gonna be a brawl like the old days, or Matt Cooke fights Shawn Thornton and it's over.'

"Again, it's the idea of policing. That game could have been an absolute bloodbath. There could have been 5,000 minutes in penalties and not a hockey play all night. I've seen it happen before and so had Glen and we decided we should go have this conversation. Billy went to Matt Cooke and said, 'You're gonna fight him. You're gonna fight him the first shift.' That fight was agreed to by both teams. When I beat him up, and it doesn't matter if I knock him out or if he comes out of it okay, that would be it.

"Did I want to knock his head off his shoulders for Savvy? You're damn right I did. I hit him and knocked him down. I didn't know if he was gonna get back up, but he did, so I hit him some more and knocked him down again. I went to the penalty box, and then I didn't have to worry about Patrice Bergeron getting decked by Eric Goddard, or they didn't have to worry about Sid [Crosby] being run by Zdeno Chara."

There's a fine line between gratuitous violence and necessary physicality. Hockey toes that line all the time. In this case, I was glad the situation was defused without anyone else getting injured. And, if anything, the Matt Cooke incident brought the Bruins closer together and taught them a lesson about team toughness.

CHAPTER 16
PATRICE BERGERON

It's hard to believe, now that I've seen him mature into one of the great all-around players in the NHL, a four-time Selke Trophy winner, and a Stanley Cup champion, but Patrice Bergeron once flew under the radar.

The Bruins drafted Bergeron with a second-round pick, 45th overall, in the 2003 NHL draft. This wasn't some flashy lottery pick like the Bruins had had six years earlier when they landed Joe Thornton No. 1 overall and then selected Sergei Samsonov seven picks later. This was a second-round pick selected weeks before his 18th birthday with little to no expectations thrust on him, coming off his second season in the Quebec Major Junior Hockey League, where he scored at a somewhat impressive clip of 73 points in 70 games in 2002–03.

But Bergeron proved to be an overachiever right off the hop, earning a spot on the NHL roster at 18 on a team that included Thornton and Samsonov, the type of talent that had the Bruins thinking they were ready to challenge for the Cup. Bruins president Harry Sinden said he knew just three or four practices into training camp that Bergeron had the right stuff. When I saw him, I could see what Harry was seeing. The kid wasn't flashy, but you could tell he didn't make many mistakes and he was always in the right spot at the right time. Little did we know that would be the foundation for his career.

Patrice has often said he was surprised he was able to make the jump to the NHL so quickly. He was at training camp just hoping to learn and grow, not start a rookie NHL season that featured him finishing sixth on the Bruins and fifth among NHL rookies in points (39, in 71 games). Sparked by Bergeron and fellow rookie Andrew Raycroft, who won the Calder

Trophy as Rookie of the Year for his 2.05 goals-against average and .926 save percentage, the Bruins were a force and they won the Northeast Division title. Along the way, general manager Mike O'Connell made some rare in-season trades to bolster the lineup, adding defenseman Sergei Gonchar and forward Michael Nylander.

Heading into the playoffs, the Bruins were the No. 2 seed in the Eastern Conference. However, they ran into their archrival Montreal in the first round. Patrice, a Quebec Nordiques fan who could never bring himself to root for the Canadiens (even after the Nordiques bolted for Denver) growing up, didn't wait long to thrust himself into the rivalry. With Game 2 of the best-of-seven series tied 1–1, Patrice skated with the puck from the red line into the offensive zone before cutting a little to his right and catching the goaltender leaning the wrong way for the game-winning goal 1:26 into overtime. I yelled "score!" as the Garden crowd celebrated a 2–0 series lead.

The Bruins lost that series in seven games and didn't return to the playoffs until 2008. Bergeron's career, though, was launched that season. He didn't just thrive on the ice; he was adapting to life off the ice in a strange city with little grasp of the local language. Patrice is as articulate as they come now but back then, just like Ray Bourque, he was just learning.

Patrice will tell you he was helped immensely by teammate Martin Lapointe, whom many fans remember as a disappointment because the Bruins made the mistake of signing him to a four-year, $20 million contract as a free agent after he scored 27 goals for Detroit in 2000–01. Marty only scored 40 goals in 205 games for the Bruins, but he was a quality guy off the ice and the type of mentor a teenaged Patrice needed. Patrice lived with Marty that year, and the Bruins didn't have to worry about their wunderkind going off the tracks. It helped that Bergeron was a model boarder for the Lapointe family. I asked Marty once if it was hard having an 18-year-old kid living with him. He said, "Not at all; he's great. My kids love the guy, my wife loves the guy."

Patrice had 73 and 70 points the next two season, respectively. Things got dicey for his career, though, when he was hit from behind by Philadelphia defenseman Randy Jones in a game in the fall of 2007. A Grade 3 concussion kept him out for the rest of the season. He started the next season but had to shake off some rust, and he even missed a few more games with a second concussion suffered in a collision with Carolina's Dennis Seidenberg, who ended up becoming a valuable teammate. Bergeron had 91 points in 137 games in 2008–09 and 2009–10. In 2011–12, he had 64 points and led the league with a plus-36 rating. He was rounding back into form, and of course, he saved his best for last with 20 points in 23 postseason games (he missed two with yet another concussion) during the Bruins' run to the Cup championship.

Patrice avoided becoming one of the all-too-many players who've had their careers concluded by concussion problems. Although he looked confident doing it, there was always uncertainty in the back of his mind.

"I was just trying to get better and get healthy, regardless of the hockey end of it," Patrice said. "At the same time, it took a long time for me to feel better. I always felt that I would come back and play and that I would still have a good career. I always believed

Patrice Bergeron, one of the best two-way forwards in the game, helped lead the Bruins to the Stanley Cup in 2011. *(AP Images)*

in that.... But it's sometimes tough to know. Every concussion is different from one another. There is so much uncertainty that goes along with it. At the time, I was trying not to think too far ahead, just be in the present and try to find a way to feel better from one week to another."

Patrice's greatest act of overcoming physical issues, though, might not have been conquering his early season concussion troubles. His greatest physical feat might've been making it through to the end of the 2013 Stanley Cup Final, which the Bruins lost in six games.

I mentioned earlier that I was walking with my broadcast partner Billy Jaffe and head coach Claude Julien after Game 6 when Julien got the call that Patrice was headed to the hospital. Patrice's perseverance in that series wrote his name into Bruins folklore.

"There was a lot that went into that entire playoffs," Patrice recalled. "I guess I hurt myself in Game 3. It sort of got worse and worse. I had hurt the ribs and cartilage, and they weren't going to get better while we were playing. But you get to Game 6, and it's kind of do or die, and you've battled through two and a half months of playoffs with your teammates. Everyone is going through various bumps and bruises and injuries. It's not like I was the only guy. I was just trying to find a way to get on the ice. I talked to trainers and doctors, and we talked about doing a nerve block, and it seemed like it would help alleviate some of the pain. It helped some, but things got worse. I knew my ribs were broken, and I knew the issue with the cartilage.... Then the collapsed lung made it hard for me to even breathe. I was gasping for air and just trying to find a way to breathe. That's when I knew things were really bad."

Patrice wound up pulling through from all those ailments and we were all able to look back at his performance in awe. He had played 17:45 of ice time in Game 6. No one personified toughness more than Patrice in that series and in that game.

I don't know how he did what he did. I don't know how any human being could do what he did under the circumstances of when he did it. It still boggles my mind.

Of course Patrice and the Bruins would've never faced the Blackhawks that year had he not capped one of the greatest comebacks in NHL history. The Bruins were trailing 4–1 in the third period of Game 7 of their first-round playoff series against Toronto. In my role as postgame show host, I had been preparing my postmortems—who's going to be traded, who's going to be back next year, that sort of stuff. Needless to say, everything we prepared had to go in the crapper.

I remember that when the Bruins scored to make it 4–2, the feeling was, "Well, at least they've made it more respectable." Then they cut the lead to one goal and the whole building began to believe they could actually pull this off. People who had started to leave were scrambling back to their seats.

Somehow the Bruins came back to tie the game with three goals in the final 11 minutes. Patrice tied the game with 51 seconds remaining. That goal nearly brought the Garden down. I had never in my life experienced anything like that at a sporting event.

After the drama of the comeback, there was no doubt in my mind they were going to win in overtime. And Patrice proved me prescient when he scored again 6:05 into overtime to send the Bruins to the second round.

That was certainly his most famous goal and one I was appreciative to have witnessed in person.

As I mentioned, Patrice has come such a long way since he was an 18-year-old rookie. He's one of the most respected athletes in his sport and in Boston. He's the type of person you might not be close to, but when you talk to him he makes you feel like a friend. He's a lot like Ray Bourque in that he grew up with a Bruins sweater on and in Boston despite coming from Quebec and not even being proficient in the language at the beginning. The comparison to Bourque isn't lost on Patrice.

"Ray's always been someone I've looked up to," Patrice said. "I was a French Canadian growing up, and I followed his career. He was already someone I respected as a player, and once I got to know him when I got to Boston, I was just so impressed by his personality, and by the way he handled himself. He was already a legend of the game, and I was impressed by him always wanting to help people, and help me, and show me things he had learned. He was always open to teach me things. It's a huge compliment just hearing you even compare me to a guy like Raymond. He's a true professional, on and off the ice."

No one is held in higher regard by his teammates than Patrice, as Shawn Thornton, a Bruins forward from 2007 to '14, explained.

"He is the heart and soul of that organization," said Thornton. "He is the grit, he is the sandpaper, plus he is also the skill and the finesse and the hardest-working guy in the room. He is the ultimate team guy, the ultimate leader. I've always said, Bergie might be the only guy I've ever played with I would probably let date my sister when I was younger. He's just the perfect human being."

CHAPTER 17
ZDENO CHARA

I'm fairly certain the first time I ever saw Zdeno Chara play in person was April 9, 1998.

As a 21-year-old rookie defenseman, Chara skated 13 shifts and had one shot on goal but no points in a 4–1 Bruins win against the New York Islanders at what was then the FleetCenter. He had been drafted in the third round (No. 56 overall) in the 1996 NHL draft and, to be kind, he looked nothing like a Norris Trophy–caliber defenseman. In 25 games that year, he had no goals and one assist to go along with 50 penalty minutes, although he did finish a plus-1 for the year.

But I will never forget Gord Kluzak, my broadcaster partner that day, saying, "That guy could be the best defenseman in the NHL someday!" Let's just say Gord knows more about hockey than me.

Chara played four rather insignificant seasons for the Islanders, including back-to-back seasons of minus-27 ratings in 1999–00 and 2000–01. He scored two goals per season for his final three seasons in New York, and never had a power-play goal. He was traded to the Ottawa Senators during the 2001 NHL draft with forward Bill Muckalt and the Islanders' first-round pick (which Ottawa turned into Jason Spezza at No. 2 overall) for Alexei Yashin in a trade that makes everyone's list of 10 best trade steals in NHL history. (Apologies to my buddy and then-Islanders GM Mike Milbury).

The Senators knew they were acquiring a large defensive presence, but I'm not sure they understood what they had, either.

In his first season in Ottawa, Chara blossomed, scoring 10 goals, including four on the power play, and went from minus-27 to a plus-30 in one season. He earned the first of 12 All-Star selections, and suddenly the largest defenseman in the NHL was also one of the best, just as Gord predicted.

The thing to know about the 6'9" Chara, the tallest player in NHL history, is that he hasn't had to fight as much as you think he would considering his size and toughness. Let's face it; there aren't many NHL players in his weight class (255 pounds). He had 10 regular-season fights in 2001–02 and followed that up with nine in 2003–04. He didn't top four in the next 14 seasons, and that just means NHL players are smarter than they're given credit for.

It was former Bruins defenseman Andrew Ference, Chara's teammate for several seasons, including the 2011 Stanley Cup championship season, who once said to me, "The thing you've got to remember is that Zee could literally kill someone if he wasn't careful."

Zdeno's father was an Olympic Greco-Roman wrestler for 11 years, and Chara always said his father was his role model and inspiration. Zdeno said it was his father who taught him the discipline needed to succeed.

"No one gave me much of a chance because of my height, but my dad told me if I could master the basics of gymnastics and acrobatics, I could master hockey as well, because it's all about being mobile, being able to make use of my explosive power in combination with my height."

Chara's height can be measured and writes him into the record books. If there was a way to measure his overwhelming fitness, that would probably also top the NHL charts. His offseason regimen is legendary and includes prodigious cycling workouts along with Greco-Roman wrestling workouts and training in the martial art of aikido. He was once featured in the Body Issue of *ESPN the*

Magazine, posing nude with a hockey stick perched on his shoulders. He looked like he took the phrase "washboard abs" to a new and ridiculous level.

Imagine a guy Chara's size doing 31 consecutive wide-grip pull-ups. Ray Bourque was always the benchmark for the Bruins' strength and conditioning testing in his day—until Chara came along and blew all of Bourque's team records out of the water. That wasn't by accident.

"When I came to Boston and was named the captain, I wanted to set the bar and wanted to establish certain standards going forward. The first standard had to do with fitness. We were going to have a certain attitude, and we were going to be one of the most fit teams in the league."

In addition to setting incredible benchmarks for fitness levels, Chara also quickly developed a reputation around the league when it came to fighting. Even noted, successful fighters like Shawn Thornton took note.

"I've hit a lot of people in my day, and I've wrestled with a lot of people and fought a lot of people," Thornton said. "When me and him used to mess around in practice I knew that if we ever fought, I would be fighting for my life if he ever got mad. If he was angry, and wound up and hit you, he could kill you. He broke a guy's face, when he was playing for Ottawa, from his back. He was lying on his back. To have that much power with nothing of a wind up. For someone who has boxed his whole life, I can tell you, that's absurd to have that kind of power and snap from your back, on the ice, when someone is on top of you. It's crazy."

Peter Chiarelli was hired to be Boston's general manager but was still working for Ottawa because of contractual obligations on

July 1, 2006, when the Bruins signed Chara away from the Senators to a five-year, $37.5 million contract—the largest contract in franchise history at the time. Chiarelli was a big reason Chara decided to sign with Boston. He also wanted to follow in the footsteps of some of the Bruins' greats—from Eddie Shore to Bobby Orr to Bourque, all of whom were defensemen and cornerstones of the Bruins.

"Ray Bourque and Bobby Orr were such huge icons in the city of Boston. They are two defensemen that I really look up to," Chara said. "They both left such huge shoes to fill. I really wanted to be someone who followed in that tradition. Ray and Bobby are two players, and people, that I wanted to emulate as far as what they accomplished."

Chara and Chiarelli's first year, though, was a disappointment, with coach Dave Lewis leading them to a 35–41–6 record and a second straight season out of the playoffs.

But then Chiarelli brought in Claude Julien to coach, and the Bruins went to the playoffs every season for seven straight years. Chara's level of play continued to soar with the Bruins' improvement. Chara had a career-high 19 goals and was plus-23 when he won the Norris Trophy as best defenseman in the NHL after the 2008–09 season. In five of his first eight seasons with the Bruins, Chara was at least in the top three in Norris voting.

Chara and the Bruins endured some team-wide disappointments their first three seasons under Julien, never getting past the second round of the Eastern Conference playoffs. But at the conclusion of the 2010–11 season, Chara finally got to experience the ultimate as a player and captain in the NHL, on June 15, 2011. After the Bruins defeated the Vancouver Canucks on the road in Game 7 of the Stanley Cup Final, commissioner Gary Bettman

Zdeno Chara has been a foundational member of the Bruins since he came to Boston in 2006. *(AP Images)*

made his usual speech to the usual barrage of boos. And then Bettman called for the Bruins' captain to come take the Cup. With a playoff beard reminiscent of the burliest mountain man, Chara raised the Cup above his head and let out a primal scream that could've been heard all the way back in Boston even if the NBC microphone had been off.

"I was very fortunate. We had built a championship team, and accomplished our goal. When you are the captain, you get to hoist the Cup first. There is nothing like it. As a player it is probably the best memory you will ever have. But at that moment, the best memory I have is turning back toward my teammates as I skated toward the commissioner and pointing at my guys and they were all pointing back at me. It is an unbelievable feeling when you accomplish so much as a team. There is so much hard work, and so much goes into it. It's actually hard to describe."

During his second season as Bruins head coach, Bruce Cassidy said Chara was still the best even-strength and penalty-killing defenseman in the league, which is remarkable considering Chara had turned 40 years old the previous March. Coincidentally, there was a 40-year-old quarterback playing at the highest level just 25 miles away, in Foxboro, Massachusetts. Tom Brady has rewritten the book when it comes to what an athlete of that age can do, and Chara has watched with great interest.

"I am a big fan of Tom. I follow him, actually, very closely. I purchased his book [*The TB12 Method*]. He surrounded himself with such a good team, as far as nutritionists, trainers, people who take care of him both before and after games. I'm very interested in his theories about muscle pliability and soft tissue work. He keeps very fit and motivated, and I'm loving it because I'm in the same position. Of course, I want to keep going and keep playing as long as I can. I'm trying to do the same things."

Chara told me he had never spoken to Brady, but would love the opportunity to talk with him about his programs and ideas. In my position as radio host, I work at Gillette Stadium every Monday during the football season, co-hosting Bill Belichick's weekly radio appearance. It also means I'm able to make connections with the team. I assured Chara that someday I'll get him his opportunity to speak directly to Brady.

After a decade-plus with the Bruins, Chara ranked in the top five in games played, goals, assists, and points by a defenseman in Bruins history. The Hall of Fame will surely beckon not long after he retires. But throughout his stint, Chara has often fallen victim in Boston to what I dubbed Big Man's Syndrome. I've seen it happen with Chara and other big men, like Hal Gill, a 6'7" defenseman who played 1,108 regular-season games (including 626 with the Bruins). There's a vocal minority of Bruins fans who feel that a player of Chara's size should be putting opposing players through the boards every shift. I get the calls on my talk show all the time: "Chara sucks! They've got to get him out of here! He can't play anymore!" I got the exact same calls about Gill. They were wrong about him too. If Zdeno Chara tried to decimate every opponent around him every time on the ice, more often than not he'd be out of position and hurting his team (not to mention risking suspension based on his overwhelming edge in strength). What Chara does is play the game the right way, the smart way, using his strength and reach to his advantage but not putting his teammates in a position where they would have to cover up for him—in fact, he's almost always the guy doing the covering up.

Let me just say this: if the Bruins made Chara available, there would be 30 other teams in the NHL who would be interested in acquiring him. Ask his teammates or his opponents and the answer is almost always the same: Zdeno Chara is one of the best and most feared defensemen in the league even as he's gotten older and has had to adapt his game based on his skills and the changing style of the league.

Meanwhile, Chara is still as enthusiastic about the sport now as he was when he first laced up his skates.

"I want to be the hardest-working player every day in the practice and in the gym," Chara says. "I want to be a player that my teammates can rely on, to do my job and play against the top lines every night. I'm not the flashy guy; I'm not the sexiest player who is going to do toe drags and spin-o-ramas and so on. I just want to play that hard style, who understands the game and will always be there for my teammates. I never shied away from standing up for a teammate, or changing the momentum of the game."

Chara doesn't just cause fear with his size and ability to physically dominate; he instills fear when he shoots the puck as well. He won the NHL Hardest Shot competition five times in a row from 2007 through 2012 and topped out at 108.8 miles per hour. A shot like his scares opposing players and goaltenders, but it also scares his own teammates. I've been told on a number of occasions that players on his own team don't like to stand in front of the opposing goaltender when Chara shoots, both because of the speed but also because he doesn't always have complete control of that shot.

Over the years, I've also heard things about Chara being hard on younger players. Some said Chara was one of the primary reasons that Dougie Hamilton wanted to leave Boston and eventually was traded to Calgary on draft day in 2015. They say Chara is cold and aloof. I've heard the stories, the descriptions, but I'm not sure I really believe them.

During the 2016–17 season, I watched Chara nurture and develop his defense partner, Brandon Carlo. Carlo surprised many when he made the team as a 19-year-old and spent almost the entire season partnered with Chara. He prospered as a result. In the Stanley Cup playoffs that same season, when 2016 first-round pick Charlie McAvoy made the leap from Boston University to the NHL, he spent most of those first games as Chara's defense partner. McAvoy also prospered. If a player like Hamilton found it hard to handle Chara's demands and expectations, perhaps the problem wasn't Chara.

As of last winter, Chara had worn the "C" for the second-longest time in Bruins history after Bourque. Chara told me about his leadership style and how he expects his teammates to follow along.

"It is so important that you have support from your core players, probably your best players. That's going to make any leadership role easier, and your leading will be stronger. You need to surround yourself with players on the same mission, players who understand what you're trying to accomplish, and they have the same attitude. When I got here, Patrice [Bergeron] was in his second year, and then we had the arrival of guys like Shawn Thornton, Mark Recchi, Andrew Ference—all guys who were in leadership roles with other teams. We talked about how we wanted to go about the business, and we never shied away from what had to be done. We weren't just holding our teammates, but we were holding each other accountable. Sometimes you have to separate personal agendas from where the team is going. A few times, I had to address things I didn't like with Mark or Jaromir Jagr. Those guys are Hall of Famers, guys who have given so much to the game. But when it came down to team business, my job as captain was to not shy away from what had to be done, whether the guy was playing five games in the NHL or played 1,500 games. You have to be responsible and honor your role. You can't play favorites. That's how I go about doing the job. I never separate the younger guy from the older guy. I hold everyone accountable and you have to be fair."

Boston hasn't always been kind to Chara. But he'll never be forgotten given his contributions to the Stanley Cup championship team, his Norris Trophy win, and a lot of other great moments. It's his desire to be thought of in the same vein as Brady, David Ortiz, and Paul Pierce, his historic contemporaries on the other Boston sports teams when he was wearing the Black and Gold.

And Chara has embraced Boston, the site of his many accomplishments and some of his disappointments, as a home as comfortable as his hometown of Trencin, Slovakia.

"Boston is home. It's a place where I find people are very hardworking, people that are very passionate. People talk to you on the streets about life. They just want to know how you're doing. They care about you. People are very welcoming. When I walk around, it feels like I'm home. My three children were born here. It really became my first home, actually. I was born and raised in Slovakia, and I've spent more than half of my life in North America. Boston is my home, it's the place I want to stay and keep raising my kids. I love Boston, and the people of Boston, and everything about it. It's a city, but kind of on a smaller scale."

CHAPTER 18
ANDREW FERENCE

As I worked on this book, it didn't seem to matter who I spoke to; everyone brought up Andrew Ference.

Patrice Bergeron, Shawn Thornton, and Zdeno Chara all talked about leadership, guts, and determination, and all brought up Ference's name separately and totally without prompting.

Ference was a rather non-heralded defenseman for the Calgary Flames when, on February 10, 2007, he and Chuck Kobasew were acquired by general manager Peter Chiarelli in a trade for Brad Stuart and Wayne Primeau. Ference was unimpressed and disappointed.

"I was a few years into my NHL career with Calgary, and I was playing close to my parents' home in Alberta," Ference said. "I had a house in the mountains and a bunch of family there and we had actually gone to the Final the year before the lockout. Getting traded was a shock to the system, and I was pretty upset about being traded to Boston. In hindsight, it was the best thing that ever happened to me, but at the time I was a bit immature about being traded and had a bit of a chip on my shoulder. And, let's be honest, I was coming to a team that was so far out of the playoffs, and had been a failure for several seasons."

Andrew noticed that the building had a bunch of empty seats, and he also noted that he didn't see a single Bruins hat or t-shirt anywhere in the city. He was coming from Canada, where hockey was king, and he arrived in Boston at a time when the Patriots were in full-blown dynasty mode, and the Red Sox and Celtics were also well ahead of the Bruins in terms of popularity. But as he put it, a giant reset button got hit in the offseason, and he bought in for his first full season in 2007–08.

Ference said that, believe it or not, he felt the seeds of a possible Stanley Cup run in that first full season. And he said expectations for him were set early on.

"My first meeting with Peter, I just wanted to ask about my role, and what was expected of me. He made it clear early on that he wasn't worried about passing the puck, or moving the puck out of our zone, or scoring goals. Peter was interested in the type of culture we had in Calgary, and how we could build that in Boston. Those teams in Boston weren't necessarily super talented, but we were building a team that would do anything for the team. It was an absolute buy-in from everyone on the roster, and that's a credit to our coach [Claude Julien] and the veteran leadership on the team."

Ference also saw Chiarelli continue to make moves with his roster. Phil Kessel was a future star, but made it clear he wouldn't re-sign with Boston as a restricted free agent in 2009. He was dealt to Toronto for draft picks. Ference told me he knew the team was at times trading away star players, but he also saw the overall plan of what Chiarelli was doing and what the ultimate goal was.

"To simplify a lot of the moves, it comes down to one basic thing: Peter was trying to get rid of negativity, push back about what was being built, and getting rid of 'why guys.' You know who they are. 'Why are we doing this? Why are we staying there? Why do we have to go now?' After a while those guys wear the others down with their attitude, and the team was trying to get everyone pulling in the same direction. If you're going to be somewhat negative, then you better be a helluva player."

Ference, and many of his teammates, emphasized to me that it didn't matter if a player was a first- or fourth-liner; every guy was important to the success or failure of the team.

"Zdeno was just awesome with that attitude. Bergie was pretty shy, but he was a leader in the making. We were all about building pride back up in the city for a once proud organization, and putting hockey back on the map. We wanted to put people back in the seats, and get fans to stop talking about the past teams, and how great they were. We wanted them to talk about us."

Leadership was not just a vague concept for Ference. He studied the idea, from some probably surprising angles. He attempted to bring information from other sports and the business world to the idea of leadership and team building.

"I wanted to learn about the success stories in corporate America. I wanted to know what Google was doing, or what Amazon was doing. And I really wanted to know if those successes were applicable to professional sports."

When Ference wanted to study something closer to home, like professional sports, he didn't turn to the triumphs of the New England Patriots, the Boston Celtics, or the Boston Red Sox. Andrew studied the worldwide successes of the New Zealand All Blacks, a rugby union team generally acknowledged as one of the best in the world.

"They have a big sign in their locker room that simply says, No DICKHEADS. They have a 15-point philosophy on how their team will be run, but humility is probably their No. 1 on the list. Every player on the team acts the same. The superstars on the team clean up the team locker room. Guys take turns sweeping out the equipment shed. When the entire team not only does that stuff, but actually believes in it, there is no end to what you can accomplish. They'll take the person above the talent."

He wanted to make it clear to me that not all the players who got moved were horrible people, but in some cases it was simply to get rid of what he calls the "infection of negativity."

Ference, like Thornton, became a Bostonian through and through. His family settled in the North End, and he returns frequently. He'll tell you his best friends are in Boston and he always felt comfortable here.

"Living in a neighborhood like the North End was an incredible experience. You go out to get some fresh pasta and it takes you an hour because you have 25 conversations along the way. You try to get your hair trimmed up and it takes you two hours because you're having all these great interactions with the neighborhood. It's just good people. I could call on anyone I know from there and they would drop everything to help me. And I would do the same for them."

Ference is also a guy who wears his heart on his completely tattooed sleeve. He told me he doesn't cry easily, but he cries at times that mean the most. He cries when he sees an athlete win an Olympic gold medal and then tear up at the playing of his or her national anthem. But he felt that same thing when fans at TD Garden belted out the national anthem before the team's first game after the Boston Marathon bombing in 2013.

"Man, when you just mention that to me, I get goosebumps and emotional and my throat constricts. There were so many emotions that whole week. So many guys on the team lived in the same general area, around the North End and Charlestown. I mean, if you went to that Whole Foods you would run into like nine of us at any one time. There was that pent-up tension in the city, and anger, and we all just wanted to let it loose before that game. We're no different than the guy sitting up in Section 301. He wanted to let his emotions loose, and so did we."

I told Ference that I considered him underappreciated by Bruins fans—at least until the night of April 21, 2011. The Bruins had dropped the first two games of their first-round playoff series at home to the Montreal Canadiens. The Bruins won Game 3 and gained a sliver of life. Then, in Game 4, Ference scored a huge goal in a game the Bruins went on to win in overtime to even up the series. Ference celebrated the goal the way many Bruins fans probably celebrated back home: by flipping Canadiens fans the bird.

Oh, at first he blamed his flipped middle finger on an equipment malfunction, but later admitted it was intentional. He had to deny the gesture in the early going to avoid a severe punishment from the NHL. He was out $2,500 after the league considered his actions. He told me he let his emotions get the better of him, and he acted in a primal scream and gesture. Bruins fans suddenly loved Ference all the more.

"I always thought I was a little overrated as player. I was a lower-rung defenseman who was just trying to stay in the league. When people were critical of me I actually got it. But all of a sudden, I come home from Montreal and word was I was going to be fined for my gesture. I got home to my apartment in the North End and on my door buzzer were several envelopes. People had left notes to thank me and even money to help me pay my fine. I knew right away it was the best money I ever spent."

When I think about the Bruins' 2010–11 Stanley Cup championship team, one of the first words I think of is selfless. It was guys doing whatever it took to win—fight, block a shot, kill a penalty, or score a goal. Guys such as Thornton and Ference, and others like Chris Kelly, Rich Peverley, and Adam McQuaid, always got that. It was a quote from Thornton that brought it all into focus: "Dale, sometimes it's not the glitter, it's the glue." He was speaking specifically about Ference, but could have been speaking of any of them.

When I told Ference what Thornton had said, he paused as if to collect himself, and said emotionally, "Oh, man. That means a lot coming from a guy like Thorty, that's for sure. Well, he knows. He's cut from the same cloth. He's just describing himself. You can't just talk about your culture, and what you want your team to be, you have to live it too. You can talk about valuing guys, doing everything for the team and sticking up for each other. You can say all that, but it's a whole other level when guys actually believe it. I was one of those guys who really, really believed it. I would do anything for that team and those guys. I would do anything that the coach said. I was only one of those guys, and I was joined by others, who also believed it. The glitter part is nice, and we had superstars, but the glue part comes from that belief in what you're doing. The glue guys are responsible for infecting the other guys with that belief system, and making that culture strong. The glue guys know how to pat themselves on the back; they don't need that confirmation from others. And we had a bunch of guys like that."

Ference told me, like others have, that he really didn't appreciate what winning the Cup meant to Boston until the team won. As he said, you kind of get tunnel vision during the chase, and he isn't proud that during that time he was probably a poor husband, a poor father, and a poor friend. It's the sacrifice that every player is willing to undertake to get his name engraved on the Cup.

And Ference told me he hoped he made up for it when he got his day with the Cup.

"I was the last guy with the Cup, and I had it in the city of Boston. I was proud to bring it around and share it with so many others. I hope they enjoyed it as much as I did."

CHAPTER 19
GOALIES

Goalies are weird. That's not to say that every goalie is weird, but at that position there is more weirdness per pound than any other position in any other sport anywhere.

I'll give you an example. When I was with the Maine Mariners of the American Hockey League, we had a goalie named Robbie Moore. Now, Robbie was a pretty good AHL goalie who was part of three consecutive Hap Holmes Award goaltending duos, the minor league version of the William Jennings Trophy. He played in the NHL for the Philadelphia Flyers and the Washington Capitals.

Moore was pretty good, but pretty strange, too. How strange? He had a habit of throwing up...a lot. Robbie threw up into a large garbage bin before every period he played...every single night. Think about throwing up three times a night, every night you ever played. The game would lose some of its allure, wouldn't it?

Among my favorite people ever to have worn a Bruins uniform was goaltender Gerry Cheevers, better known to his teammates as Cheesie. He sported the iconic mask that simulated all the stitches he might have received had he not been wearing the mask. He also had a terrific sense of humor.

He used to tell me things like, "Do you know what it means if they hit the post, Dale? They missed the f—g net!"

He also liked to joke about the league's great shooters—guys like the Golden Jet, Bobby Hull. Cheese would tell me, "Three things can happen when Hull is shooting at you: he can score or he can miss the net. The worst of the three might be that he could hit you!"

Cheevers finished his playing career in 1980, and he was named Bruins head coach by Harry Sinden before the 1981 season.

Before being replaced by Sinden in the middle of the 1984–85 season, Cheevers put together a record of 204–126–46 (.604), which is the seventh-best record all time among NHL coaches with 250 games or more.

It comes as no surprise that someone as glib as Gerry Cheevers was a terrific hockey color announcer. He worked for the Hartford Whalers from 1986 to 1995 and for the Bruins from 1999 to 2002. During those years, I had the pleasure of getting to know and work with Cheesie.

The Bruins have had some incredible goaltending through the years. They have had Vezina Trophy winners and Stanley Cup champions. They have had Rookie of the Year winners and one-hit wonders. When I wanted to talk about goaltenders, I felt I had the perfect panel. I spent a night sitting with former Bruins goaltender Andrew Raycroft, a very good goalie, and Barry Pederson, a very good goal scorer. It was interesting getting their take on the position that I think is closest to quarterback in the NFL.

Andrew is a very normal person and was a relatively normal goaltender. The problem is that there is just no such thing as a normal goaltender.

Like most who play the position, Andrew started at a very young age.

"It's something you just always did. Look, it didn't hurt when you were eight years old, but when you're 28, it hurts like hell... but you're already in the position," Andrew laughed.

"Martin Lapointe hurt me the most I've ever been hurt. I remember it like it was yesterday. Robbie Ftorek got fired that morning, and Mike O'Connell is coaching the team on the ice, and it's like World War III out there. It's just nuts. The puck comes out into the slot, and Marty is mad, and big and huge, and he takes a slapper. Now, Mike O'Connell is right in front of me, but he managed to get out of the way. The puck hits me in the collarbone, and I felt like everything was over for me. I felt like my bone just exploded. He was inside the hash marks, and it was not something a teammate would ever do on a normal day. But Marty was just mad, and I paid the price. I was a rookie, so I didn't think I could get off the ice, so I had to skate with everyone at the end, basically with one arm."

Raycroft has catalogued the superstitions that seem to go with his position. As I said, he's a pretty normal guy, but even he was not immune to developing his own quirks.

"I got really particular on the timing of getting dressed. With 33 minutes left before warmup, I would start. By 29 minutes left I would have my skates on. That sort of became my thing. I felt like the game actually started when you started getting dressed. The time made me focus, and no matter when happened leading up to that point, when I started getting dressed 33 minutes before going on the ice, I started focusing on what I had to do. As I got older, it kind of started to go away, but when I was younger, it was essential for me to perform well."

But, again, compared to many, Andrew was pretty normal. He remembered Kari Lehtonen beginning every morning with two Red Bulls. But, as Andrew also pointed out, Lehtonen was talented enough that coaches were willing to let him do whatever he felt was needed to prepare himself to play.

Jeff Hackett was a goaltender who had a cup of coffee with the Bruins, but he was also part of a goaltending duo in Toronto with Eddie Belfour.

"[Hackett] was pretty particular about everything," Andrew recalled. "He wouldn't talk to anyone, just kind of salty. He was known as being a hard teammate. Eddie Belfour just hated him! Those two guys together were just hard to get along with. By that time there weren't too many crazy guys left playing in goal, but those two guys were on the same team at the same time. That was difficult for everyone."

Pete Peeters was another goaltender for the Maine Mariners of the AHL, but he really made his mark playing for the Bruins in 1982–83 after being traded by the Philadelphia Flyers for defenseman Brad McCrimmon. Peeters had a record of 40–12–9 with a 2.37 goals-against-average and eight shutouts. At one time during the season he went 31 consecutive games without a loss and was awarded the Vezina Trophy, was a first-team All-Star goalie, and finished second to Wayne Gretzky in the balloting for the Hart Trophy as league Most Valuable Player.

Barry Pederson said that while Reggie Lemelin and Andy Moog comprised the best Bruins goaltending tandem he ever saw, Peeters had the best season he's ever seen. The Bruins had the best regular-season record in the league that year, and Pederson said Peeters stole a lot of wins for the team during that stretch.

"Our goalies that season were Pete and Marco Baron. Marco was just a character," Pederson recalled. "The contrast between him and Pete Peeters was unbelievable. If Pete even spoke, you would end up finishing his sentence for him, because he would take forever to put it all together. But, boy, he was a great goalie for us that year."

For many Bruins fans, the gold standard for goaltender play in the modern era belongs to Tim Thomas. Thomas played four seasons at the University of Vermont and was drafted No. 217 over-all by the Quebec Nordiques in the 1994 NHL draft. He kicked around the minor leagues and Europe before finally making it to the NHL with the Bruins in the 2002–03 season. He played four games in the NHL and went back to the Providence Bruins for several more seasons. He finally earned the starting spot for the Boston Bruins in 2005–06 at the age of 32. Beginning with the 2006–07 season, Thomas simply became one of the best goalies in the entire NHL.

Tim won the Vezina Trophy as the league's top netminder in 2009 and 2011 and was a member of the U.S. Olympic hockey team in 2010. It was his work as Bruins goalie in the 2010–11 season that solidified his spot in Boston sports folklore. His playoff run, like his team, began inauspiciously.

The Bruins dropped the first two games of the opening play-off series against the Montreal Canadiens, losing at home by 2–0 and 3–1 scores. The team was able to even the series with 4–2 and 5–4 (OT) decisions in Montreal. The Bruins took a 3–2 series lead with a 2–1, double-overtime decision in Boston in Game 5. After Montreal grabbed Game 6 2–1 it set up a winner-takes-all Game 7 back in Boston.

Raycroft remembers Game 7 vividly.

"Think about that first series against Montreal. Hal Gill almost scored in overtime of that seventh game; screened shot from the point, and he just barely misses the net in like the first two minutes of that Game 7 overtime. If that goes in, it's a year after they blew a three-nothing series lead to the Flyers. Claude probably gets fired, and the whole thing gets blown up. Heck, if they lose that Montreal series, Tim Thomas might be out of town too. The line between success and failure is just so razor-thin."

The Bruins avenged their seven-game series loss to the Flyers in the 2010 playoffs, sweeping the 2011 series in four games, although Thomas didn't have as much to do with the series win as overwhelming offense. The Bruins won their four games by 7–3, 3–2 (OT), 5–1, and 5–1 scores.

Even in the Eastern Conference finals series against the Tampa Bay Lightning, Thomas played solid if unspectacular goal. In splitting the first six games of the series, Thomas allowed five, five, zero, five, one, and five goals, but the Bruins faced a second decisive Game 7, and there Thomas was otherworldly.

The Bruins outshot the Lightning 38 –24 at the Garden, and Nathan Horton scored the only goal of the game at 12:27 of the third period, to send Boston on to the Stanley Cup Final against the heavily favored Vancouver Canucks. Barry remembers that particular game well.

"The best goalie game I've seen involving the Bruins was that 1–0, Game 7 playoff game against the Tampa Bay Lightning. That game by Tim Thomas was as good a game as I've ever seen."

In the seven-game Stanley Cup Final series, Thomas faced 246 shots, allowing just eight goals in seven games. Two of his three losses were by 1–0 scores, and the other was 3–2 in overtime. On the other hand, Thomas won games by scores of 8–1, 4–0, 5–2, and, in the deciding Game 7, another 4–0 shutout.

He became the oldest player to win the Conn Smythe Trophy as playoff MVP at the age of 37. He is also one of only four Americans to win the award, along with Brian Leetch, Jonathan Quick, and Patrick Kane.

But in the case of Tim Thomas, his fall from grace was as unlikely as his ascension to best goalie in the NHL. That fall began the following January when the Bruins were invited to visit the White House at the invitation of President Barack Obama. Despite the urging of team president Cam Neely and general manager Peter Chiarelli, Thomas was the only member of the Bruins to skip the traditional visit by the Stanley Cup champions.

While Thomas said he did not want to talk about his decision, he released a statement on his personal Facebook page, which read:

I believe the Federal government has grown out of control, threatening the Rights, Liberties and Property of the People.

This is being done at the Executive, Legislative, and Judicial level. This is in direct opposition to the Constitution and the Founding Fathers' vision for the Federal government. Because I believe this, today I exercised my right as a Free Citizen, and did not visit the White House. This was not about politics or party, as in my opinion both parties are responsible for the situation we are in as a country. This was about a choice I had to make as an INDIVIDUAL. This is the only public statement I will be making on this topic.

I always said that after his heroic performance in the "bloody sock" game against the Yankees that Curt Schilling would never have to buy a meal or a drink in Boston ever again. I was wrong. Curt's somewhat abrasive style and right-leaning political views turned a number of Red Sox fans against him, and there are those who don't even acknowledge how important he was in breaking the 86-year World Series drought.

In the aftermath of Thomas' White House decision, there were Bruins fans who seemed to turn against him as well. Many were grateful for his part in recapturing the Stanley Cup, but many felt he should have left his political viewpoints out of the Bruins' locker room. There were teammates who even admitted that Thomas could be a divisive influence off the ice.

The following season, Thomas beat out Tuukka Rask as the Bruins' starting goaltender and started 59 games. The Bruins were eliminated by the Washington Capitals in seven games in the first round of the Stanley Cup playoffs, and shortly after the season ended, Thomas announced on his Facebook page that he would sit out the 2012–13 season. The Bruins ended up suspending Thomas for not reporting to training camp, and in February 2013 he was traded to the New York Islanders for a conditional draft pick. He never played a game for the Islanders, and finished his career with the Florida Panthers and the Dallas Stars. Last I heard, he and his family were living on a secluded ranch in Colorado that was described by some as a bunker. He has not, as far as I know, returned to the Boston area since.

His starting spot in the Boston net was taken by Rask, who has manned that position since the 2012–13 season. Interestingly, his rights were acquired by the Bruins from the Toronto Maple Leafs in exchange for Raycroft, who thinks Rask might end up being the best of the bunch.

"At the end of it all, I think Tuukka is going to be right there. He's probably going to be No. 1 in all stats, in all everything. If he had found a way to beat Chicago, he's a no-brainer. If he had won that Cup in 2013, people would already think of him as the best Bruins goalie ever. Right now, when you look at it, he's probably close."

While Barry agreed that Rask would be viewed differently if the Bruins had captured that second Stanley Cup in three seasons, he doesn't think much of the blame belongs to Rask.

Tuukka Rask took over in net from the controversial Tim Thomas in 2012. *(AP Images)*

"I put part of that blame on Claude. He almost coached like he didn't want to win. When the Bruins gave up those leads, he just tried to pull the reins back in all the way. Bruce Cassidy coaches entirely differently. Now his teams are still responsible, but he wants them to go...go...go! Claude's teams just sat back and waited for Chicago to make a mistake, and they just wouldn't make it."

Rask has the stats and the records to back up Raycroft's confidence. In the 2009–10 season he was the only goalie with a goals-against average below 2.00 and a save percentage above .930. Despite that, he was inexplicably not named a finalist for the Rookie of the Year Award. He followed that up by being named the Vezina Trophy winner as the league's best goaltender after the 2013–14 season. He still holds the all-time record for highest save percentage in league history. As I discuss in Chapter 24, I'm not sure he gets the credit he deserves among Bruins fans, and it's likely as simple as missing that Stanley Cup title on his résumé.

We had just watched the Bruins and the Washington Capitals engage in a shootout decision, and it got me thinking about penalty shots, shootouts, and goaltenders. Andrew was playing when the shootout first began.

"I was playing in the first year of the shootout, the year after the lockout. The first couple of years, I just felt I would just go with it, and 'see-it-save-it.' Fortunately, I started really getting into the video. Once there was enough video on guys it made a huge difference. In many shootouts, I knew exactly what the guy was going to do as soon as he hit the blue line. I never remember being surprised by a move a guy would make after I started studying video. Now, I might still get beat sometimes, but it wasn't because I wasn't ready for what he was going to do."

Barry agreed with Andrew that pre-scouting gives the goaltender a decided advantage.

"I think I only had one or two penalty shots in my whole career at the most," Barry said. "They didn't call it very much back in those days. Unless your leg was broken, the other guy was just going to get a two-minute minor. When I watch the shootouts today, I think the most difficult part of it is the repetitiveness of it. You're doing it so often you feel like you've got to come up with something new almost every time out there. I'm not sure I could have been creative enough."

While our conversation that night centered on the goaltending position, and the quality of play from those stars, I had to take advantage of the chance to see the goaltender from the perspective of the guy trying to score the goal, and Barry agrees that sometimes it simply involves a head game.

"There were a couple of Buffalo guys who I felt I had things going pretty well against. Mario Gosselin in Quebec was one of those guys. On the other hand, there was a guy like Patrick Roy, and he always had a way of making you think too much, instead of reacting. Mario Lemieux would say, 'What are you guys doing? Just go down there on him, and whatever he does, you just do the opposite.' If only it was that easy for all of us. Great goalies just make you think too much. Heck, for years we just couldn't beat Montreal. They were in our heads. Just like the Washington Capitals and Braden Holtby have been in the Bruins' heads over the last few years."

A total of 106 men have played goaltender for the Bruins in their history from 1924 to the present. They include names like John Blue, Jim Carey, Jon Casey, Jim Craig, Byron Dafoe, Gilles Gilbert, John and Ron Grahame, Doug Keans, Blaine Lacher, Bernie Parent, Jim "Seaweed" Pettie, Jacques Plante, Felix Potvin, Pat Riggin, Terry Sawchuk, Tiny Thompson, Marty Turco, and Rogie Vachon.

They were all unique, and I've been priveleged to be around some of the best ones.

CHAPTER 20
TOUGH GUYS

If I'm being honest about it, there should be no less likely defender of fighting in hockey than me. First of all, I'm about 5'8" tall. (Okay, those are my Sports Information Director numbers. I'm really only 5'7".) Other than the occasional tussle with my three brothers, I've never actually been in a fist fight in my life. And I first learned the sport of hockey at the Division III college level, where fighting is not only disallowed, it's flat-out frowned upon. I never saw a hockey fight until I moved into the professional hockey ranks, but I made up for that very quickly.

As I mentioned earlier, after I graduated from Bowdoin College I began my career with the Maine Mariners of the American Hockey League. Back in those days, fighting was not only allowed, it was expected, and bench-clearing brawls were still a staple of the sport. It was practically unheard of to have a game without a fight, and it was not unusual to see two or three bench clearers per week.

I also worked for the top minor league affiliate of the Philadelphia Flyers, an organization that celebrated fighting and fighters. I worked with, and called the battles of, some of the best brawlers to ever play the game—names like Dave Brown, Glen Cochrane, John Paddock, Daryl Stanley, Allan Stewart, Archie Henderson, and Mel Hewitt. More important, I got to know these players as people and quickly learned what almost anyone in the sport will support: as a group, tough guys might be the nicest and most approachable players in the game. I grew to like and appreciate nearly every one of them. I even liked and appreciated some tough guys who played in other organizations.

I once saw Paul Stewart (later an NHL referee, but at that time a rough-and-tumble player for the Syracuse Firebirds) challenge the entire Mariners bench, much like Bruins pugilist John Wensink once did to the Minnesota North Stars. Unlike the North Stars, who probably intelligently declined Wensink's invitation, the Mariners accepted Stewart's challenge. Stewart ended up fighting three different Mariners, earning his game misconduct and ejection, plus a bloodied game sweater.

After Stewart was ejected, he went to the Firebirds' dressing room and gathered all of his personal belongings. As the game officials were coming off the ice at the end of the busy period and going to their own dressing room for a well-deserved rest, they were surprised to see a dripping wet Stewart coming out of their shower. He informed the officials (just one referee and two linesmen in those days) he would not shower and change in a room with teammates who would watch him take a beating like that and not come to his aid.

When the Firebirds climbed on their bus after the game for the seven-hour bus ride back to upstate New York, Stewart checked himself into the hotel across the street and paid for his own plane ticket home the next day. A number of years later, when Stewart had become a referee, he seemed thrilled when I gave him a photo of himself from that night. He was battered and he was bloodied, but he was unbowed. That's what the minor leagues were like in those days.

Another incident from my Mariners days involved Blake Wesley, whose brother Glen was a mainstay on the Bruins defense for a number of seasons. Blake was involved in a full-blown battle on the ice, and evidently felt that the officials erred when they gave him a misconduct and sent him to the dressing room while his opponent was allowed to head for the penalty box.

Blake went off the ice and headed down the walkway toward the Mariners dressing room, but he didn't stop there. He kept going down the hall to the doors that entered onto the ice behind the penalty boxes. Suddenly the doors behind the boxes slammed open and Wesley came charging back toward the ice. For some reason, he couldn't get the back door to the box open, so he began to climb the boards and glass, skates and all, to begin Round 2. The redheaded Wesley had a bit of a temper, and that's the way the game was played back then.

I once watched two notorious fighters—Archie Henderson of the Mariners and Jeff Brubaker of the Nova Scotia Voyageurs— stage an epic. They fought, toe to toe, in the middle of the ice, trading shot after shot before punching themselves to exhaustion and earning a rest in the penalty box. Fans could clearly see them exchanging words, but we had no way of knowing they were simply reaching an agreement.

When their five minutes had been served, they stepped from their respective penalty boxes without their sticks and gloves, and staged Round 2. It was another minor league classic with a second straight trip right back to the penalty box. If you think that ended it, you would be mistaken. The two again left their sticks and gloves in the box and fought for a third and final time. I truly think they didn't fight a fourth time only because they both received game misconducts.

Ask any player in any dressing room in the NHL and he will almost always point to the tough guy as one of the most popular people in the room. The players know how important the tough guys are, and appreciate their "hard way to make a good living."

Some of the most popular players to ever wear a Bruins uniform were also some of the toughest. Besides Joe Thornton and Cam

Neely, you could add names like Terry O'Reilly, Stan Jonathan, John Wensink, Lyndon Byers, Jay Miller, and P.J. Stock.

Stock only played 130 games in a Bruins uniform, primarily over two seasons, and topped out at 160 penalty minutes in 2002–2003. He had seasons of 386 and 432 penalty minutes with the Victoriaville Tigers of the Quebec Major Junior Hockey League. Stock was claimed off waivers by the Bruins and became beloved in Boston because of his willingness to fight when he sometimes shouldn't have. He was listed at 5'10" and 190 pounds, but those numbers might be exaggerated.

"The weight one was a little inflated—I'm probably 195 pounds now," Stock said, laughing. "I've got a story about the height part. When they first measured us for height and weight, they've got you there in your socks and your little underwear. I actually stuck a little Kleenex in the bottom of the heel of my socks to get something extra. Hey, it makes a difference, you know! If you're 5'9", you're short and even if you're 5'10", you're still a little short. But 5'10⅛" gets rounded up to 5'10½" and 5'10½" becomes 5'11". And, heck, that's almost 6'0"! At least in my head, that's how I figured it."

Stock never passed up on a fight invitation, and almost always topped it off with a wave to the TD Garden crowd as he made his way to the penalty box. But when I asked Stock where the wave came from, he had a hard time explaining.

"You know, I'm not really sure. You get so excited in the moment. Guys score, and they celebrate. I've done a few stupid things after fights, and it's all because of excitement. It's like scoring a goal. Maybe I got too excited. Heck, I don't know what I was doing! Then I started getting a reaction from the fans, and I'm thinking, 'Well, they like it, so now I've got to do it again.'

The hardest part is, I've got to survive the fight, so I can actually do the wave. It became so much pressure on me to make sure I didn't get destroyed so I could do the wave. It became fun for the fans and my teammates. But I never did it as disrespect for my opponent. It was never meant as putting up the middle finger or the No. 1 finger or putting on the belt. It was a thank you to the fans for the way they cheered me on and it was kind of, right back at them. At the end of the day, no matter what anyone says, sports are part of the entertainment business, and we do whatever we can to win, and make it exciting so fans want to keep coming back."

You can find Stock sweaters in the seats even today, even though his last game in Boston was in 2003.

The Bruins currently have 10 retired numbers. One of those is No. 24, retired in honor of Terry O'Reilly. O'Reilly played in 891 games in the National Hockey League, and had 204 goals and 402 assists for 606 points. He leads only one Boston Bruins career list—penalty minutes, with a total of 2,095. By his own admission, O'Reilly did not possess the skills to have his number retired, but he is also arguably one of the most popular personalities in the history of the organization. As Shawn Thornton said of O'Reilly, "He worked harder than anyone and never backed down from anyone. He led by example. He deserves to have his number retired. You don't always have to be the flashiest."

Thornton was talking about himself, but he spoke for every tough guy who ever played when he said, "We put more work into trying to become a player, and trying to become more than one-dimensional, than anyone else. You don't see skill guys working on their fighting for six hours a day, but you see every tough guy working on his skills for six hours a day."

In every sport, players talk about policing themselves. In hockey, fighting is a big part of that policing. Hockey tough guys, at least the legitimate ones, play by what is known as The Code, which I've learned about through my quarter century around the sport and some of the toughest guys to ever play it.

It's not written down anywhere, but it is passed down from hockey generation to generation. Tough guys will tell you that The Code is a very real thing.

Playing by The Code means a real tough guy will never take a run at one of the game's skill players. A tough guy almost always fights in defense of a teammate, and usually that means fighting the other team's tough guy, even if that tough guy was not necessarily the guilty party. You will often see tough guys in conversation before a fight. The conversation is often an invitation, an acceptance, and a quick setting of ground rules. When the battle is done, you will often see a pat on the backside or a nod of the head—an acknowledgement between combatants of a battle well and honorably fought.

There was an embarrassing incident involving a Bruins tough guy: Marty McSorley. McSorley played 961 games in the National Hockey League, although only 27 of those with the Bruins. He could play both forward and defense, and was known as an enforcer and protector of skill players like Wayne Gretzky. He had 108 goals and 251 assists for 359 points, but accumulated 3,381 penalty minutes. His single-season high was 399 while with the Los Angeles Kings in 1992-93. His reputation was flushed in a moment on February 21, 2000.

The Bruins were playing the Canucks in Vancouver, and with 4.6 seconds left to play in the game, McSorley swung his stick and hit Donald Brashear, another well-known tough guy, in the head. Brashear fell, hitting his head on the ice, knocked unconscious with what was described as a Grade III concussion. McSorley was suspended by the league for the rest of the regular season, plus playoffs, missing 23 games. He was charged with and found guilty of assault with a weapon in a British Columbia Provinicial Court. Judge William Kitchen sentenced McSorley to 18 months probation, and the NHL extended his suspension to a full year, through February 21, 2001. He never played another game in the National Hockey League.

As the years have gone on, and we've learned more about the effects of head trauma and CTE, I admit my thoughts about fighting have begun to evolve. Gord Kluzak and I have had some of our most animated disagreements about the place of fighting in the game; Gord would like to see it eliminated, and I've always been in favor of it. As they say, no one ever goes for a beer or popcorn during a fight. Especially in Boston. But I've thought about it, and I even asked P.J. Stock if he's ever been concerned about what the toll has been for the way he made a living.

After a long pause, Stock said, "No…no. It's funny; I just had this conversation recently. I have four kids and I'm 42 years old, and probably don't get as much sleep as I should. I'll forget something, and I'll go to my wife and say, 'Is it just me or is it because I've been punched in the head?' And she'll say, 'No, honey. You're 42 and you forget things.' But you just don't know. I just lost a brother to ALS. Sometimes you just question yourself—am I supposed to hurt when I wake up in the morning? Am I supposed to forget things every now and then? My mom is in her seventies and she never got punched in the head, and sometimes she forgets things too. Am I scared of any of the ramifications on what I did? I just can't live my life that way. I knew what I was doing at the time. I was pretty confident while I was doing it. I was never really, really hurt while I was doing it, which I'm really lucky about."

So the obvious follow-up question was simple. I asked Stock, but I could have asked any of the "tough guys" and I have a feeling their answers would be similar—*If you had to do it all over again, would you?*

"Oh man, there is nothing like the rush standing in the Fleet Center [now TD Garden] on a first-place team, with an unbelievable crowd behind you. For me, it wasn't necessarily about making a great play, or making a great pass, it was about you and another guy going mano a mano, trying to get your team and 17,000 people to go crazy. Would I do it again? You're damn right I would do it again! I just might not let the other guy hit me as much.

"I might have dodged a little bit more or been a little more defensive! I was very lucky. Maybe even the eye injury and getting out when I did was even lucky. There is definitely wear and tear to do that job. There is risk and reward that goes with it. But I would do it again in a heartbeat!"

Talk to any tough guy and eventually you get around to the same question. Sometimes they answer, and sometimes they dodge, but they know it's coming. So I asked Stock flat out—*What was the best fight you ever had?*

"I had a really good fight with Stephen Peat one time. It was a Saturday afternoon matinee game at the Garden, and we had a really good go. That led to probably one of the best nights I ever had in the Boston bars after the game. We were at this place, and they kept showing the highlights of the fight over and over, and it was awesome! My experiences in Boston were something you can't explain to other people. You wish every kid could experience what I experienced from Bruins fans. It was an amazing feeling."

CHAPTER 21
SHAWN THORNTON

Shawn Thornton always knew where he would've been had he not made it as a professional hockey player. His grandmother, father, and mother had all made their livings in the factories of blue-collar Oshawa, Ontario, and Shawn even spent one summer working in a steel mill. "I said I'd never go back," he once said shortly after arriving in Boston.

Shawn never did and instead enjoyed a 20-year professional career, including 14 seasons in the NHL. He won the Stanley Cup twice—with Anaheim in 2007 and the Bruins in 2011. He accumulated 1,103 penalty minutes, mostly with his fists. He was the type of player who stood up for his teammates, whom he considered family, and held opponents to account. Sometimes there was pain, sometimes there was even fear (or at least nerves, because I'm not sure Thornton ever admits to fear), but let's face it: it beat working in the steel mill.

Fresh off winning the Cup with the Ducks in 2007, Thornton became an unrestricted free agent. It sort of floated under the radar at the time, but Bruins general manager Peter Chiarelli signed Thornton as part of the rebuilding of the Bruins' character and toughness after a two-season playoff drought. I didn't think much of the signing at the time. I knew he was a tough, hard-nosed guy but figured he'd compete for a fourth-line role and do some of the dirty work. As soon as he got to training camp, though, Shawn proved he was more than just some pug enforcer; he could play. As Bruins legend Terry O'Reilly explained it, Shawn "could skate and had great hands."

The Bruins hadn't had a fan-favorite tough guy maybe since P.J. Stock left. Well, here came Shawn Thornton to fill the void and then some, as a love affair between Shawn and Boston began.

"When I signed in Boston in 2007, Cam Neely called me and said, 'I've played in this town, I've seen players like you that come here, and I don't think you'll be loved any more, any place in the world than Boston,'" Shawn recalled. "And that might have been the understatement of the entire conversation.

"Boston has always had a soft spot for tough guys. People still talk about P.J. Stock, and he played, like, 70 games there. Stan Jonathan, Taz [Terry O'Reilly], L.B. [Lyndon Byers], and so many others were all incredibly popular in Boston. They were all embraced by that city, and I was definitely embraced as well. Boston is a fairly blue-collar, hardworking kind of city at heart, and I think they appreciate that kind of effort on the ice."

It soon became clear to anyone that Shawn not only was a hard worker and tough guy but could also play on the ice. Sure, he was willing to fight or throw a big hit to change the momentum of a game. But off the ice he was the type of player that could keep a dressing room in line. His Cup-winning pedigree spoke for itself, and he became a driving force behind the Bruins' resilience in the years ahead. He was a gigantic piece of the Bruins winning the Cup in 2011. It was no coincidence that in the 2011 Stanley Cup Final against Vancouver, the Bruins' comeback from 2–0 down in the series began in Game 3, when Thornton was re-inserted into the lineup after he was scratched for the first two games. Obviously there were a lot of contributors to that historic turnaround, but Thornton played his part and his presence and efforts made a huge difference.

On March 7, 2010, skilled Bruins center Marc Savard suffered a horrific open-ice elbow to the head from Matt Cooke of the Pittsburgh Penguins in the third period of their game in Pittsburgh. Although Savard attempted to come back in the playoffs that season, he was never the same player, and ultimately was forced into an injury retirement.

Thornton was more than willing to respond to Cooke's vicious hit, but he never got back on the ice that night. He got his chance a few weeks later when the Penguins visited TD Garden.

Thornton and Glen Murray went to Billy Guerin of the Penguins before the game to discuss the rules of engagement. Rather than Eric Goddard going after Patrice Bergeron or Zdeno Chara going after Sidney Crosby as retribution, both teams decided that Thornton and Cooke would fight in the first shift, and that was that.

For most of his career, Thornton was known as an "honest" player. When he fought, he did it the right way. He'd face an opponent head-on. He'd let up if a guy became off balance or entangled in his equipment. It meant a lot to Shawn that, for most of his 14 years, he didn't have any run-ins with the league office.

Often around hockey we hear about The Code that players who make their living the way Shawn does all claim to live by. He said he learned the code from guys like Greg Smith, Al MacAdam, Trent Yawney, and Brian Sutter. For the most part (with one exception), Shawn lived by The Code, which isn't the easiest thing when you're playing a violent sport and playing the role Shawn filled.

"I think The Code is very real thing, and was something that I was taught at an early stage by teammates and coaches who knew what it was as well," Shawn said. "I don't think I ever took a run at someone considered a skill player, and I almost always fought in defense of a teammate. I've always believed that if you threw that extra punch when the linesmen were coming in, if you hit a guy when he's down, you bury somebody when their back is turned, that [stuff] will happen to *you* eventually."

Shawn was the first player of his ilk that I can remember actually training for what he did beyond hockey. He actually did boxing training. There's no doubt some of it came in handy, even if it was just the stamina aspect of it. And he needed all the training he could get, considering he was somewhat under-sized at 6'2", 217 pounds. When he fought someone like John Scott, who was 6'8", 260, you had to worry at least a little bit. If Scott lands one good one, Shawn could get hurt. But Shawn was able to hold his own, beat up some bigger guys, and use his skills to avoid injury.

I mentioned above the one time The Code got away from Shawn. It was an unfortunate incident that cost him 15 games because of a suspension and tarnished his reputation.

"I will probably take the Brooks Orpik hit to my f—g grave," Shawn admitted to me.

The December 7, 2013, Bruins-Penguins game was chippy from the start. These two teams had bad blood going back to Cooke's cheap shot on Savard in 2010 and then the dial was turned up on the rivalry during the Bruins' four-game sweep in the Eastern Conference finals in 2013.

Early in the game, Orpik leveled skilled Bruins forward Loui Eriksson with a predatory hit at the Pittsburgh blue line that went unpunished. Later in the first period, when Penguins forward James Neal "accidentally" kneed Bruins forward Brad Marchand in the head while he was down, all heck broke loose. Orpik was down at the other end of the ice with a teammate engaged in trash talk with two Bruins when Thornton intervened.

Shawn pulled Orpik down from behind and unleashed a series of punches that left Orpik prone on the ice after Thornton was removed from the fracas. Orpik went off on a stretcher and Shawn's initial punishment was a match penalty.

Watching it live, my first thought was, "Oh no." Because it was clear that what had happened wasn't what Shawn intended. After all, he'd toed the line his entire career for more than a decade. But he crossed the line there and you knew he was going to have to pay the price.

"My intention was never to hurt him. What's ironic is I really liked Brooks; we hung out together," said Shawn, who was also an offseason workout partner of Orpik's. "I tried to make sure he didn't hit his head when he fell to the ice, but the entire situation was one of my biggest regrets, and something I wish I could take back. It's my own fault. I take complete responsibility for it."

I felt bad for Shawn because I knew him well enough to know how much it was bothering him that he had lost control. He was obviously a bit embarrassed, as any of us would've been, both for himself and the team. I was surprised he got 15 games and that the commissioner upheld the length of the penalty on appeal. This wasn't Cooke or some other player with a reputation and a rap sheet. This was Shawn Thornton, and he had simply made a mistake. He paid the price in games missed and money docked from his paycheck. Although his reputation may have dipped a rung around the league, in Boston the Orpik incident was just a footnote and he was just as beloved from then until he left the Bruins after that season.

There was so much more to Shawn's endearment to Boston than what he did on the ice and in the dressing room. He immersed himself in the city like few players from out of town ever before. He bought a place in Charlestown and became a "Townie." You'd see him at the Warren Tavern or milling about town. If Shawn missed his blue-collar hometown of Oshawa, he definitely found a second home in Charlestown. Everyone crossed paths with him and felt like they knew him after one encounter.

He dove right into the charity appearances and hospital visits. Sometimes he'd go unannounced to visit sick kids. My friend Lisa Scherber, the director of patient and family programs at the Jimmy Fund, has a list of what she calls "her guys." I like to think I'm on that list, and I love visiting the kids at the Jimmy Fund Clinic, but Shawn probably could have had an office there as many times as he visited. The kids loved him, the staff admired him, and Shawn still makes visits when he comes back to Boston.

After the 2013 Boston Marathon bombings, he made sure he did his part to console the victims without looking for any credit. "I had told [Bruins director of community relations] Kerry Collins that I didn't want people to know I was going to the hospitals. It was just the right thing to do, to visit people and try to cheer them up," Shawn said. "They had been through something terrible, and I couldn't look myself in the mirror if I didn't do whatever I could to help. I was on like my 14th visit of the day, and Gerry Callahan of WEEI was visiting [bombing survivor] Jeff Bauman when I walked in. I had never met Gerry before then, and if he hadn't been there, no one would have found out I had visited. I was adamant that no one knew. I just wanted to visit those people, and I learned that so many other athletes and actors did the exact same thing, and they did it anonymously too. I just wish we could have done more."

Over the course of his time in Boston, Shawn started his own foundation in part to raise money for Alzheimer's research. Every

At the Jimmy Fund Radio-Telethon with my radio partner, Michael Holley, and Shawn Thornton.

year he visited us during our WEEI/NESN Jimmy Fund Radio-Telethon to drop off the foundation's donation. It is always very, very generous.

I personally felt Shawn's kindness one year when I wanted a signed jersey for my nephew who was home on leave from the Air Force and was visiting me at the game. He was a big Shawn Thornton fan. I got the jersey to him through a coworker just before game time. He didn't just sign it; he wrote a really nice message to my nephew thanking him for his service. That's just the type of person Shawn was here and continues to be.

He's retired from playing now and he went to work for his last NHL employer, the Florida Panthers, in their marketing department. He returns to the Boston area every summer, though, and his foundation's golf tournament is a sellout every August.

Shawn loved it here because this place loved him back. I have a feeling he'll always be considered part of this town.

CHAPTER 22
PATRIOTS' DAY

Patriots' Day is a uniquely New England event. It is officially a state holiday celebrating and commemorating the Revolutionary War battles of Concord and Lexington. But unofficially, Patriots' Day is a "get out of jail free" card for workers and schoolchildren in the state of Massachusetts. Patriots' Day is a rite of spring, especially in the city of Boston, and always falls on the third Monday of April.

One of the highlights of Patriots' Day is the Boston Marathon, and hundreds of thousands of people cover the route from Hopkinton to Boston, cheering on friends and relatives who are running and offering support to total strangers from around the world. As a sports reporter in Boston, I've had the pleasure of covering the race from the start line in Hopkinton, from the bridge over the finish line, and the from the pool truck in front of the race leaders. I've seen the Marathon from every aspect, with the exception of participant. I've seen for myself that the crowd gets especially congested as you near the finish line on Boylston Street, next to the Boston Public Library.

That gigantic gathering gets a booster shot from the Boston Red Sox, who always play an 11:05 AM game and spill another 35,000 people into the streets of Boston as the game ends and the runners continue their march to the finish line. Regardless of where they're from, Bruins players either know about Marathon Monday, or they quickly learn about it once they move to the Hub.

"I had heard about Marathon Monday before," Shawn Thornton told me. "I played in the minors with Jeff Farkas, who had played at Boston College, and all he ever talked about was Marathon Monday being the best day ever. It was on my radar before I ever even played in Boston.

"We always seemed to be playing, usually on the road, so I never got a chance to partake, but obviously you're aware of how big a day it is. The Sox are playing, the Marathon, the history—even though you're not from Boston, you know it's a big day from the minute you arrive."

On April 15, 2013, the Bruins added a third big sporting event to the calendar with a game scheduled at TD Garden against the Ottawa Senators. However, the game wouldn't be played until two weeks later.

Dzhokhar and Tamerlan Tsarnaev were Chechen-American brothers who grew up in Cambridge but had become radicalized. They planned to strike a blow at the heart of America. Their target was the finish line of the Boston Marathon.

The Tsarnaev brothers manufactured homemade pressure cooker bombs in the kitchen of their Cambridge apartment based on plans they found online. They hatched a plan to plant and detonate their bombs near the finish line of the Marathon, hoping to kill or maim as many people as they possibly could. Ultimately, security camera footage pieced together by a dogged Boston Police Department and the FBI showed the brothers calmly and coldly setting their backpack bombs at the feet of innocent men, women, and children, and simply walking away. The two bombs detonated at 2:49 PM, some 200 yards apart, killing three people and wounding hundreds, including 16 people who lost limbs as a result of the attack.

Bruins players usually begin arriving at the Garden around 4:30 PM for home games, and many lived close enough that they could actually walk to work. They arrived that day with varying levels of awareness of what had unfolded mere miles from the Garden.

"I always get up from my pre-game nap at 3, 3:15 PM, and I always turn on the Golf Network or music videos before a game, so I didn't really understand what was going on at first," Shawn recalled. "I don't have social media, and I received a few text messages, but I didn't truly understand. I was kind of sheltered from it, to be completely honest."

When I first heard about the bombings, I was driving to the Garden on the Southeast Expressway. Like everybody else, I was stunned. When I arrived, we didn't know if there was going to be a game and, as always, our NESN crew was busy constructing our TD Garden set, but we were also glued to the televisions in our Garden studio suite as well. It was definitely difficult to prepare for a hockey game—whether you were a player or a broadcaster—and the bomb-sniffing dogs that came walking through with the bomb squad that afternoon didn't make the circumstances more comfortable.

A manhunt for the perpetrators ensued. The city was on edge, and there were numerous false reports about other possible attacks throughout the area. A fire had broken out at the JFK Library in Dorchester, but that turned out to be unrelated to the bombing. It quickly became clear that it was going to be next to impossible to play a hockey game that night. The fact was no one knew which areas were safe and which were not. Bruins players were in the building and the Ottawa Senators had been bused from their Copley Square hotel just blocks from the attack zone at the Marathon finish line.

Ultimately, common sense prevailed. There was simply no way to pull police resources from the rest of the city and ask them to protect Bruins fans at the Garden. The roads and streets of Boston were a ghost town, and asking people to leave their homes to attend a suddenly meaningless hockey game was out of the question. Players from both teams were relieved when the NHL postponed the game and told the players to head back to their homes or hotels.

"I got to the Garden around 4:00, and there were just a few of us there at that point. [General manager] Peter Chiarelli came down to the room and said, 'The game is cancelled. Go home and be with your families,'" Shawn said. "There was so much stuff going on out there, and you didn't really know what was real and what was rumor. It really wasn't until Peter told us that it really started to sink in. We just didn't know yet how catastrophic it truly was. Knowing the situation, you know there isn't going to be a f—g game—it was a no-brainer."

Shawn recalled that teammate Andrew Ference, a defenseman who might've been second to Shawn in the amount he made himself part of the Boston community despite being from Canada, had some family that was at the finish line. They had known some runners. That made it hit home for the Bruins. Almost everyone in Boston knew of someone related to the attack in some way, shape, or form.

I went home via those deserted streets and watched television the rest of the night as all of Boston, all of New England, all of the United States waited to hear what the authorities had to say. I remember seeing the video of two New England Patriots players, Joe Andruzzi and Matt Chatham, who I had gotten to know in my role on WEEI and its Patriots Monday programming, carrying victims out of a restaurant. It was a day for fear in Boston, but it was also a day of unity and courage.

The Bruins' next game was scheduled for two nights later, and the Buffalo Sabres were in town. Although the city was still on edge and the perpetrators were still on the lam, the game was played as scheduled. It would be one of the most emotional ones most could remember. The night ended with a shootout loss that didn't seem to mean much to Bruins fans, but it started in a way no Bruins fan would ever forget.

There were three fatalities on Monday at the Marathon finish line (and a fourth would follow two days later, when MIT Police Officer Sean Collier was gunned down in the front seat of his squad car by the Tsarnaev brothers). All were heartbreaking and devastating to their families and all were taken to heart by the entire city.

Twenty-nine-year-old Krystle Campbell was from Medford and had gone to the finish line with her best friend to take photos. Twenty-three-year-old Lingzi Lu was from China and a graduate student at Boston University. She simply wanted to experience the local color and pageantry of the marathon.

Excruciatingly, eight-year-old Martin Richard was also killed. He was at the finish line with his family, enjoying the sunshine and cheering the finishers. Dzhokhar Tsarnaev had placed his backpack directly behind the Richard family. The blast injured both parents, Bill and Denise Richard, and Martin's younger sister, Jane, lost her left leg. Martin suffered devastating injuries that ended his life at the age of eight. As a father of three, Martin's death really struck me. All the deaths were heart-wrenching, of course, but there was something about the death of an eight-year-old kid that really knocked me for a loop. I wasn't alone.

The Bruins and the hockey community took Martin's death to heart. To this day, a Google image search for Martin Richard shows the young boy at a Bruins game at the Garden. Martin is wearing his Bruins cap and team sweater and smiling broadly during warmups for Military Appreciation Night, held earlier that season. Martin loved his Bruins, and on this night, two days after his death, the Bruins and entire city of Boston loved him and his family right back.

"All of the victims were heartbreaking, and I don't want to take anything away from the families of the other victims as well, but Martin Richard was a hockey fan," Shawn said. "I got to know his family a little bit, after that, and they're such good, good people, and way stronger than I would ever be. But that image of Martin wearing his Bruins sweater was very real, very shocking, and hit so close to home. That image just stuck, and it hit so close to home. It hit us all hard."

The Bruins game that night was the first mass gathering of people in the city since the attack 48 hours earlier. Fans arriving at the game were greeted by a massive police and security presence and helicopters circled overhead. The crowd was somber but resolved, determined to return to life as they knew it, even if just for a night.

The One Fund Boston had already been established to assist the victims of the attack, many on a long road to recovery. Bruins owner Jeremy Jacobs pledged $100,000, and TD Garden, the NHL, and the NHL Players' Association added $50,000 each.

Bruins players came onto the Garden ice for warmups, not wearing their usual hockey helmets but sporting baseball caps representing the Boston Police Department, Boston Fire Department, Massachusetts State Police, and Boston EMTs. Shawn remembered players divvying up those hats with pride and playfully arguing over who got to wear which one. Those caps stayed in every player's locker the rest of the season and are still worn during some post-workout or postgame media availabilities.

When the teams lined up for the national anthem, the arena was darkened and a large blue and yellow "Boston Strong" ribbon was projected onto the ice. The Boston Fire Department Honor Guard, representing the city's first responders, marched onto the ice along with the team's longtime anthem singer, Rene Rancourt.

After a moment of silence was observed in honor of the victims Rancourt raised the microphone to sing. He began an a cappella version of the anthem and got as far as "what so proudly we hailed" before he was drowned out. The sellout crowd of 17,565 wanted to send a message to the bombers (still unknown) and to the world: the city of Boston would not back down, and would not be silenced. They raised their voices as one and sang as loud and proudly as they possibly could. Players on the ice were shown with tears streaming down their faces, and fans watching either at the Garden, or as part of a national television audience, were overcome as well.

With the game on NBC, I was not working that night. Like the rest of the country, I was watching from my couch, and I cried like a baby. I wished I could've been there, but it was still a cool spectacle to see as Bruins fans showed their patriotism and their resilience.

Standing on artificial legs, Boston Marathon bombing victim Jeff Bauman and Carlos Arredondo, wearing the hat, waves the Boston Strong banner before Game 6 of the Stanley Cup Final in 2013. *(AP Images)*

Bruins fans were the first, but soon all of Boston showed the world what President Barack Obama observed the next day when he told a somber gathering at an interfaith service at the Cathedral of the Holy Cross, "Whoever committed this heinous act... picked the wrong city." As a lifelong New Englander and long-time Massachusetts resident, I felt anger, I felt anxiety, and I felt depression. In the same way a hockey player would put it, we were hurt but we weren't injured. It didn't matter what political party we belonged to, we needed to hear what our president had to say, and we needed to get those emotions out.

"It was very emotional, but different than any kind of emotion I've ever been a part of playing hockey," Bruins center Patrice Bergeron told me. "This was beyond hockey; it was beyond anything sports related. It was about being unified, and about the people of Boston, and the city itself. It was about rallying and finding a way to show support for the victims and their families. It was the most emotional I've ever been on the ice. You almost didn't want to even play the game, because of the loss suffered by so many. But at the same time, you realized what playing a game meant to the city. I hope none of us ever have to go through anything like that ever again, but it's also something none of us will ever forget. We were living downtown, and for days after there was so much unknown—who were the bombers, where were they? There was military and police everywhere."

The next night the gutless suspects took a fourth victim, MIT police officer Sean Collier, as they attempted to steal his gun while he was sitting in his police car. Later that same evening, in a scene that played out just blocks from our NESN studios in Watertown, the beginning of the end took place.

Many of my NESN colleagues were working that night when Watertown police entered the building. The police felt certain that the perpetrator was in the area, but they weren't sure of the exact location. They asked my colleagues in the building to lock themselves in an inside room and stay there until given the all clear. They were asked to stay off their phones and off social media. It was a long, long night—not just for them, but for the entire city of Boston.

The drama played out on a quiet residential Watertown street, and during a police shootout that included hand-to-hand combat and more pipe and pressure cooker bombs being tossed, Tamerlan Tsarnaev was killed. His younger brother, Dzohkar, averted capture. The manhunt went on all day Friday without anyone knowing if there would be a second phase of the plan or if there were other accomplices. A shelter-in-place order was issued for most of the Greater Boston area by Governor Deval Patrick. The Bruins game that night against Pittsburgh was postponed until the next day.

I watched the events unfold from my home in the suburbs. Several Bruins, including Shawn, were closer to the action and managed to find ways to cope with the uncertainty.

"My wife and I were just sitting in our living room in Charlestown, and there were a million different rumors and a million different stories," Shawn recalled. "We heard they had been spotted down by the Schrafft Center, we heard they were in Watertown and that they were in Brookline. Everyone was just sitting on the edge of their seats.

"Finally, we just decided we're not going to let this asshole ruin another day. We ended up going down to the Warren Tavern, and it was like a blizzard had happened, and everyone wanted to just be together and have a beer and show that neighborhood camaraderie."

Dzhokhar Tsarnaev was captured that night in a standoff with police as he hid in a boat in a backyard in Watertown. He was taken into custody, survived the wounds he suffered in the shootout, and eventually received the death penalty after trial. I cheered the guilty verdict and even the sentence, as so many others did in the commonwealth.

The Bruins lost to the Penguins in the rescheduled game, but the city needed a lift after all it had been through. The Bruins provided just that. They finished 28–14–6, second place in the Northeast Division and fourth in the Eastern Conference, at the conclusion of the lockout-shortened regular season.

Famously, they came back from three goals down in the final half of the third period of Game 7 in the first round against Toronto to force overtime. After winning in overtime on Patrice Bergeron's goal, the Bruins defeated the New York Rangers in five games and swept Pittsburgh to reach the Stanley Cup Final for the second time in three seasons.

In the Final, however, the Bruins ran into an ultra-talented Blackhawks team. The Bruins led the series 2–1 but lost in overtime in Game 4 and dropped Game 5. They were less than two minutes from forcing Game 7 when the Blackhawks tied Game 6 with 1:16 remaining and then scored the game winner 17 seconds later. It was a heartbreaking defeat, but the unexpected run that lasted until late June gave Boston a much-needed distraction and a lot of fun.

That spring the Red Sox were coming off one of their worst seasons, a 69–93 2012 campaign. Despite a change in manager and the addition of some new players, not much was expected of that squad. But it was almost as though the emotion of the aftermath of the bombings and the Bruins' run sparked the Red Sox. They rolled all the way to their third World Series title in 10 seasons in October 2013.

Part of Shawn Thornton's embrace of Boston was his affection for the Red Sox and he was a frequent visitor to Fenway Park, including several times that magical season.

"What the Red Sox were able to do, rallying the city and winning the World Series, was amazing," Shawn told me. "The speech that David [Ortiz] gave [on Opening Day] was unbelievable. He's like the only guy who can drop the F-bomb in front of a full stadium and on national television, and have the FCC say, 'You know, we're okay with that.'

"We really wanted to do that for the city too, but we just couldn't get it done the way they did."

The Stanley Cup didn't come back to Boston, but the Bruins' help in healing the city both with their play and their dedication to the community was every bit as inspirational as if they had raised the Cup.

CHAPTER 23
GREATEST GAMES

I've been so blessed to see so many incredible Bruins games over the years—regular-season games, playoff games, games with a lot on the line, and games with nothing on the line. But I couldn't write a book like this without reflecting on a few of the best Bruins games I've ever seen. Two of these three I attended only as a fan, and one I was working, but I'll never forget any of them.

March 21, 1991: Quebec Nordiques at Boston Bruins

I was not yet working for the Bruins, and I was sitting in the press box at the old Boston Garden ostensibly as a member of the media, but truthfully just because I was a hockey fan and wanted to see a game.

The Nordiques came to town in last place, with no hope for the remainder of the season. An indicator of the team's futility was that they used five starting goaltenders over the course of the season—Jacques Cloutier, John Tanner, Stephane Fiset, Scott Gordon, and Ron Tugnutt.

Tugnutt got the start for that March game at the Garden, but no one was expecting what they saw that night. The Nordiques were dead last in the NHL in goals against, and the Bruins were an offensive juggernaut, with no fewer than five players who finished the season with 50 or more points.

As expected, the Bruins launched an assault on the Nordiques net in the first period, firing 17 shots on Tugnutt. They then had 44 more shots on the Quebec goal over the next two periods. The Bruins trailed 1–0, 2–1, and 3–2 before Ray Bourque tied the game halfway through the third period.

The Bourque goal set up sudden-death overtime, and the Bruins had 12 more shots. Think of that—a five minute overtime period and 12 shots on goal. Bourque nearly ended the game in the closing seconds of the extra session.

With eight seconds left in overtime, Ken Hodge, Jr., sent a pass to Bourque in the slot. Raymond unleashed a blast from about 15 feet away that seemed ticketed for the back of the net. But Tugnutt flashed out his glove and snared the shot for his 70th save of the game. That's right; the Bruins had 73 shots on goal, and Bourque himself had 19 shots on goal, including that final opportunity. As the final horn sounded, even Raymond had to skate over to tap Tugnutt on the pads.

I sat in the Garden in awe, as did the sellout crowd of 14,895. In the overall scheme of things, the game didn't mean anything, but it gave an individual an opportunity to shine, and Ron Tugnutt had the single best goaltending performance I ever had the privilege to witness.

May 27, 2011: Tampa Bay Lightning at Boston Bruins

I was once again simply a hockey fan at this game. It was the season before I returned to the Bruins telecasts on NESN, and I just wanted to watch a deciding Game 7 between the Bruins and the Tampa Bay Lightning. On the line was a trip to the Stanley Cup Final. It was the best hockey game I've ever watched.

The Bruins dominated play in the first period, outshooting the Lightning 15–9. But goaltender Dwayne Roloson was incredible, preserving a 0–0 tie. The best scoring chance for either team was a Milan Lucic breakaway, but Roloson turned it aside. Zdeno Chara led both teams with nearly nine minutes of ice time in the first period alone.

The benchmark moment of the second period wasn't a goal or a save or a penalty. It was Steven Stamkos showing just how tough a hockey player can be.

A Johnny Boychuk shot caught Stamkos in the face, hitting much of the plastic shield, but also exploding his nose. He missed exactly one shift, returning with a full cage and a nose that could cause people nightmares. Television showed a close-up of the shattered nose, but Stamkos of course finished the game, earning the respect of the TD Garden crowd that continues to this day.

The Bruins outshot Tampa Bay 14–8 in the second period, and led 29–17 in shots through two periods, but the game was still in search of its first goal. Roloson was again immense, stopping Mark Recchi, point blank, with the best scoring chance of the period.

Finally, at 12:27 of the third period, the scoring dam was broken. David Krejci and Nathan Horton finally beat the tenacious Tampa Bay defense and broke in on Roloson, 2-on-1. Krejci slid the puck to Horton who tapped it into a vacant net for the game's only goal.

The Game 7 featured incredible scoring opportunities, unbelievable goaltending, unmatched intensity—and zero penalties. Referees Stephen Walkom and Dan O'Halloran were the heroes of the game. They did not call a single minor penalty, and allowed two tough, hard-nosed teams to fight to the very end for a chance at a Stanley Cup Final.

I've seen hundreds if not thousands of hockey games in my life. This game between the Bruins and the Lightning will probably always be the best I've ever seen.

May 13, 2013—-Toronto Maple Leafs at Boston Bruins

This game, forevermore, will simply be known as The Comeback. And I would be lying if I told you I saw this one coming.

The Bruins and Maple Leafs were playing Game 7 of their Eastern Conference playoff series, and the Leafs were making life difficult for the Bruins on their home ice, at the TD Garden. The Bruins were exhausted and injury-depleted and the Leafs had a 4–1 lead halfway through the third period. Then came The Comeback.

Milan Lucic set up Nathan Horton at 9:18 of the third period, and the Bruins had a pulse (although weak and thready), trailing 4–2. Coach Claude Julien pulled goaltender Tuukka Rask with a little more than two minutes left. Patrice Bergeron fed Zdeno Chara, who shot from the point, and Lucic buried the rebound with 1:22 left to play, making the score 4–3.

Patrice was 16-for-22 in the faceoff circle for the game, and of course, he won the ensuing draw, sending Rask back to the bench for the extra attacker. The Bruins swarmed back into the Leafs defensive zone, and this time Chara set that 6'9" screen in front of goaltender James Reimer. The puck went to Bergeron in the high slot, and his goal with 51 seconds left tied the game at 4–4.

Barry Pederson and I were watching from our TD Garden set just above the AT&T Sportsdeck. We had begun working on our Game 7, (series-losing), postgame show when The Comeback began. When Bergeron scored the game-tying goal, Barry hugged me, saying, "I've never seen anything like this!" To which I replied, "Barry, *no* one has ever seen anything like this!"

It just felt like overtime was destiny for the Bruins at that point, and when Bergeron beat Reimer at 6:05 of OT, the Bruins crowd was in an absolute frenzy.

There will always be moments I will never forget from that Game 7. Many of the team's fans began leaving the Garden when the score went to 4–1 in the third period. I'm not even saying I blame them, because I felt the cause was lost as well. As the Bruins began sneaking back into the game, fans started sneaking back into the building. As long as they hadn't made it out of the Garden, and only onto the concourse or stairways levels, they could get back in. But those who had made their way out of the building proper were left begging with security guards, who weren't letting people back in.

I will also always remember a shot we showed on NESN of the plaza outside of the Air Canada Centre. When the Leafs led 4–1 in the third period, that plaza was absolutely crazy with Toronto fans beside themselves as they got ready to move on to the next round of the Stanley Cup playoffs. As Bergeron scored the game-tying goal in the third period that plaza got very, very quiet. When Patrice scored to end Game 7 in sudden-death overtime, that plaza was as depressing as Boston was after Aaron Boone's home run left Yankee Stadium in 2003.

It's incredibly difficult to narrow hundreds of Bruins games down to the three best, but these are the games I will always remember from my years with the team.

CHAPTER 24
CURRENT PLAYERS

IF THESE WALLS COULD TALK: BOSTON BRUINS

What follows are some of my thoughts and anecdotes about some of the Bruins' most recent starring players.

Tuukka Rask

Jack Edwards coined the phrase, "Two U's, two K's, two points! And the Bruins win!"—something Jack will bellow out after the horn sounds on a Bruins win that was enabled in large part to the efforts of their goaltender. Given Rask's résumé between the pipes for Boston, that happens more often than not.

Tuukka was drafted by the Toronto Maple Leafs in the first round, No. 21 overall, in the 2005 NHL draft. He never wore the Leafs uniform, and was traded one year later for goaltender Andrew Raycroft. He left his native Finland and signed with the Bruins in May 2007.

He began the 2007–08 season with Providence of the American Hockey League, earning his first recall to Boston in November. The following season he was in a training camp battle for an NHL spot, but the two Boston jobs were given to Tim Thomas and Manny Fernandez, and Rask again began the season in Providence. He was recalled to replace an injured Fernandez after the All-Star break, and never looked back.

During the 2009–10 season, Rask actually beat out Thomas as the starting goaltender, and promptly became the first rookie in league history to post a goals-against average of less than two (1.97), to go along with a sizzling .931 save percentage and a record of 22–12–5. He also played in 13 playoffs games, but unfortunately was in net when the Philadelphia Flyers came back from a 3–0 series deficit, winning four straight to knock the Bruins out of the playoffs.

Rask backed up an injury-recovered Thomas during the 2010–11 season that ended with the team's sixth Stanley Cup championship. Thomas played every minute of the playoff run, but Rask became just the second Finnish netminder to have his name on the Cup, following Antti Niemi.

Eventually, Rask took over the starting goaltender role full time, and Thomas was traded to the New York Islanders. After a lockout shortened the 2012–13 season, Rask led the Bruins to their second Stanley Cup Final berth, this time against the Chicago Blackhawks. But it was his third-round performance that might be as good as any I've ever seen, including the incredible performance by Thomas in the 2011 playoffs.

The Bruins played the Pittsburgh Penguins in the Eastern Conference finals, and the Penguins were an offensive juggernaut, led by Sidney Crosby, Evgeni Malkin, and Jarome Iginla. I watched Tuukka stop 134 shots in four games, and allow only two goals—*total*! He had a 0.50 GAA and .985 save percentage, and the Bruins swept the mighty Penguins, in large part because of the play of Rask.

He continued his strong showing against a strong Blackhawks team, until the closing minutes of Game 6 at the Garden. The Bruins had a 2–1 lead late in the third period, looking to force a deciding Game 7. Chicago pulled goaltender Corey Crawford for the extra attacker, and Bryan Bickell scored the game-tying goal with 1:16 left to play. Any thoughts of a fourth overtime game in the series were erased, however, when Dave Bolland scored only 17 seconds later. Chicago won the game and the Cup, and Bruins fans voiced a little concern about Rask's play.

You might have thought those doubts would have been erased the following season when Tuukka won the Vezina Trophy, as the league's top goaltender. He had a 2.04 GAA and .930 save percentage with a record of 36–15–6. The team captured the Presidents' Trophy for the league's best record, and fans expected another long playoff run. After defeating the Detroit Red Wings in six games, fans settled in for another playoff battle with the Canadiens.

The Bruins had a 3–2 series lead, but were shut out in Montreal 4–0, tying the series. Two days later Montreal won 3–1 at the Garden, capturing the series, four games to three and more doubts about Rask's play in the "big games" festered.

The next season ended the Bruins' run of playoff appearances. Rask was the workhorse in net, but in the minds of many fans, failed when the team needed him the most. Tuukka, and the Bruins, lost their last three games 3–0 to the Washington Capitals, 4–2 to the Florida Panthers, and 3–2 in a shootout to the Tampa Bay Lightning, missing the playoffs by two points.

In the 2015–16 season, the Bruins' playoff possibilities again came down to the final weekend. The Bruins needed a win in Game 82, and a Flyers loss to return to the playoffs. Rask reported he was ill for the final game, and his backup Jonas Gustavsson lost 6–1 to the Ottawa Senators and the Bruins missed the playoffs by three points.

Taking calls on my radio shows from Bruins fans during the entire course of Rask's career, there is a common theme: he's a good goaltender, but not good enough to take your team to a championship. All this despite Rask's résumé: a Vezina Trophy, NHL First All-Star berth, NHL All-Star team, Olympic team, and World Cup roster. His eight-year, $56 million contract signed in July 2013 brought certain expectations, and many fans feel he has fallen short of those expectations.

His calm demeanor probably doesn't help, either, as Bruins fans want their players to show the same emotional connection they have. Ironically, Rask was a firebrand earlier in his career, and there is a classic YouTube clip of Rask having a minor league meltdown while playing for the Providence Bruins. It was something he felt he had to change in his game, and I think fans misread his calm demeanor as lack of caring. They are dead wrong.

Until Rask leads the Bruins down the same path Tim Thomas did, the doubts will always be there. He needs to have his name on the Stanley Cup a second time, but this time as the starter.

Brad Marchand

Brad Marchand is that unique kind of player—unless he plays for your team, you probably don't like him very much. And even if he does play for your team, there are times he can frustrate you.

Brad was a late bloomer. He was drafted in the third round, No. 71 overall, in the 2006 NHL draft. Following his junior hockey career, and a couple of seasons with Providence, he became a fulltime member of the Bruins for the 2010–11 season. His timing was perfect, as the team earned the Stanley Cup championship.

That season, Brad had 21 goals and 20 assists for 41 points in 77 games. He added another 11 goals and 8 assists in 25 playoff games, including two goals in the Cup-clinching win in Vancouver, and was a key cog in the Bruins title.

He has made himself into one of the best two-way players in the National Hockey League, thanks in large part to his pairing on the team's top line with center Patrice Bergeron. He led the NHL in shorthanded goals in 2013–14, with five, and has been a consistently strong plus/minus player. He has, quite simply, made himself into an All-Star, and represented Canada in the 2016 World Cup, scoring the championship-clinching goal for his country.

But I mentioned he is also frustrating, and there have been many times when Brad's "close to the edge" game went, well, over the edge.

Brad has been fined or suspended by the NHL 10 times through the 2017–18 season. He has drawn suspensions of two, five, two, three, and two games. Included in that list was the three-game suspension for clipping Mark Borowiecki that kept Marchand from the Winter Classic game on January 1, 2016, at Gillette Stadium in Foxboro. His longest suspension, of five games, was for a low bridge hit on Sami Salo of the Canucks. Marchand matched that number when he was hit with five games in January 2018 for elbowing Devils forward Marcus Johansson in the head.

At 5'9" and 185 pounds, Brad may feel he has to play on that razor's edge in order to be successful. He just can't always reel things in before teetering over that edge. Ask around the NHL and you'll be told he is a dirty player. He is generally protected by Bruins fans, because they love how feisty and competitive he is. But sometimes even Bruins fans have trouble defending his actions.

During the 2017–18 season—especially during the Stanley Cup playoff run—Marchand ran off the tracks again.

I'm not sure if it began during the All-Star break or even earlier, but Brad had decided the way to counteract the impression fans had of him was to do the opposite. Instead of slashing, high-sticking, slew-footing, or low-bridging opponents, Marchand started to get more affectionate.

He had been suspended—again—by the NHL before the All-Star Game in Tampa, but was allowed to participate in the surrounding festivities. He was introduced to a chorus of boos from the crowd, and responded by blowing kisses to the fans. Brad had become what's known in professional wrestling as a "heel," and he took that act into the second half of the season. In an apparent attempt to get into his opponents' heads, Brad began cuddling up to them in heated moments, and even kissing them on the cheek. Then in the playoff series against the Tampa Bay Lightning, Marchand took it to another level.

During Game 4 at TD Garden, with the players pushing and shoving during a scrum, Marchand licked Ryan Callahan of the Lightning. And I'm not talking about a simple little lick on the cheek; Brad licked Callahan's face from his chin right up to his nose. I'm not going to lie—it was kind of gross.

After the game, Marchand said he'd done it because he had been punched "three or four times in the face." Lightning coach Jon Cooper had said at the start of the series that he'd really enjoyed coaching Marchand at the All-Star Game. In fact, he said, he'd hoped to find out Marchand was a bit of an idiot but had actually grown to like him. After this incident, Cooper's tone had changed, and after the game he said, "There is no place in our game for that stuff."

As it turned out, the league agreed, and before Game 5, NHL director of hockey operations Colin Campbell spoke to Marchand and said the behavior had to stop. The Bruins went on to lose that game, ending their season.

A few days later, the Bruins had their final media availability at Warrior Arena, and Marchand didn't dodge the questions about his actions.

"I took a pretty hard look in the mirror, and you realize the actions, some of the things I'm doing, have much bigger consequences than I may ever think," he said. "The last thing I want to do is bring embarrassment to my teammates and the organization that I did. I have to be a lot better. I know I've said that in the past, but I think that's gotta be the thing I really work on the most. I think I've gotten my game into a pretty decent spot, but I've got some character things that clearly need fixing."

Then, as only Brad could do, he boiled it down to a bumper-sticker slogan: "I gotta figure some shit out."

Make no mistake about it, Marchand can play. I've called him one of the five best forwards in the NHL, and I'll stick with that. During the 2017–18 season, the line of Marchand, Patrice Bergeron, and Dave Pastrnak was the best in the NHL, with three 30+ goal scorers. He had a spectacular playoffs, with four goals and 13 assists in 12 games. He says he has to play with an edge to be successful in the league, but he has to be sure to not step over that line.

I can tell you very honestly that Brad is a hugely popular teammate. He has one of the quickest wits on the team and an acid-tongue trash-talking game that is said to be all-world. I really appreciate how hard he works on his game, and how much effort he has put into making himself one of the best forwards in the National Hockey League.

Adam McQuaid

I have a real affinity for players who might fly under many fans' radars. One of those players is defenseman Adam McQuaid.

McQuaid is the very definition of a "stay at home" defenseman. But at 6'5", 210 pounds, that "home" he's staying at is a little larger than most. What attracts me to McQuaid's game is a toughness that is hard to measure. He is fearless and will throw his body in front of any shot, at any time, from any shooter. He missed games early in the 2017–18 season when he suffered a broken leg. I'm not sure if he broke his leg on the first shot he blocked on his final shift of the game or the second, because he stayed on the ice for both of them.

Adam always is one of the first players to come to the defense of a teammate. He is a willing combatant, even if many opponents aren't as willing to battle with him. As I write this, he has had 51 NHL fights, including 12 in the 2010–11 season. For some reason, the Washington Capitals really get him going, as he has fought the Caps five times. Virtually every fight he has ever had has been with a true NHL heavyweight, including John Scott, and even former teammate Shawn Thornton.

I've told you that tough guys hold a special place in my heart, and McQuaid is positively one of those players. He is soft-spoken off the ice, but a true battler on the ice.

I have a friend named Ben Coes, who is the *New York Times* bestselling author of the popular Dewey Andreas series of thrillers. I knew Ben and I would get along famously when he "blew up" the Bath Iron Works from my home state of Maine in his first book, and when he named a general Torey Krug in another. He recently asked me to deliver a signed copy of his latest bestseller to his favorite player—Adam McQuaid. Maybe Adam will make an appearance in a future *New York Times* bestseller as well.

David Pastrnak

David Pastrnak might be the most talented player I've seen in a Bruins uniform in a long, long time. I know Bruins fans still talk about the ones who got away, such as Joe Thornton, Tyler Seguin, and Phil Kessel, and I honestly think Pastrnak may be as talented as those players.

Pastrnak was drafted in the first round, No. 25 overall, in the 2014 amateur draft. He may end up being the best pick ever for Keith Gretzky, Wayne's brother, who was the Bruins Director of Amateur Scouting from 2013 to 2016.

The story from Pastrnak's Czech Republic is that his father wanted him to be a hockey player. After his father passed away from cancer, David rededicated himself to playing hockey. That effort led to his being selected by the Bruins.

David has already become a fan favorite at a very young age. He makes a habit of passing pucks over the glass to young fans during warmups for every game, and will suddenly interject himself into fans' selfies, or break into dance moves while the music is playing before the game. He has a permanent smile and, much like Joe Thornton, who preceded David by almost 20 years, never seems to have a bad day.

Pastrnak has declared teammate David Krejci to be one of hockey's heroes, and he seems to relish the opportunity to skate on a line with him. But he also has held down a wing on the Bruins' top line, with Patrice Bergeron and Brad Marchand. He is unbelievably creative offensively, but his primary weapon is a bazooka-like one-timer from the left side on the Bruins power play. It is not dissimilar to the shot Alex Ovechkin has from almost the identical spot.

He has already become the youngest Bruins player to score on a penalty shot; he became the first teenage player in team history to score an overtime, game-winning goal; and he became the youngest Bruins player to score 30 goals in a regular season when he accomplished the feat at 20 years and 291 days.

His 2016–17 season may be a true indicator of the talent still to come. Pastrnak played in 75 games, scoring 34 goals and amassing 36 assists for 70 points. He added another two goals and two assists in six playoff games.

The Bruins have All-Star and possibly even Hall of Fame caliber players in Zdeno Chara and Patrice Bergeron. But, in my opinion, David Pastrnak may well be the face of the Bruins franchise for many years to come.

CHAPTER 25
BRUINS IN THE COMMUNITY

Professional athletes have the power to help and the power to present a positive example. The Bruins not only understand those responsibilities, they embrace them. And they have truly made a difference in many lives.

The people who've spearheaded the Bruins' efforts in the community over the years have been Kerry Collins, director of community relations, and former Bruin Bob Sweeney, the executive director of the Boston Bruins Foundation. They often lay the groundwork for the ultimate connection between the team and the community, and they work tirelessly on behalf of people in need.

This chapter is dedicated to the efforts of the Bruins to help those in need. They've got some amazing stories to tell.

Lisa Scherber

Lisa Scherber is the director of patient and family programs at the Jimmy Fund Clinic, but to the kids who are undergoing cancer treatment at the Dana-Farmer Cancer Institute, she is known simply as the "play lady." Lisa is the constant smile, and perpetual cheery presence, who is always trying to make life better for people who are seeing life at its worst. Sometimes that means reaching out to the professional sports teams in Boston, and the Bruins have become one of her go-to sources.

"We can all remember what it was like to be a kid and having your sports heroes and watching them fly down the ice," Lisa said. "Now imagine you're in the Jimmy Fund Clinic getting your treatment and you look up, and it's one of those guys standing there. I think the kids don't think the players are real people in a way, but then they find they are just regular guys, and they're making you laugh or they're just listening to you. It's such a simple thing when these players come in, but it's really not. You know, because you're in here all the time, too, but it's really hard to see kids going through the worst of times. I don't think I've ever met a Bruins player that didn't make my kids feel just amazing."

Lisa has a group of athletes she calls "her guys." These are players from basically all the pro teams in Boston whom she can call on when needed. But she also remembers that her first encounter with one of "her guys," Shawn Thornton, was not what she expected.

"I remember the first time I was told Shawn Thornton was coming in, and I'm thinking, 'Great! Just what I need! This big, tough, mean guy coming to see my kids!' Then he came into the clinic and all I could think was, 'Are you kidding me? This guy is a marshmallow!' You saw immediately how big his heart was, and I never looked at him the same again. He would just pop in. He would call me, and say, 'Hey, I'm in the area. Is it okay if I come in to see the kids?'

"The fact that he was thinking of our kids, and knowing that his visit could change someone's day tells you all about him."

Lisa also says that what a Bruins player brings to a Jimmy Fund kid isn't just important to the child, it's important to the entire family.

"The benefit isn't just for the kids, it's also for the parents. They get to see their kids smile, and feel regular and normal again. For the kids, it just lights them up! Obviously, it doesn't take medical pain away, but it's amazing what the mind does and what the heart does.

"These guys tug at the kids' hearts, and they change what we can't do with medicine, even if it's just for a brief moment, and helps them get through that day."

In December 2017, the Bruins invited a Jimmy Fund patient named Kyle Koster and his mom, Melissa, to join them on a trip to Detroit to face the Red Wings. The game was on NBC Sports Network that night, and you might have seen the shots of the two of them cheering the Bruins on to an overtime victory.

"Kyle's mom has already texted me a million times about how much this made the worst time of their life feel normal again," Lisa told me not long after that night. "I know what Kyle has been through. The doctors would say, 'Well, you might experience this side effect,' and Kyle has had every single one of them. He's only eight, and he used to play hockey. He's watching his older brother playing and winning tournaments, and he's having trouble walking because of his treatment for leukemia. All of a sudden he's in the dressing room with the Bruins, and watching them get ready for their game that night. And he's just experiencing this magical moment, and finally feeling, 'You know what, I'm going to make it through this.'"

Another one of Lisa's "guys" is Patrice Bergeron. He pays for a luxury suite at the TD Garden which has the name "Patrice's Pals." Patrice makes it available almost exclusively to children in need and their families. And it's not just a ticket for the game that comes with an invitation; it's an entire experience.

"He offers up his suite, with food, for these families. Then, after the game, he meets all of them. And he's just a regular guy. The guys come in and they're wearing their nice suits, and sometimes I think the kids need a moment to realize who they're talking to. He doesn't just come in, sign an autograph, and leave. He's with them; he's a part of their night. Patrice is absolutely one of 'my guys!'"

While it's the kids who are being treated for cancer at the Jimmy Fund Clinic, Lisa never loses sight of the fact that the entire family is going through the experience as well, and she tries to help the entire family when she can.

"When Kerry calls from the Bruins and says, 'We've got some seats in Patrice's suite open, can you find someone who needs them?' *Yeah*, I can find someone. You know, it's not just for my Jimmy Fund kid, it's also for the parents and it's also for the siblings. All of a sudden the siblings don't see their parents a lot, because their parents are in the clinic with the child needing treatment. So for that one moment, for that one night, when the family is all together and experiencing the same joy and the same happiness and the same excitement—that's magic."

What Lisa knows is that players like Thornton and Bergeron—and many, many others—are always there for her and her kids at the Jimmy Fund Clinic. She knows that if she ever needs something for a kid facing medical crisis, help is just a phone call away.

"No doubt. And I have called. I would never bother Kerry for anything trivial, and I would only ask if I felt something was really needed. But it means so much to know the Bruins are part of our Jimmy Fund team. We can't do it all here, as much as we like to think we can, and sometimes we have someone who needs something as simple as a quick visit, or a stick or a puck. And they're always there for us."

Sam Berns

Sampson Gordon Berns had progeria, but he never let it define who he was. He was simply one of the most remarkable people I've ever had the pleasure of meeting.

Progeria is a very rare genetic condition. Its official name is Hutchinson-Gilford progeria syndrome, or HGPS. Its primary characteristic is what appears to be premature aging in children. Within the first couple of years of life, children with Progeria begin to show signs of the disease, such as growth failure, loss of hair, an aged appearance, stiffness of joints, and hip dislocations. They inevitably develop heart disease and generally pass away at an average age of 14.

Sam's father, Scott, said the first connection between the family and the Bruins came when Sam was just eight.

"We were at an event in Las Vegas in 2004 for the Garth Brooks Teammates for Kids Foundation and Kerry Collins was there. She ended up inviting Sam to come to a Bruins game, and the relationship developed from there. We began going to some of the team events, like the Wives Carnival, and it went from there."

I need to add a word or two about Sam's remarkable parents. Scott and his wife, Leslie Gordon, are both pediatricians. After learning of Sam's diagnosis when he was two, they established the Progeria Research Foundation, and they've worked tirelessly since then. Leslie is the medical director of the foundation and Scott serves as chairman of the board. They have been working since that time trying to determine the cause of the disease and developing treatments.

"I think Sam just struck up a friendship with the whole organization. The Bruins Foundation gave several grants to our Progeria Research Foundation, which we were very grateful for. They have supported us every year. It ultimately led to that night, November 9, 2013, when the Bruins hosted Progeria Awareness Night. Of course, we didn't have any idea that night that Sam would pass away two months later."

That was the night I had the opportunity to meet Sam. He appeared with me on set at the Garden, and we talked about progeria, and the importance of continuing funding and research. We generally have a rather large studio audience for many of these interviews, and I can say that in the six-plus seasons I've been doing them, there have been less than a handful of times when the audience responds. One of those was when New England Patriots Rob Gronkowski and Chandler Jones appeared after winning the Super Bowl. Another was the night Sam was with me. The fans were eerily quiet as they watched and listened. When the interview ended, they erupted in applause.

For Scott and Leslie, that night was also highlighted by a generous gesture from Bruins captain Zdeno Chara.

"It is still one of my favorite photos. When Sam was going to go on the ice to drop the puck, I asked Zdeno to please hold his hand so he wouldn't fall. In the photo their backs are to the camera, and you see Zee, holding Sam's hand and wearing the Progeria Research bracelet that we had given him. As Zdeno was escorting Sam off the ice, Patrice Bergeron and Brad Marchand were there to give him a fist bump and a pat on the back."

The relationship with Chara dated back to 2006, his first season with the Bruins.

"I believe the Bruins were playing the Islanders in 2006 and Zdeno scored a goal to help the Bruins win the game. After the game, Sam met Zee for the first time and said something like, 'You're the hero!' Zdeno responded with, 'No, you're the hero!' And their friendship just continued from then on."

It's been an honor to get to know Sam Berns, and his wonderful parents, over the years.

Sam had a project he was working on and enlisted his new friends on the Bruins to help him. Because progeria is such a rare condition, there are generally only about 1,000 children with the condition at any one time in the entire world. Sam wanted to produce a series of public service announcements to air in various countries to help with awareness. Players such as Tuukka Rask, Chara, Milan Lucic, and others donated their time and filmed these PSAs with Sam to air in their native countries. It was a gesture Scott remembers to this day.

"I think Tuukka was only a rookie when Sam first met him, and he personally came up to me after Sam's passing to express his regrets. I got a phone call from Zee the day after Sam passed away. Hockey players are just so real. Sam had filmed a public service announcement for progeria research with those guys, and some others, like Milan Lucic, and they donated their time and helped Sam do this, and they never forgot him. It was a warm, generous, loving relationship."

For Sam, his friendship with the players was just that— friendship.

"He understood that perhaps his initial contact was because he had progeria, but that quickly went away, because he made that personal connection with each individual player. We were watching the movie *Ted* and Sam elbowed me in the theater and said, 'Hey, that's my friend Shawn!' He and Shawn Thornton had struck up a friendship, and they were in constant contact."

Sam knew full well what he was up against, and what his prognosis was. In 2013 he recorded a video at the TEDxMidAtlantic entitled "My Philosophy for a Happy Life." It has been viewed almost 30 million times. He was approached by HBO about an idea they had for a documentary.

"When the HBO people first asked if they could produce the documentary *Life According to Sam*, he was hesitant to do it. He knew what progeria was and he knew what he was up against. He said all the things he had seen with other kids and progeria were kind of sad, and he didn't want people to take pity on him or feel bad for him. He said he had a really happy life, and that progeria was just a part of who he was."

Sam had a profound impact on everyone he came in contact with. His classmates at Foxboro High School clearly adored him and his Bruins friends never forgot him. Scott says he still hears from former players like Andrew Ference and Chuck Kobasew even today. When Sam saw his Bruins jersey, with the number 13, hanging in a locker stall in the team dressing room, he knew he was being welcomed as a member of that team. The players who got to know him have never forgotten him, and Sam's family has never forgotten the kindness of those players and the organization.

Sam was only 17 years old when he passed away, but perhaps his father put his impact in the simplest of terms:

"He loved life and he loved people, and he wanted to change the world."

Liam Fitzgerald

Bill and Christine Fitzgerald are the proud parents of a remarkable young man named Liam. Liam has been through more than most, especially at his age, but he's funny and excitable and loves the sport of hockey and his Bruins. And he's friends with most of them.

Liam was born with Down syndrome, but Bill describes him as "high functioning." Down syndrome is a genetic disorder and is known for characteristic facial features, delays in physical growth, and intellectual disability. The Fitzgeralds were dealing with Liam's condition, and moving forward in life...until he developed cancer. He was diagnosed with acute lymphoblastic leukemia, which involved a completely different set of treatment modalities and challenges.

Liam was five years old and in the midst of his cancer battle when the family was invited to attend a Bruins game as part of Brad's Brigade—a program developed and funded by Bruins forward Brad Marchand. Christine said Liam's first meeting with Brad did not go exactly as planned.

"The first time they met, Brad came into the room and Liam had a puck and a picture for Brad to sign. Brad was in shorts and flip-flops with his hat on backward and a t-shirt that said NOSE

FACE KILLAH. He walked up to Liam and said, 'Hey buddy, that's awesome. Is that for me?' And Liam said, 'No, that's for Brad Marchand.' Brad said, 'But that's me!' And Liam just said, 'Oh, okay. Can you please sign this?'"

That was the beginning of a long and wonderful relationship between the Bruins and Liam. With the assistance of Kerry Collins, Liam was eventually invited back to another Bruins game and given the chance to sit on the bench during warmups. When the team was coming off the ice, and heading back into their dressing room, Liam began putting his small fist out to each player, inviting a fist bump in return. Bill said that was something Liam came up with on his own.

"No one told Liam to do that. No one instructed him. As a little guy with Down syndrome, I think people expected that we had prompted him. But the uniqueness of that moment is that no one needed to. He knew to do it himself. He was either copying, or he had an idea that this was what you did when players came off the ice. It was totally his idea."

What neither Bill or Christine knew, and certainly Liam didn't realize, was that a camera caught all of his fist bumping, including when Bruins forward Gregory Campbell apparently got too exuberant, and Liam was seen shaking his hand afterward. A group called Hockey Webcast posted the video online, and suddenly, after 5.5 million views, Liam was a household name.

"We started getting messages from around the world...from Europe, from New Zealand, from Australia. The tie for many people was, 'I have a brother with Down, I have a nephew with Down.' Sadly, many people were older and their Down relative had passed, and Liam seemed to bring back a lot of memories for people. We had no idea that somebody was taping Liam on the bench. It wasn't until the next morning that we realized that Liam had gone viral around the world."

I did an interview with Liam on our NESN set, and there are two photos of Liam and me that I will cherish forever. In the first he is staring intently as I am reading a highlight package. And in the second we are posing and smiling into the camera. When I tweeted out that photo of me and "The Fist Bump Kid" it got retweeted by Bob McKenzie, the dean of Canadian hockey reporters, to his 1.5 million followers. Liam's story spread even farther and people in TD Garden were taking notice, too. Christine was touched by the number of people who reached out during and after games.

"We met so many people that night at the Garden. There were so many people around us that seemed so excited to meet Liam. We met a guy who was sitting behind us who was an Army Ranger, and he gave Liam a Combat Action Badge that was his. He said, 'This has kept me safe. It should keep Liam safe, too.' Then we met another woman who was infatuated with Liam and wanted to know his story. When we told her, she took her necklace and medal right off of her neck, that she had blessed by the Pope, and she handed it to Liam and said, 'This will keep you safe.'"

While fans were just beginning to know Liam's story, the players on the team had known about him for some time. Liam dressed as Adam McQuaid for Halloween, and Adam's sister, Michelle, saw the photo and told her brother, "You've got to meet this kid." McQuaid extended an invitation to attend a game and another friendship was born. Liam was suddenly a member of the

Liam Fitzgerald has been an inspiration to everyone who's gotten to know him.

extended McQuaid family, and that included an invitation to a birthday party for Adam.

"Adam's mom wrote to me and invited Liam to her son's 30th birthday party. So we meet up with the family at Mike's Pastry (in Boston's famous North End). It was just Adam's immediate family, and us, in the back room at Mike's. He's sitting with Adam, and we're singing and he's blowing out candles. Then in comes Patrice [Bergeron] with his wife and the baby and the dog. And suddenly Brad [Marchand] comes in with his family, and Marchie is wearing his Ninja Turtle pajamas, and he says, 'Liam,

337

do you like my Ninja Turtle pajamas?' They acted like they were just old friends. We just feel like we're family with them."

As the relationship has continued over the years, the Fitzgeralds learned what many within the hockey community have always known: the toughest guys have the softest hearts.

"Guys like Adam and Milan Lucic and Shawn Thornton have been the absolute best with Liam. Shawn was carrying him around at the Buchholz Bowl [a charity event hosted by former Red Sox pitcher Clay Buchholz and his wife, Lindsay Clubine] and Liam fell asleep in Shawn's arms. He just walked around with him like Liam was his own kid."

Bill and Christine say the Bruins have changed Liam's life, and they are forever grateful for it. Bill says it allows his family to help make a difference.

"We always appreciate the chance to showcase Liam and his story, in the interest of inclusion and awareness. We want people to see a child, that they might have a preconceived idea about, but then they get to see a Down child who is so aware, who is so with it. They get to know a child who is generous and fun, and who just so enjoys the game. And the Bruins get that. He's always treated as one of the guys. The more people see him, it's 'that's just Liam.' It's not a kid with Down syndrome."

Matt Brown

Matt Brown was a sophomore hockey player for Norwood High School playing against Weymouth High School on January 23, 2010. He was bumped behind the net, lost his balance, and fell headfirst into the glass. His coach, Bill Clifford, described the play as a freak accident, and was quick to point out there was no blame or malicious intent. But as a result of the accident, Matt suffered a broken neck.

"I was in a medically induced coma for a couple of days. One of the first things I remember was kind of opening my eyes and not really knowing where I was. But in my hospital room was a Patrice Bergeron jersey that was signed, To MATT—STAY POSITIVE. What came with it was a handwritten note. Patrice was probably only about 24 years old, and he took the time out of his day to handwrite me a note and send the jersey. Before my accident, he was my favorite player, but then I grew to love him even more."

Matt continued to hear from Bergeron from time to time, but he still had a long, grueling rehabilitation to come. Patrice didn't lose sight of where Matt was.

"After Children's Hospital, I went down to the Shepherd's Center in Atlanta for three months, and the Thrashers were still playing down there at the time. One night we get a call in my room, and someone says, 'Patrice Bergeron is here. He's wondering if you mind if he comes up.' My mom was like, '*Do we mind?*' Then he spent an hour with me there. He brought some sweatshirts, and he brought his Olympic gold medal for me to see."

If you think a visit from a professional hockey player is no big deal, especially one Matt had emulated as a player, think again.

"When he walked into the room, my chest got tight, my spirits rose through the roof, and just for that hour, life wasn't as dark. It wasn't until he left that the other thoughts and emotions came in. The Bruins just flew in that day, and Patrice took time out of his day to come over to see me. It was the first time that we realized Patrice is a special, special guy."

Over the years, the relationship between Matt and Patrice has grown.

"*Friends* is the perfect word. It's weird to talk about him with people who don't know him or know my story, like you do, but that's what we are—we're friends. Every time I see him, I realize that it's not like, 'Oh my God, what am I going to say to him?' It's now, 'How is your family, how are you feeling?' We laugh, we talk about the game. It's like seeing a buddy after the game.

"He is easily the nicest man I've ever met. People just don't understand how nice he is. I get to go downstairs sometimes with the kids and the people who go to the game in the Patrice's Pals Suite, and to see the smile he gives to these kids and these families— well, words just don't describe. I mean he started Patrice's Pals when he was like 21 or 22 years old. He's just a down-to-earth, great, great guy."

Patrice was the start of Matt's relationship with the Bruins, but he certainly wasn't the only one who made the connection, and then stayed connected.

"Another guy who I've gotten to know is Andrew Ference. I might even have a more brother-like relationship with Andrew than I do with Patrice. We goof, we rag on each other. When he left to go to Edmonton, he shot me a text and said, 'Can I come by and say goodbye?' When he came in he brought the Army Ranger jacket that the Bruins gave to the player of the game during the Stanley Cup run. He gave it to me, and it still hangs above my bed at home. He was such a rock in that locker room, for that team, and in the community. When he left it was so sad, but I understand it's a business. When he brought me that jacket, I, couldn't muster up the words. I finally just said, 'Thanks.' I really hope he comes back to Boston eventually."

Like Liam, Matt feels like a part of the Bruins family now.

"I do actually feel like I'm part of the team now. It stood out to me when I was at the season Face-Off Gala [in 2017]. It's no longer going in and thinking, 'Oh my gosh, it's the Boston Bruins!' Now it's going in to see Tuukka, and seeing Zdeno, and seeing guys that you know and you can feel that they care for you too."

Zdeno Chara may appear to have a cold façade, but to Matt he's much, much different. He remembers back to when he was injured, and the tough times his Norwood High School teammates were going through as well. Zdeno wanted to reach out to help.

"When I was first hurt, and I was in the hospital, my team had a pasta dinner at a friend's house. Suddenly, there's a knock on the door, and in walks Zdeno. Everyone stopped eating, and for a second it was dead quiet, and then everyone freaked out! He just spent time with them, and talked about what it's like to be on a team and how everyone has to come together. I finally had a chance to thank him this year at the Face-Off Gala."

In 2017 Matt had the opportunity to make connections with the Bruins "Fist Bump Kid," and not surprisingly, he and Liam hit it off immediately.

"I fell in love with Liam when I met him at the Face-Off Gala. When I got to go to a game with him, and his family, it was the highlight of my year. He's such a special kid, and just lights up a room. It was an honor to watch a game with him."

If Matt Brown sounds like a special young man, you don't know the half of it. He graduated from Norwood High School in 2012 and then graduated from Stonehill College on May 24, 2016. He has advocated for others who have suffered spinal cord injuries and has spoken on behalf of Boston Children's Hospital.

Matt Brown thanked me for giving him the opportunity to talk about his relationship with the Boston Bruins. I felt like I should thank him for the chance to speak with him.

Denna Laing

Quite simply, Denna Laing is a hockey player. The Marblehead, Massachusetts, native played for four years at Princeton University and was the Tigers captain in both her junior and senior seasons, scoring 77 points during her college career. That led to Denna being an eighth-round draft pick of the Boston Blades of the Canadian Women's Hockey League. She helped the Blades win the Clarkson Cup as league champions.

The following season, Denna signed with the Boston Pride of the brand new National Women's Hockey League and she played on a team with such national and international stars as Hilary Knight and Brianna Decker. When the NHL Winter Classic came to Foxboro Stadium on January 1, 2016, the Pride were part of the hockey festival. The Pride played Les Canadiennes of the CWHL on December 31. It was Denna Laing's last hockey game.

It was a brilliantly sunny, but cold, day when the two teams lined up to play. In the first period of the game, Denna stepped on a stick behind the net and fell awkwardly, headfirst, into the boards. As the crowd watched silently, she was taken from the ice on a stretcher and transported immediately to a Boston hospital. Her parents, Dennis and Jerilyn, issued a statement with the worst possible news:

> Denna was thrilled to be taking part in the inaugural season of the National Women's Hockey League and was absolutely delighted to be one of the pioneers in a breakthrough moment for her sport—the

Outdoor Women's Classic. Tragically, Denna suffered a severe spinal cord injury playing the sport she loves. As of today, Denna has limited movement of her arms and no feeling in her legs.

The hockey world, and the Bruins in particular, jumped into action and began an ongoing show of support. Denna says she was first visited by the team just two weeks after her injury.

"The Bruins were involved right away, or as soon as they could be, after my injury. On January 14, I first met Bob Sweeney and Kerry Collins, and I would imagine that was the very first time they were allowed to come see me. They were there right from the beginning. They brought me a Bruins jersey, with my number and LAING on the back. I still had my neck brace on, so we had a very difficult time getting the jersey on me, but we were determined. It was the first jersey that I received and the Bruins contacted Terry O'Reilly to ask his permission to give me a jersey with No. 24 on the back, because they retired that number for him. It was so cool that Terry allowed me to wear his number."

Needless to say, O'Reilly not only gave his wholehearted permission to have Laing wear his retired No. 24, he was proud to have her wear it. They have since met, and Denna was able to express her thanks to him directly. But Terry wasn't the only Bruins player to meet Denna. Soon after the contact from Sweeney and Collins, Denna had another visitor in the hospital.

"Not long after that, Zdeno Chara came to see me in the hospital. He brought with him a pair of special Bruins high-heeled shoes. Now if you know me, you know how much I love wearing heels, so that was a very special gift. It was really funny to see Zdeno having to duck to get through the door and bringing me high-heeled shoes."

But that hospital visit, with the special gift, was not a one-time thing for Chara. It became just the first contact in what has become an ongoing friendship.

"Since that day, whenever I come to a game or if I'm at a Bruins event, he always makes sure to come and say hello to me. When he first came to visit me, I had lots of things up on my wall that people had sent me to cheer me up, and one of the things was a box of butterflies that a youth organization had sent me from a tournament. They were all beautiful, handmade paper butterflies. I was showing them to Zdeno. The next Bruins game I attended, Kerry brought me a butterfly from his daughter to add to my collection."

As I said, the Bruins were just part of a huge show by the entire hockey world to support Denna in her recovery and rehabilitation efforts. The popular and energetic Laing suddenly found herself an honorary member of the National Hockey League.

"The Bruins and the Canadiens were the first teams to send me a jersey and show me their support, but the rest of the NHL definitely got involved after they did. I was invited out to the NHL All-Star Game in Los Angeles. I was also invited to the NHL Awards Night in Las Vegas. It has been great to have the NHL's support. Gary Bettman came to visit me in the hospital, and he brought the Stanley Cup. Every time I see him at any event he is always so nice to me and makes sure to say hello. He came to the Bruins' Face-Off Gala in 2016, and he presented an award to me. Cam Neely was also there with Gary Bettman."

And sometimes it was a subtle show of support that meant so much. The Bruins had special hats made that included both their own logo, but also a nameplate that had LAING and the No. 24 on the back. My daughters were among the thousands of hockey fans who bought and wore the hats with pride.

"The challenges I face are really difficult, but I've never felt alone, and I've always felt I was part of a team. The Bruins made those winter hats with the team logo and my name and number on them. I can't tell you how cool it was to see people out and about in the city of Boston wearing my hat."

While Denna continued her rehabilitation and made incredible progress, she didn't abandon her athletic career. Former Bruins star Bobby Carpenter, father of U.S. Olympic star Alex Carpenter, had a plan for Denna to take part in another athletic event—the Boston Marathon.

"Bobby and my dad have known each other for years. They grew up playing hockey with each other and against each other. And I've known his daughter Alex through playing against her. In the hockey world we've known each other. He called my dad and had this idea to run the Boston Marathon and push me in a wheelchair. At first I wasn't sure about how I felt about that. I wasn't comfortable playing such an inactive roll, just sitting in the chair and being pushed. But then Bobby suggested we run as a fundraiser for Journey Forward, which is the organization I work out at every day, so I was willing to help them out.

Sometimes in any sport, you have to be willing to take on a different roll than you might want. Bobby definitely took on the more physical aspect of the marathon, but I was there assisting him and pushing him. And the marathon ended up being an incredible experience. It was great to get to know Bobby, and we'll be friends forever."

Everyone at the Bruins jumped into action to support Denna Laing after she suffered a terrible injury.

Fans in New England know all about the famous Hoyt family—Rick and Dick Hoyt. Rick has cerebral palsy, and the father-son team became famous for competing in marathons and Ironman competitions. The Hoyts loaned one of their special competition wheelchairs to Bobby and Denna.

When I was with the Maine Mariners, one of the arena workers was a Yarmouth, Maine, native named Lee Roy. His son, Travis, was always around the Cumberland County Civic Center, the towheaded youngster picking up tape and broken sticks, and working on a hockey game that earned him a Division I scholarship to Boston University. Travis had his hockey career end just 11 seconds into his first game when he fell headfirst into the boards and was paralyzed. He has been a remarkable example of courage and perseverance and is still a tireless worker on behalf of others like him. His accident happened on October 20, 1995, and medical advances have been remarkable since then.

Denna has been one of the beneficiaries of those advances, and she continues her own efforts to not only survive, but to thrive.

"The space I'm in right now is just so hopeful. There are so many medical breakthroughs coming down the line. Being injured was not lucky, or anything I would wish for anyone, but being injured when I was, with the advancements in medicine, does make me feel lucky. There is a lot of hope going on for people like me.

The sky is the limit. I hope to continue with my therapy, gain back as much as I possibly can, and keep living my life the way I want to live it."

Denna Laing is another inspirational figure. And the Bruins have been great to play a small part in her recovery and life.

In ways both big and small, the Bruins have made an indelible mark not only on the city of Boston and its residents, but on Bruins fans around the world.

ACKNOWLEDGMENTS

There are so many people to thank as this book comes to press. If I leave anyone out, it is simply a mistake on my part, not an intent.

First and foremost, I have to thank Triumph Books. I've always wanted to write a book, and when they approached me a year ago and asked if I was interested, I couldn't say yes fast enough. Thank you for the opportunity. I also want to thank my co-author, Matt Kalman, who was always a source of encouragement and positivity. I have to add sincere thanks to *New York Times* bestselling author (and huge Bruins fan) Ben Coes, who encouraged me and gave me terrific tips on how to tell a compelling story.

There are so many people to thank within the hockey world. I start with my friend and mentor, Tom McVie, who did so much to teach me the game. From the Bruins organization, I have to start with Harry Sinden, Nate Greenberg, Kerry Collins, and the people from within the team when I began my association with the Bruins. Every single person I asked to talk with me said yes—and I mean everyone. I won't go listing names for fear of forgetting someone, but I promise I will always remember and appreciate your help and cooperation.

Current members of the team were exceedingly helpful as well. It starts with head coach Bruce Cassidy, and goes to Zdeno Chara and Patrice Bergeron. In fact, Patrice was the first interview I did in preparing this book, and he was the total gentleman he has always been. I sincerely appreciate the help of all.

I have to take a moment to thank my co-workers: Rich Keefe from WEEI Radio, and more specifically, Barry Pederson and Billy Jaffe from NESN. All those guys were always supportive and helpful. I also have to thank management from NESN, especially Sean McGrail, who hired me back and made this possible.

Please let me also take a moment to thank Boston Bruins fans. They are known as the most passionate fans in the National Hockey League, and I can attest to that. They also have always treated me as member of the family, and I'll never forget it.

I hope you like this. I know I loved the chance to tell these stories to you.